Music in
the Cultured
Generation

 PI KAPPA LAMBDA *Studies in American Music*

Music in the Cultured Generation

A Social History of Music in America, 1870-1900

JOSEPH A. MUSSULMAN

NORTHWESTERN UNIVERSITY PRESS · EVANSTON · 1971

Joseph A. Mussulman is Professor of Music at the University of Montana, Missoula, Montana.

Contents

	Foreword	ix
	Preface	xi
	Introduction	3
Chapter I	The Gentle Tradition	7
Chapter II	The Cultured Generation	24
Chapter III	The Power of Beauty	36
Chapter IV	Music and Morals	52
Chapter V	The Progress of Taste	70
Chapter VI	Meliorism through Music	84
Chapter VII	Cosmopolitan Nationalism	104
Chapter VIII	Opera for America	124
Chapter IX	Wagnerism in America	142
Chapter X	Music in the Sanctuaries: Parlor and Church	169
Chapter XI	The Legacies of the Cultured Generation	193
Appendix I	*Articles Pertaining to Music in the* Atlantic Monthly, *1857–1900*	200
Appendix II	*Articles Pertaining to Music in* Harper's New Monthly Magazine, *1850–1900*	226

Appendix III   *Articles Pertaining to Music in* Scribner's Monthly–Century Illustrated Monthly Magazine, *1871–1900*   250

Appendix IV   *Articles Pertaining to Music in* Scribner's Magazine, *1887–1900*   270

Bibliography   275

Index   287

List of Plates

Plate 1   Pen drawing of Birmingham, England, by Felix
          Mendelssohn   61
Plate 2   *Matinee at the Academy of Music,* by Thomas
          Worth   73
Plate 3a *The Voodoo Dance,* by Edward W. Kemble   112
Plate 3b *The Bamboula,* by Edward W. Kemble   113
Plate 4   *High C, and How They Take It,* by Henry Mayer   126
Plate 5   Chromolithographs by Maxfield Parrish illustrating
          Das Rheingold   153
Plate 6   Opening bars of "Song," by George L. Osgood   178

Foreword

IT HAS BEEN my pleasure and privilege to have been closely associated with the Pi Kappa Lambda Studies in American Music since the idea for such a series was conceived in 1964. Since that time two important works have appeared under the series imprint: *The Anthem in New England before 1800,* by Professor Ralph T. Daniel of Indiana University; and *Andrew Law, American Psalmodist,* by Professor Richard A. Crawford of the University of Michigan. It is with a renewed pride that the Society herewith presents its third publication.

While the Society of Pi Kappa Lambda is an honor society (the only music group to be a member of the Association of College Honor Societies), we feel that the responsibility of the organization lies beyond the mere recognition and rewarding of academic achievement. Our ultimate ideal is to develop a means through which not only scholarship but all scholarly and artistic communication can be furthered. It is hoped that the present series of publications has approached this goal to some degree.

This is not intended as the final volume of the Studies in American

Music. The high standard set by the series has indicated a path to be followed, and we are eagerly looking forward to the future.

WILLIAM J. WEICHLEIN
President
Pi Kappa Lambda

Ann Arbor, Michigan
March, 1971

Preface

THIS BOOK IS DIRECTED toward two types of readers. First, I hope it will be found worthy by those whose connection with music is not primarily academic or professional and whose interest in the history of American musical life is no greater than might be expected of any person who is a product of general education at the present time. Second, I would especially cherish the attention of those spiritual descendants of the "thoughtful" music-lovers of a century ago, who, no doubt, are again to be numbered among the readers of the *Atlantic* and *Harper's*. No special effort has been made to capture their attention, of course. Living legatees of the Cultured class, their drastically altered aims and ideals notwithstanding, would neither expect nor require any concessions to their intellectual capacities and would never tolerate vulgar, sophistical artifices of logic or language. In any case, the implications of the presupposition which this study embodies—namely, that music is a *social act*—should cumulatively serve to dispel the anticipations of effeteness which histories of music have heretofore aroused in most readers of humanistic disposition.

The period under consideration, no less than the subject matter and the approach, is very much an open field for students of music and Americana at the present time, and much material of unique interest and import remains to be examined and interpreted. To satisfy the second type of reader, therefore, I have deliberately sought to be as thorough as possible in my documentation of the facts and opinions found in the four literary magazines upon whose contents this book mainly relies. To be sure, I have done this at the risk of annoying the reader who expects his curiosity about the subject to be more or less fully satisfied by this book and who does not really care to be interrupted by the scholarly amenities, but I am confident that the spirit of charity will suppress that objection.

In order to conserve the time and the patience of both types of readers, abbreviated references to the four literary magazines have been placed in parentheses in the body of the text wherever the source has not otherwise been made sufficiently clear and wherever circumstances do not demand a formal footnote. The magazines are designated by the initials *A* for *Atlantic,* *H* for *Harper's,* *C* for *Century,* and *S* for *Scribner's.* The initials are followed by the volume and page numbers. The titles of the articles cited and the authors, if known, can be ascertained by referring to the four appendixes, which comprise an exhaustive bibliography of references to the subject of music in those periodicals during the period under consideration. As a favor to the serious scholar, musical articles in the *Atlantic* and *Harper's* that appeared from their beginnings up to 1870 have been included, even though little if any use has been made of them in this book.

The bulk of the data employed was originally gathered for a dissertation (Ph.D., Humanities, Syracuse University, 1966) under a series of Danforth Teacher Study Grants from the Danforth Foundation of St. Louis, Missouri, for which my profound gratitude is hereby once more expressed. In addition, some references have been made to material now being assembled for a projected biography of the Boston music critic William Foster Apthorp under grants from the National Endowment for the Humanities and from the University of Montana. Dr. Norman Taylor, Chairman of the Faculty Research

Advisory Council of the University of Montana, has generously assisted in the preparation of the final manuscript. Portions of Chapter IV have been reprinted verbatim from the *Musical Quarterly* (LIII [July, 1967], 335–64) by permission of G. Schirmer, Inc.

JOSEPH A. MUSSULMAN

Missoula, Montana
April, 1971

Music in
the Cultured
Generation

Introduction

IF MUSIC IS DEFINED simply as sonorous design, then the history of it may be studied in terms of its styles and media or even in terms of the composers and performers who create and practice it. But music may also be defined as a complex phenomenon representing an activity of, and in, society, and as such it may be studied in terms of the attitudes and judgments that people in general, or classes of individuals—including musicians—hold about it and in terms of the part those people, with their emotional and intellectual equipment, play in musical activities, either as active or as passive participants. And when we study these matters and the pertinent connections between them and all aspects of music considered as sonorous design, then we are studying the musical life of a given milieu.

The history of music as a social act has hardly begun to be written. There have been objective studies employing "operational methodologies," such as John Henry Mueller's and Kate Hevner's *Trends in Musical Taste* and the experiments described in Paul R. Farnsworth's *The Social Psychology of Music;* and there have been subjective, doctrinaire analyses of the musical tastes of the masses, such as Louis Harap's *The Social Roots of the Arts,* which is a

3

Marxist approach, and Michael D. Calvocoressi's *Musical Taste*.[1] Unfortunately, the scientific method is atomistic; it requires that a study be limited in scope to the dimensions of a manageable fund of statistical data. Thus it is difficult to project a synthetic view of a given era without completing an optimum number of separate investigations. On the other hand, the historian of music too often judges the past from the musician's bias alone, and on the basis of the prejudices of his own moment, instead of permitting the circumstances of the milieu under consideration to reveal their own causes and relationships.

For example, the musical life of nineteenth-century America has been described as being "characterized by the cult of the fashionable, the worship of the conventional, the emulation of the elegant, the cultivation of the trite and artificial, the indulgence of sentimentality, and the predominance of superficiality." Furthermore, the last generation of the century has been dismissed as "the closing of a fading era, the *fin de siècle* decline of the genteel tradition which had dominated American art music since the days of Hopkinson and Hewitt." [2] Such sweeping and eloquent indictments represent challenges to students who entertain doubts that any era can fairly be judged to have been all bad, especially by its own standards.

Then there is the hitherto unchallenged assertion that during the nineteenth century, and especially the last few decades of it, the arts in general, and music in particular, were dominated by economic determinism and the doctrine of what Thorstein Veblen called "conspicuous consumption" and that the whole basis for the judgment of quality in art then was the cash nexus. As one historian has expressed it,

> After the Civil War, the greatest single controlling influence in American intellectual life came to be that exerted by a

1. The history, methods, and achievements of the sociology of music have been summarized by Alphons Silbermann in *The Sociology of Music,* trans. Corbet Stewart (London, 1963).

2. Gilbert Chase, *America's Music,* 2d ed. rev. (New York, 1966), pp. 165, 364.

powerful small group, the big-business class. Ultimately, the ante-bellum tyranny of the majority was superseded by a new tyranny of the minority, a libertarianism much different in its crass materialism from the idealistic libertarianism of the first years of the American republic. The "almighty dollar" became the standard of value, infecting the country with contempt for things of the spirit.[3]

But the very wealthy were not the only individuals taking part in American musical life. The economic and artistic histories of the major symphony orchestras, the Metropolitan Opera, and certain schools like the Peabody Conservatory, all of which were supported chiefly by "tyrannical materialists," assuredly are important, and an understanding of them is absolutely essential to a full appreciation of the history of music in America. But it is equally certain that additional and perhaps more meaningful details are to be found in the actions and attitudes of the men and women who participated in those histories, however indirectly, but whose names never appeared in rosters of guarantors or performers. There were idealists then, too.

Furthermore, the economic hypothesis leaves unexplained the presence in certain periodicals, during the years from 1870 to 1900, of a tremendous body of critical and reportorial writing about music in which, as even a superficial inquiry reveals, the principle of conspicuous consumption is emphatically decried. If these magazines, all monthly periodicals of similar character, were organic institutions— that is, if there was a reciprocal relationship between them and the class of individuals that constituted their collective readership—then a study of them and their musical contents should lead us to a clearer understanding of a significant but long-neglected episode in American musical life.

3. Irving Lowens, "American Democracy and American Music," in *Music and Musicians in Early America* (New York, 1964), pp. 269–70.

Chapter I

The Gentle Tradition

THE AMERICAN LITERARY MONTHLY MAGAZINE originated in the colonial era with Benjamin Franklin's *General Magazine,* the prototypes of which were the English magazines developed under Defoe, Steele, Addison, and Johnson. Both the English and the American magazines were intended from the start to be vehicles of more durable literary quality and less ephemeral intellectual content than were the newspapers of the time. They were meant "to comment as well as to inform, to communicate pleasure as well as fact, to provoke speculation, and to influence belief and conduct." [1]

By the last quarter of the nineteenth century there had developed in this country, according to S. N. D. North, "several types of what may be properly styled the purely American magazine—types which are not even imitated elsewhere, and are not rivaled by the best products of the English periodical press." Their uniqueness as a class,

---

1. James Playsted Wood, *Magazines in the United States,* 2d ed. (New York, 1956), p. 9. The definitive history of the subject is Frank Luther Mott, *A History of American Magazines,* 5 Vols. (Cambridge, Mass., 1938–68), esp. III, 32–37, 223–63.

he wrote, lay in "the somewhat heterogeneous character of their contents, and the commingling in their pages of prose and verse, fiction, description, historical papers, moral or amusing essays, summaries of current events, [and] literary criticism." North singled out *Harper's* and the *Century,* and other observers, including some magazine editors themselves, included the *Atlantic* and later *Scribner's* among the leading representatives of the quality group.[2] To be sure, though they shared an audience that possessed certain traits in common, the monthlies were not carbon copies of one another; each was a distinct variety within the species, and each described the readers it intended to appeal to and its means of reaching them in its own terms.

The Quality Monthlies

The *Atlantic Monthly,* founded in 1857, was conceived as a magazine "devoted to Literature, Art, and Politics." On the cover page of the first issue it was explained that

> in the term Art [the editors] intend to include the whole domain of esthetics, and hope gradually to make this critical department a true and fearless representative of Art, in all its various branches, without any regard to prejudice, whether personal or national, or to private considerations of what kind soever.

Nevertheless, its table of contents was always dominated by literary criticism, fiction, and poetry; the years between 1870 and 1900 were among the richest of all in those areas, while arts and politics were but intermittently included, except for the existence of a Music Department from January, 1872, to July, 1877, the only such depart-

2. S. N. D. North, "The Newspaper and Periodical Press," in *Tenth Census of the United States,* 22 Vols. (Washington, 1883–88), VIII, 115–16.

ment in any of the leading monthlies. In 1877 the Contributors' Club was opened as an outlet for anonymous expositions of "intellectual grudges" of every sort, which were to be written in the style of polite conversation or personal correspondence,[3] and musical grudges occasionally appeared there.

The magazine "was not expected to appeal to the general public, but was to contain enough light literature and timely commentary to make it pay."[4] Bliss Perry, who edited the *Atlantic* from 1899 until 1909, reaffirmed that policy: "Most unreadable of all," he insisted, "is the matter written with a painful effort to be read by everybody." Each of the editors maintained for the magazine an atmosphere of studied objectivity, abjuring self-consciousness and self-analysis and seeking to make it "a readable proposition," with special appeal to the class of readers which, as Perry said, had come into existence during the magazine's lifetime—a group not identifiable by the normal distinctions of social or economic stratification but known by its affinity for the ideas the *Atlantic* represented.[5]

Auspiciously, the first volume of the *Atlantic* contained an article by Alexander Wheelock Thayer entitled "Beethoven: His Childhood and Youth (*From Original Sources*)";[6] but little else of importance concerning music was published until 1865, when a three-part series by Louis Moreau Gottschalk entitled "Notes of a Pianist" appeared.[7] Gradually, thereafter, the *Atlantic's* manifest interest in literature on music increased in volume and scope.

Harper's New Monthly Magazine was founded in 1850 as an ex-

---

3. Editorial Statement, *Atlantic*, XXXIX (January, 1877), p. 100.

4. James C. Austin, *Fields of the Atlantic Monthly* (San Marino, Calif., 1953), p. 27.

5. Bliss Perry, *Park Street Papers* (Boston, 1908), p. 43.

6. The publication of the article may have been brought about through the offices of one or both of Thayer's American patrons—Mrs. Mehetabel Adams, a friend of James Russell Lowell, who was editor of the magazine for the first two years, and Lowell Mason, the founder of music education in the public schools. If so, it was possibly a part of their aid which enabled him to return to Europe in August, 1858, to continue work on his great biography of Beethoven, the first volume of which appeared (in a German translation) in 1866.

7. The articles were also published posthumously as part of his diary, which bore the same title and which was reviewed in the *Atlantic* in December, 1881.

tension of, and a stimulant to, the Harper brothers' book-publishing business, but it quickly evolved into more than a literary journal or a house organ.[8] The *Nation* pointed out in 1866 that it had become a reliable index to the general character of the country, and by 1870 it was in every respect a great, successful middle-class magazine.[9] Proof of its success was the fact that *Harper's,* with the exception of a slump in 1865 which was reportedly caused by the pervasive economic and cultural aftereffects of the war, maintained a consistently large circulation, even under competition, in the seventies from the *Atlantic* and *Scribner's* and in the nineties from cheap illustrated reviews and from newspapers.[10]

The basic editorial policies of *Harper's* issued from a corporate rather than an individual source. As Henry Mills Alden, who was managing editor from 1869 until 1919, wrote, "If the selection [of material] follows the individual tastes or interests of any of those engaged in the making of the Magazine, it is likely to be eccentric and certain to fall short of a catholic scope." [11] The Harper brothers themselves were staunch Democrats, for example, but, through unbending adherence to the corporate policy, their personal political persuasions never seemed to affect their conduct of the magazine.

One result of the unusual editorial policy was that the magazine either avoided mention of extremely controversial issues or else assumed studiously impartial points of view. Only when an opinion had been widely accepted, or when it could be convincingly rationalized to suit the tastes of the *Harper's* constituency, was it forcibly advocated; otherwise it was proffered with gentlemanly open-mindedness. No exceptions are to be found in the treatment of music. The magazine's very agreeable spirit was in fact one of the objects of criticism from its detractors. "Every month it made its courtly bow," said a writer in

8. J. Henry Harper, *The House of Harper* (New York, 1912), pp. 84–85.
9. *Nation,* May 1, 1886, p. 550, quoted in Mott, *History,* II, 405.
10. Mott, *History,* II, 395–96.
11. Henry Mills Alden, "An Anniversary Retrospect: 1900–1910," *Harper's,* CXXI (June, 1910), 45.

Putnam's, "and, with bent head and unimpeachable toilet, whispered smoothly, 'no offence, I hope.' " [12]

Moreover, Fletcher Harper had determined from the beginning that the magazine should never approach its audience from so lofty an intellectual position that it might be forced to condescend in order to communicate; but he also insisted that it should not offend the reader by underestimating his ability to form his own opinions. Sophisticated literary journals like *Blackwood's* were designed to appeal to an extremely limited number of highly educated readers, while periodicals such as *Godey's* were energetic popular taste makers, spreading ready-made, marketable ideas. *Harper's,* however, was made a part of a social organism: it was "addressed to all readers of average intelligence, having for its purpose their entertainment and illumination, meeting in a general way the varied claims of their human intellect and sensibility, and in this accommodation following the lines of their aspiration." [13] *Harper's* was "the people's Magazine, appealing to no especial interest or taste, but adapted to the general taste of the great public." [14]

The *Century Illustrated Monthly Magazine* was founded in 1870 by three men—Josiah Gilbert Holland, Roswell Smith, and Charles Scribner. From its first issue in November of that year until the middle of 1881, when new owners assumed control, it was known as *Scribner's Monthly Magazine;* but the continuity of tradition and policy as well as of editorial and technical personnel was so strong from the one regime into the other that in the eighties and nineties the magazine was referred to throughout its entire history as the *Century,* with parenthetical acknowledgment of its original title sometimes, but by no means always, included. [15]

The immediate success of the magazine, in terms of circulation, was attributed by many of its admirers to the fact that it bore the strong impression of the character and personality of its editors,

12. *Putnam's,* IX (March, 1857), 294, quoted in Mott, *History,* II, 392.
13. "Fifty Years of *Harper's Magazine," Harper's,* C (May, 1900), 950.
14. "Editorial Policy," *Harper's,* LXII (January, 1881), 303.
15. Hereafter in this study the magazine will be referred to as the *Century* in order to avoid confusion with *Scribner's Magazine,* which appeared in 1887.

Josiah Gilbert Holland and his successor, Richard Watson Gilder. Unlike *Harper's*, the *Century* was kept under the close control of its two strong-minded editors. "Not only did we not steer the course of the *Century* by that of any of our admirable rivals," wrote Robert Underwood Johnson, one-time associate editor of the magazine, "but we never edited by having an ear to the ground." [16]

In the first issue, Holland explained that it was the firm intention of the editors and publishers "to make a magazine that is intelligent on all living questions of morals and society, and to present something in every number that will interest and instruct every member of every family into which it shall have the good fortune to find its way." [17] The key word in that declaration is *instruct;* it was the magazine's mission always to know more than its readers. Holland and his successor utilized editorial space every few years to recapitulate the history of the magazine's accomplishments and to emphasize that in specific areas of thought and action it had not obediently followed but had deliberately and sometimes courageously led trends in tastes, morals, and duties. Johnson recalled that the *Century* was unique among the middle-class magazines for its direct efforts at leadership in political, religious, artistic, and social opinion. [18] That the editors felt it necessary every few years to plead for open-mindedness on the part of their readers was possibly an indication that some readers objected to the magazine's contents now and then; but it was also good sales psychology, for it must have emphasized that the *Century* was dedicated to leadership and that extraordinary things might be expected from its pages any month.

The *Century* cultivated a type of nationalism which its editor called "a sane and earnest Americanism." A similar aim was implicit in the fundamental motives of the founders of the *Atlantic* and *Harper's*, but in the *Century* it was more clearly defined:

16. Robert Underwood Johnson, *Remembered Yesterdays* (Boston, 1923), p. 129.
17. "*Scribner's Monthly*," *Century*, I (November, 1870), 106.
18. Johnson, *Remembered Yesterdays*, p. 82.

The kind of Americanism which THE CENTURY has desired to cultivate is as far as possible from the "anti-abroad" cant of the political, literary, or artistic demagogue. It is the Americanism that deems the best of the Old World none too good for the New; that would, therefore, learn eagerly every lesson in good government, or in matters social or esthetic, that may be learned from the older countries.[19]

Throughout the seventies and most of the eighties *Harper's* and the *Century,* paced with regard to literary quality by the *Atlantic,* dominated the field of quality magazines intended for the middle-class audience. Each published approximately one hundred fifty pages per issue, exclusive of advertising, and each sold for thirty-five cents a copy, or four dollars a year. In the late eighties the *Atlantic,* which was not illustrated, claimed a circulation of only about 12,500 copies, while the other two were illustrated and, possibly for that reason, plus the fact that they dealt more fully with current affairs, could claim circulations of about 200,000 each.

In 1887 *Scribner's Magazine* joined the field, "a new publication in every sense, in no way a revival of any part of the past." [20] Within two years of its founding it was circulating 100,000 copies a month at twenty-five cents for about one hundred thirty pages plus advertising, and had assumed a recognized position as a worthy competitor with the three older "buff-covers." [21] Until it expired in 1930, it was maintained as "a cultivated magazine for an intelligent audience, a thought-provoking magazine for a thoughtful audience, without in any way making it a highbrow magazine for the select few." [22]

---

19. "The *Century's* Twentieth Anniversary," *Century,* XLI (November, 1889), 148. See also "The *Century's* First Year under Its New Name," *ibid.,* XXIV (October, 1882), 939; "To the Readers of the *Century,*" *ibid.,* XXXV (November, 1887), 160.

20. "The History of a Publishing House: 1846–1894," *Scribner's Magazine,* XVI (December, 1894), 801.

21. Mott, *History,* IV, 717–18.

22. Marion Ives, *"Scribner's*—Surveyor of the American Scene," *Quill,* XXIII (December, 1935), 12.

The Editors

The coverage that music received in the literary monthlies was often part of a calculated effort to appeal to a general readership, but sometimes it also corresponded with the inclinations of the managing editors or of the men who wrote the editorial columns. James T. Fields, who edited the *Atlantic* from 1861 to 1871, was fond of music, for instance, and frequently welcomed performers, including Ole Bull, into his home,[23] but he did not further the cause of music in the *Atlantic* to a very great extent.[24] On the other hand, William Dean Howells, who was editor from 1872 until 1881, made the magazine one of the most interesting, to music-lovers, of all its competitors at the time. Howells himself enjoyed vocal music and was a friend of one of the prominent song-writers in America, Francis Boott, whose works he occasionally sent to his song-loving friends like Mark Twain.[25] He tried to encourage American composers by commissioning a series of songs for publication in the *Atlantic* in 1877, but the results were only partly salutary for both the art-song tradition and the magazine, whose circulation the plan was intended to boost. He collaborated with the Boston composer George Henschel in the early eighties on a comic opera, *A Sea Change,* but it was not performed during his lifetime. That he had clear-cut opinions with regard to vocal music, including opera, is evident from some of the items he wrote for the *Atlantic* and, later on, for *Harper's,* though he protested that he had "the natural modesty of people who know

23. Annie Adams Fields, *James T. Fields: Biographical Notes and Personal Sketches* (Boston, 1881), pp. 129–31, 258–59.

24. Howard Malcom Ticknor, Fields's partner in the publishing firm and an assistant editor under the *Atalntic's* first editor, James Russell Lowell, was a competent music critic who wrote for three Boston newspapers. Inexplicably, he contributed nothing on music to the *Atlantic* until June, 1904, when he reviewed Elson's history of music in America. See Louis C. Elson, *The History of American Music,* rev. ed. (New York, 1915), p. 326.

25. See Henry Nash Smith and William M. Gibson, eds., *Mark Twain–Howells Letters,* 2 Vols. (Cambridge, Mass., 1960), pp. 86–87, 484.

nothing about music, and . . . [had] not at command the phrase-ology of those who pretend to understand it" (A-XXIV, 247). On two occasions, nevertheless, he reviewed books about music; twice he mentioned opera—Italian, but not Wagnerian; and he reviewed the season of Offenbach's *opéra bouffe* (1869) and the second Peace Jubilee (1872). It would seem, then, that Howells included musical subjects in the table of contents because he himself was interested. Indeed, not until the 1950s did the editors of the *Atlantic* regularly devote to music an amount of space equivalent to that which Howells had once considered appropriate. Thomas Bailey Aldrich (1881–90), Horace Elisha Scudder (1890–98), Walter Hines Page (1898–99), and Bliss Perry (1899–1909) showed little or no personal interest in music; they evidently dealt with it only as a duty to their readers.

The men whom Henry Mills Alden, of *Harper's,* depended on to face the public in the magazine's behalf—men like Howells and George William Curtis—were thought of as the real editors by many readers. Howells wrote the Editor's Study from 1886 until 1892 and used it to mount his vehement campaign for literary realism. But the leading columnist—and the music critic—for *Harper's* during most of the second half of the century was Curtis, who occupied the Editor's Easy Chair and of whom Howells said, "No one is more entirely the child of his age." [26]

In 1842, at the age of eighteen, Curtis enrolled in school at Brook Farm, where he remained for two years, studying, among other subjects, music under John Sullivan Dwight. After he left Brook Farm for Concord (where he helped Thoreau build his cabin at Walden Pond), his friendship with Dwight continued. He encouraged the latter in the beginning of the *Journal of Music,* secured subscriptions from a number of his friends, and occasionally contributed articles to it. An intimate correspondence was carried on between the two for several years; the letters from the younger man, containing clear

26. William Dean Howells, "George William Curtis," *North American Review,* CVII (July, 1868), 110.

echoes of Emersonian doctrine and diction, showed the profound impact which transcendentalism had made upon his mind.[27] "Beauty," he wrote to Dwight in 1845, "suggests what Truth only can answer and Goodness realize; and the whole circle of nature offers these three only, beauty, truth, and goodness, or, again, poetry, philosophy, religion, or, more subtly, tone, color, feeling." [28]

The Editor's Easy Chair was begun in 1851, with Donald G. Mitchell in charge. Curtis joined Mitchell on a part-time basis in 1853 and in 1859 took over complete control of the department, which he conducted continuously until his death in 1892. In general the Chair's business, Curtis explained occasionally, was the observation and criticism of the "minor manners and morals" of practical human intercourse. Curtis repeatedly stressed such topics as fire safety in public buildings, railroad safety, relations of capital and labor, dishonesty in public and private circles, European attitudes toward American culture—and American attitudes toward European culture—and the need for an international copyright law.

One of the causes which Curtis championed throughout his tenure in the Easy Chair was the refinement of etiquette among concert and theater audiences, especially among the wealthy patrons in their boxes at the Metropolitan Opera. The fact that the subject had first been brought up by Mitchell in 1852 is both an indication of the recalcitrance of American audiences and an index of the continuity and persistence which the Chair represented in the magazine over the years.

Stylistically, some of the columns have their prototypes in Thackeray's *Book of Snobs,* while others are written in the manner of Addison or Steele. Still others, such as the sprightly reminiscences of musical events in old New York, are similar in style to the French *feuilleton,* which served as the model for a great deal of American music criticism.

27. George Willis Cooke, "George William Curtis at Concord," *Harper's,* XCVI (December, 1897), 137.
28. Quoted in George Willis Cooke, ed., *Early Letters of George William Curtis to John S. Dwight; Brook Farm and Concord* (New York, 1898), p. 208.

In contrast, the few columns concerning music that were written by the *Century's* Josiah Gilbert Holland reflected his reputation as one of the most popular of all American lecturers of his time. Holland's speeches, which he delivered before lyceums throughout the United States, were actually sermons full of healthy common sense and sound moral teaching; he was "the oracle of the active and ambitious young man; of the susceptible and enthusaistic young woman; the guide, philosopher and school-master of humanity at large, touching all questions of life and character." [29] Unfortunately, there is no record of the exact nature and extent of his training and experience in music. We know only that he possessed a fine tenor voice and that "he led the excellent quartette choir of the North Church in Springfield [Massachusetts] for many years." [30] "You should have seen him sing, as well as heard him, to understand what he meant by the service of song in the house of the Lord!" wrote one eulogist. [31]

Richard Watson Gilder, who was named editor of the *Century* upon Holland's death, in 1881, was likewise "true to the tradition of moral passion, of old religious awe, of civic devotion, of manifold service to the public and the private life." [32] He was an exemplary citizen, and as a moral force in politics he was, as Henry van Dyke expressed it, a "militant meliorist." [33] Moreover, he was actively interested in music, though there is no evidence that he ever had the benefit of formal music education; he even admitted to having "no claim to musical expertness." [34]

For many years, on Friday evenings, the Gilders held informal receptions in their home, "The Studio," on East 14th Street in New York City. Some of the most famous men and women of the artistic, literary, dramatic, and musical worlds met there. Indeed, music was

29. Edward Eggleston, "Josiah Gilbert Holland," *Century,* XXIII (December, 1881), 164.
30. *Ibid.*
31. "Josiah Gilbert Holland," *Century,* XXIII (December, 1881), 312.
32. Elizabeth S. Phelps et al., "Richard Watson Gilder," *Century,* LXXIX (February, 1910), 626.
33. Quoted in *ibid.,* p. 627.
34. Rosamund Gilder, ed., *Letters of Richard Watson Gilder* (Boston, 1916), p. 420.

the most notable feature of many of those evening gatherings, one frequent guest recalled.[35] The singing of Clara Louise Kellogg and the playing of the pianist Adele aus der Ohe or the violinist Leonora von Stosch could be heard there from time to time. It is conceivable that the series of articles on great composers and virtuosos which the *Century* featured in the late eighties and the nineties was inspired by those Friday soirees. In any case, one of the musicians who impressed Gilder and his wife the most was the great Paderewski, who visited them in January, 1892.[36] The March issue of the *Century* contained a critical study of the pianist by William Mason, a biographical sketch by Fanny Morris Smith, and a poem, "How Paderewski Plays," by Gilder.

Gilder was known widely for his poems, which, Brander Matthews pointed out, "reveal his open-mindedness on every side to the influence of art in its several manifestations, painting and sculpture, architecture and music—more especially music."[37] He had, wrote one of his eulogists, "the same sympathies that MacDowell, as a musician, showed—a sense of the unity of art." For Gilder, music and poetry alike sang of the beauty of the soul.[38] His poetical approach to music was almost transcendentalist in character. He wrote to the noted music critic Lawrence Gilman that "the mind holds thoughts that are awakened only by music and are expressed only in music."[39] He referred to many of his poems as "songs" and in 1906 published a collection of musically inspired poems called *A Book of Music.*

Edward L. Burlingame was a more prosaic music-lover than Gilder

35. William Webster Ellsworth, *A Golden Age of Authors* (Boston, 1919), p. 148.

36. Helen Gilder wrote that Paderewski had "a wonderful intelligence which some artists, actors, and especially musicians (above all virtuosi)," lacked (Gilder, *Letters*, p. 216).

37. Brander Matthews, "Richard Watson Gilder," *North American Review,* CXCI (January, 1910), p. 41.

38. George Edward Woodberry, "Mr. Gilder's Public Activities: As Poet," *Century*, LXXIX (February, 1910), 626. Gilder was for a time president of the MacDowell Memorial Association. See Cecelia Beaux, "Mr. Gilder's Public Activities: His Relation to the Arts," *ibid.,* p. 631.

39. Gilder, *Letters,* p. 431.

but was nonetheless influential in that he made some significant contributions to Wagnerism in America. In 1875 he translated into English some of the more important items in Wagner's recently published *Gesammelte Schriften und Dichtungen.*[40] Subsequently, as editor of *Scribner's* from its beginning in 1887 until 1914 he offered his readers several definitive articles on the subject by William Foster Apthorp and Henry Krehbiel.

The Writers

Regarded individually, and during the editorship of any particular man, each of the literary magazines had its own musical —or unmusical—character. Yet taken together, and considering the full array of writers, the remarkable aspect of these four periodicals is the atmosphere of intellectual expansiveness which the total body of literature on music exudes. For example, whereas four-fifths of the more than sixty-five identifiable writers on music in the *Century* and seven of the nine in *Scribner's* were professional performers, teachers, composers, or critics, roughly two-thirds of the *Atlantic*'s authors and commentators and four-fifths of those in *Harper's* were merely knowledgeable dilettantes—in the rare and best sense of the word—or else just casual music-lovers with little or no experience or formal education in the art. And though the picture of American musical life one gains from a perusal of *Harper's* is dominated by one man, the *Atlantic*—except for the tenure of Apthorp—and the *Century* were marked by an over-all heterogeneity of attitude and authority. These facts alone are sufficient to justify the establishment of the chronological limits of this study at 1870 and 1900; neither before nor since has the literary side of American musical life exhibited such catholicity with respect to the backgrounds of the participants.

Furthermore, though the majority of the writers in the *Atlantic*

40. See p. 152 below.

were products of either New England or Harvard or both, and thus lent a provincial tone to its image of our musical life, a list of the *Century's* contributors on music displays precisely the opposite feature: an extremely wide variety of social, educational, regional, and even national backgrounds. Similarly, though most of the nearly forty identifiable writers for *Harper's* were sometime residents of New York City, their places of birth and education ranged from the Midwest to Europe; relatively few were New Englanders, and only four had any connection at all with Harvard University. These factors also serve to enhance the impression that the ideas contained or reflected in the literature before us are not entirely parochial, the concentration of musical activity and education in Boston and New York notwithstanding.

Unfortunately, the authors of many articles must remain forever unnamed; for though attributions were sometimes given in the indexes to complete volumes, the practice of signing critical essays and reviews was introduced but slowly into the monthlies, and the authors in the *Atlantic's* Contributors' Club and the *Century's* Culture and Progress columns, for example, remained perpetually anonymous. Other than the possibility that knowledge of their identities might alter the proportion of professional musicians to nonprofessionals, the matter is unimportant.

Among the dilettantes are such interesting personalities as Richard Grant White, a recognized authority on Shakespeare, who was self-taught in music theory and history and was a talented cellist. White not only contributed some important articles to the *Atlantic* and the *Century* but also wrote music criticisms for the *New York Morning Courier* and the *Enquirer*. Another was John Fiske, the great popularizer of Spencerism in America, a self-taught pianist and sometime composer.[41] Then there were men and women whose musical interests were evidently only passive—Charles Dudley Warner, the essayist, editor, and collaborator with Mark Twain on *The Gilded Age;* William F. Biddle, a Philadelphia patron of music (but not opera!

41. See John Spencer Clark, *Life and Letters of John Fiske,* 2 Vols. (Boston, 1917), I, 79, 84, 206, 299, 412–17, 422; *ibid.,* II, 82–84.

See A-LXXVII, 786–96); Arlo Bates, poet, teacher, editor, and novelist; Frederick A. Nast, a member of the *Harper's* business staff; and Moncure D. Conway, Freethinking clergyman, editor, reformer, and biographer. In addition, there were numerous literary figures of even more minuscule reputation, like Louisa T. Cragin, who wrote under the pen name "Ellis Gray" and whose output seems to include only two books of childhood reminiscences, a book of pictures of Palestine, and one essay on music. Finally, there were writers like Emily Royall and J. Bunting, doomed to biographical obscurity, whose lifetime efforts were limited to an article or two in a magazine.

The professionals ranged from composers and performers of world-wide renown, such as Grieg, Dvořák, Gounod, Saint-Saëns, Massenet, Richard Hoffman, Moritz Moszkowski, Bernhard Stavenhagen, William Mason, Sir Julius Benedict, and Theodore Thomas, to historians like Frédéric Louis Ritter and teachers like Waldo Selden Pratt, H. E. Holt, William L. Tomlins, and J. Spencer Curwen. Critics of substantial repute, earned either in the daily press or in the music periodicals, included Henry Krehbiel, Henry T. Finck, John Rose Green Hassard, William J. Henderson, Gustav Kobbé, the Englishmen Francis Hueffer and Hugh Reginald Haweis, and finally, in 1900, James Huneker.

If there was one critic whose stature was fully commensurate with the best standards of the magazines for which he wrote and the highest ideals of the class he represented, it was, without a doubt, William Foster Apthorp. His writing displayed, as Max Graf has noted, all the criteria of good literary style that were enumerated by Matthew Arnold.[42] He did not wear his erudition effetely but fitted it to himself and used it as every conscientious Cultured reader would have liked to have been able to use his own: to enlighten his audience, not merely to sway it. He never lost control of his intellectual equilibrium like Richard Grant White; he never preached like Josiah Gilbert Holland. He was more serious than George William

---

42. Max Graf, *Composer and Critic: Two Hundred Years of Musical Criticism* (London, 1947), pp. 307–9.

Curtis; less superficial than Gustav Kobbé or Rupert Hughes; wittier than John Sullivan Dwight, but never flippant or superficial.

Apthorp was definitely aristocratic in outlook, but he was also convinced of the melioristic potential of musical beauty. He never assumed an attitude of superiority; he never accused his readers, as Henry Krehbiel did, of not living up to the standards of "a cultured Greek of the classical period" (H-LXXX, 530). Unlike Henry T. Finck, a passionate advocate who believed in the power of "contagious enthusiasm," [43] Apthorp maintained a judicious balance between objectivity and a sense of the urgency of Cultural aims and values. Altogether, Apthorp's ideas were not merely subjective opinions, and his writings were not simply skillful rephrasings of old a priori assumptions. Both were, in effect, prescriptions for the act of choosing among options on the basis of a useful fund of disinterested knowledge. His contributions to the intellectual life of musical America from 1871 until the end of the century represented the lifework of a superior individual among individualists.

After the turn of the century the volume of musical writing in the quality monthlies diminished, for the dilettantes retired from the scene, perhaps intimidated by the professionalism of the others. Moreover, in the early eighties Apthorp, Krehbiel, Finck, and Henderson, the leading critics of the period, joined the staffs of great newspapers in Boston and New York. Immediately the quality of daily music criticism improved, and its character soon grew to be unique. Henderson, who considered himself "a reporter with a specialty," [44] while remaining a child of his generation intellectually, became one of the first and best writers in the new genre of criticism. With its demand for stylistic terseness, breeding epigrammatic formulations of opinion concerning specific musical events, this genre became less and less hospitable to profound, prolonged ruminations about the past or about principles.

---

43. W. S. B. Mathews and Granville L. Howe, eds., *A Hundred Years of Music in America* (Chicago, 1889), p. 370.
44. Edward Downes, "The Taste Makers: Critics and Criticism," in *One Hundred Years of Music in America,* ed. Paul Henry Lang (New York, 1961), p. 232.

Nevertheless, during the last generation of the nineteenth century the quality monthly literary magazines fulfilled a needed function not satisfied by either the strictly musical periodicals or the newspapers—the serious, reflective treatment of musical topics of permanent import in a superior, leisurely, literary style. They were laboratories for experimentation with ideas, forums for discussions, educational media, and tally sheets of progress. Critical histories of orchestras and theaters, analytical biographies of composers and performers, extended expositions of aesthetic theories, and massive reactions to epochal trends found the monthlies to be their best media.

Chapter II

The Cultured Generation

THE CLASS OF INDIVIDUALS who read the literary monthlies was not large. If only the subscribers to the four typical magazines are counted, it numbered between five and six hundred thousand individuals in 1887; if the "rule of five" was valid, the total was perhaps three million—less than 10 per cent of the white adult population. Yet the size of this class actually was disproportionate to its own sense of importance, for it did not evaluate its vitality and success in terms of numbers. Instead, it looked toward the possibility of meliorating, according to humanistic principles, the rude effects of mindless nature, the demoralizing tendencies of materialism, and the degrading influences of democratic equalitarianism upon life in the United States. It judged its success according to the degree of integrity with which it kept faith with its own ideals.

At first the precise identity of the class seems as mystifying to the historian of today as it was to the editors of the magazines then. One writer described it merely as "the most undisciplined and disorderly host in the world—the thoughtful classes of the United States," whose "nearest approach to intercourse is the reading of the same periodicals."[1] Yet there clearly was present, in the literature published in its behalf, an underlying matrix of ideas which, taken together, define the class as an intellectually organic entity.

If there is a single word by which the substance of the class's thoughtfulness might best be described, that word is *Culture*. Unfortunately, it has acquired so many different meanings among social scientists that it no longer denotes any clear-cut ideas.[2] Among social critics it has perhaps never been entirely free from the shadow of reproach. However, the cluster of ideas that seems to have adhered to it in the literary monthlies can be analyzed with considerable precision and clarity. Therefore, the word will be capitalized in this study in all references to the concept we are dealing with, in order to avoid confusion with the connotations that sociologists, anthropologists, and critics of the period have given to it.

Ralph Waldo Emerson was the conscience and guide to late-century American Culturists; his ideas helped to give their outlook a focus: "The word of ambition at the present day is Culture," he wrote in 1860. "Whilst all the world is in pursuit of power, and of wealth as a means of power, culture corrects the theory of success."[3] Culture, said Emerson, prompts in a man "a catholicity, a power to see with a free and disengaged look every object"; it makes him a member of a select class, an elite, "this great knighthood of virtue" in whom reside high personal worth, rich information, and practical power.[4] That is, Culture was not a mere fastidiousness of taste; on the contrary, "the end of culture is . . . to train away all impediment and mixture, and leave nothing but pure power."[5]

Emerson's aphoristic definitions were sometimes difficult for even

1. "The Organization of Culture," *Nation,* June 18, 1868, p. 487.
2. See A. L. Kroeber and Clyde Kluckhohn, *Culture: A Critical Review of Concepts and Definitions,* Papers of the Peabody Museum of American Archaeology and Ethnology, Harvard University, Vol. XLVII, no. 1 (Cambridge, Mass., 1952); Frank Richard Cowell, *Culture in Private and Public Life* (New York, 1959), p. 237.
3. Ralph Waldo Emerson, "Culture," *Atlantic,* VI (September, 1860), 343.
4. "Ralph Waldo Emerson, "Aspects of Culture," *Atlantic,* XXI (January, 1868), 95.
5. Emerson, "Culture," p. 344.

the thoughtful class to grasp. Matthew Arnold eventually supplied the mottoes that bore the ring of truth and effect. Indeed, it has been convincingly shown that Emerson was "both Arnold's teacher and Arnold's preparatory force in America." [6] The *Essays in Criticism,* published simultaneously in London and Boston in 1865, contained the famous definition of criticism as a "free play of the mind," obeying an instinct "to try to know the best that is known and thought in the world, irrespectively of practice, politics, and everything of the kind; and to value knowledge and thought as they approach this best, without the intrusion of any other considerations whatever." [7]

The term *Culture* acquired all the meanings that Americans learned to associate with it following the publication of Arnold's most famous work, *Culture and Anarchy,* which had first appeared in England in the late sixties and had become well known in the United States long before its first appearance in a New York imprint in 1880. As Henry James, one of Arnold's principal advocates in this country, said, the critic had not invented the idea of Culture, "but he made it more definite than it had been before—he vivified it and lighted it up." [8] Culture came to mean "criticism" itself and a "disinterested" dedication to "the authority of right reason," to Jonathan Swift's "two noblest of things, *sweetness and light,"* and to "totality." Moreover, it was marked by the polarity of "Hebraism and Hellenism," on which point Arnold addressed himself pointedly to the United States: Americans, he said, were failing of a true concept of Culture; they needed Hellenizing, meaning the expansion and enrichment of the life of the mind.[9] The responsibility for leadership, he said later, belonged to "the remnant." [10]

6. John Henry Raleigh, *Matthew Arnold and American Culture* (Berkeley, Calif., 1957), p. 11.

7. Matthew Arnold, *Lectures and Essays in Criticism,* ed. R. H. Super (Ann Arbor, Mich., 1962), p. 268.

8. Henry James, "Matthew Arnold," *English Illustrated Magazine,* I (January, 1884), 246.

9. Matthew Arnold, *Culture and Anarchy,* ed. R. H. Super (Ann Arbor, Mich., 1965), pp. 87–256.

10. See Matthew Arnold, "Numbers, or the Majority and the Remnant," in *Discourses in America* (New York, 1894); see also Matthew Arnold, *Civilization in the United States* (Boston, 1888).

The education that "the remnant" considered necessary for the life of the mind was characteristically "disinterested," no matter what profession one chose to follow after graduation. It was oriented toward the classics in language, literature, philosophy, and science, including mathematics. Whether it was sought at Harvard or at Yale or at nearly any other American college or university, it was certain to be formalized into what Arnold termed an "institution," a systematic conservator of tradition. Thus all well-educated young American men could predictably have knowledge of precisely the same subjects and share precisely the same intellectual pleasures. Theodore T. Munger, a Congregational minister, summarized the basic educational philosophy of the thoughtful class in one intense Emersonian paragraph:

> To think, to reason, to feel nobly, to see the relations of things, to put the ages together in their grand progress, to trace causes, to prophesy results, to discern the sources of power, to find true beginnings instead of unknowable causes, to perceive the moral as governing the intellectual and both as dominating the material, to discern the lines along which humanity is moving and distinguish them from the eddies of the day—such is the end of education.[11]

Specifically, its function was to raise the standards of life by calling forth the powers of reason, moral feeling, and artistic taste.

The Social Idea

The education of a Cultured gentleman was not intended to lead him to success but to equip him for service. The conscientious members of the thoughtful class were supplied by the nature of American socioeconomic structure with an opportunity for service which amounted to a calling: they were summoned to be the Culture-

11. Theodore T. Munger, "Education and Social Progress," *Century*, XXXIV (June, 1887), 272–73.

guardians of the Culturally underprivileged, the economically over-privileged, and the un-Cultured majority of the middle class; or, in Matthew Arnold's terms, the Populace, the Barbarians, and the Philistines.[12]

In this role the thoughtful individual represented what Emerson called "Society's Gentleman," whose duty was to employ his education and his talents not only to conserve the good life but also to enhance the lives of the greatest possible number of people.[13] Specifically, Culture was to be disseminated by its guardians because it had the capacity to reconcile antagonisms among classes "by a commonness of thought and feeling and aim in life." [14] Matthew Arnold termed the Culture-guardian's duty "the passion for doing good." Yet, he contended, Culture is never condescending:

> It does not try to teach down to the level of inferior classes; it does not try to win them for this or that sect of its own, with ready-made judgments and watchwords. It seeks to do away with classes. . . . This is the *social idea;* and the men of culture are the true apostles of equality.[15]

The guardians of Culture were equally determined to refine the too-public life of the rich. They waged a relentless campaign, not against the acquisition of wealth and power, but against the substitution of the power of wealth for the power of Culture. They were willing to put up with a certain amount of recklessness: "The rich can," remarked one critic, "in a pecuniary sense, better afford to throw away money on unrefined amusements and vulgar display than workingmen can, for their means are sufficient to admit of some waste." [16] The

12. Arnold, *Culture and Anarchy*, pp. 137–62.
13. Edwin Cady, *The Gentleman in America: A Literary Study in American Culture* (Syracuse, 1949), pp. 168–75. See also Emerson, *The Works of Ralph Waldo Emerson*, 5 Vols. (New York, n.d.), III, 64, 91.
14. Cady, *Gentleman*, p. 475.
15. Arnold, *Culture and Anarchy*, p. 113.
16. "The Greatest Need of the Working Class," *Century*, XXVI (August, 1883), 470. See also Aline Gorren, "American Society and the Artist," *Scribner's*, XXVI (November, 1899), 628.

Remnant were grateful, of course, for any largess received from the rich in the form of art museums, libraries, schools, orchestras, and opera houses. Yet they could be righteously indignant if they believed a philanthropy had been selfishly motivated or too ostentatiously bestowed. One of the chief obligations of the wealthy class, it was held, was to pay the big bills of Culture—and to do so with dignity and humility.

The majority of the growing middle class, who, appearing to have little interest in intellectual or aesthetic exertions, sought to emulate the Remnant by merely securing the outward evidence of Cultured life, constituted perhaps the most serious threat and the greatest challenge. Their motives seemed shallow and materialistic. They continually misappropriated the aims and methods of Culture and consequently attracted adverse criticism, which, by association, redounded upon genuinely Cultured individuals. Because of their intellectual and economic inflexibility, as well as their numerical strength, they required the most careful guidance in the refinement of their tastes.

The implicit contradiction between the "social idea," which transcended class differences, and the doctrine of individualism, which supported class stratification, was easily circumvented. George Washington Cable, for example, believed in the beneficent influence of Culture, claiming that "to leave the unfortunate to fight ill-fortune with only their handicapped merit is to leave them to an unintelligent and merciless natural selection." He insisted, however, that, in order for the proper result to be brought about, "the masses" must be regarded as a group of individuals and Culture must not be doled out in large quantities and broad generalizations to groups of passive recipients but rather must be taken into the very homes of the poor.[17] Cultural altruism could also be reconciled with natural law by appeals to the teleological doctrine of progress.

17. George Washington Cable, "Home Culture Clubs," *Century,* XXXVI (August, 1888), 497. See also Washington Gladden, "Christianity and Popular Amusements," *Century,* XXIX (January, 1885), 384–92.

The Idea of Progress

The idea of progress, like the idea of Culture, was not new to the postwar era. As "the flower of the doctrine of human perfectibility," it had been an important element in the philosophy of the founders of the nation, and during the first half of the nineteenth century it gained momentum and became a dominant mode of thought.[18] In fact, it has been shown that a distinctly American reading of the idea of progress helped to differentiate the whole complex of American thought and behavior from that of Europe.[19] Progress, in America, was both a law of history and the will of a benign Providence; the country both *had* progressed and *was* Progress.[20]

> On the classic European view, the conflict of opinions produces truth; in the light of the idea of progress truth will be constantly accruing new meanings. But in the United States neither conflict nor innovation was deemed necessary. Indeed, all that was necessary, according to a commonly held view, was the education of all children in the accepted truths of their parents.[21]

Thus the American idea of progress was essentially conservative; it reflected a sense of possession and self-identification rather than yearning, and it predicted that future progress would be a continuous advance and improvement upon the present, not a revolutionary leap upward.

The idea remained basically unaltered after 1865, except that

18. Arthur Alphonse Ekirch, Jr., *The Idea of Progress in America, 1815–1860* (New York, 1944); Charles A. and Mary R. Beard, *The American Spirit* (New York, 1942), pp. 248–53.
19. Rush Welter, "The Idea of Progress in America," *Journal of the History of Ideas,* XVI (June, 1955), 407.
20. *Ibid.,* p. 406.
21. *Ibid.,* p. 413.

additional support for it was then at hand. "With the rise of an in-dustrialized, urbanized society, science, with its theory of evolution and its law of thermodynamics, became the chief authority for a belief in the idea of progress." [22] In particular, Herbert Spencer's popular philosophy radically strengthened the conservative and optimistic fea-tures of the idea.[23] Simultaneously, there was a growth of skepti-cism regarding the certainty of progress, with the result that the idea was systematically explored and, consequently, defined. Charles Dud-ley Warner, for example, expressed a consensus on the subject in the early seventies:

> When we speak of progress we may mean two things. We may mean a lifting of the races as a whole by reason of more power over the material world, by reason of what we call the conquest of nature and a practical use of its forces; or we may mean a higher development of the individual man, so that he shall be better and happier. If from age to age it is discover-able that the earth is better adapted to man as a dwelling-place, and he is on the whole fitted to get more out of it for his own growth, is not that progress, and is it not evidence of an intention of progress? [24]

Clearly, progress toward "a higher development of the individual man" was not a mechanism which operated only through passive creatures. Rather, it permitted the rational manipulation of selected circumstances supplied by Nature. Therefore, evidence of progress, when discovered, could readily be employed to demonstrate that what had specifically and measurably improved prospects for a better world was Culture.

22. Ekirch, *Progress in America,* p. 267.
23. Welter, "Progress in America," p. 414. See also Richard Hofstadter, *Social Darwinism in America,* rev. ed. (Boston, 1955), chap. 2.
24. Charles Dudley Warner, "Thoughts Suggested by Mr. Froude's 'Progress,'" *Century,* VII (January, 1874), 351-59.

Cosmopolitan Nationalism

As a result of its dedication to the pursuit and dissemination of Culture in the name of progress, the educated class was faced with the opportunity and the impulse to shape the form and character of American civilization and especially to clarify its relationships with its European heritage. Confronted on the one hand with a widespread antagonism toward Europeans, their ideas, and their products and on the other with a clear need for the continued assimilation of the best of the European heritage, the only reasonable course for the Culture-guardians to pursue was a temperate nationalism balanced by an objective, discriminating cosmopolitanism. In any case, an attempt to create a completely new civilization in every detail in America would have been considered a blind and potentially catastrophic disregard for the best that had been known and thought throughout the history of European and Mediterranean civilization. It would have been, in a word, immoral; almost any disturbance of the rational equanimity and progress of Cultured life was immoral.

Morality

"The foundation of culture, as of character, is at last the moral sentiment," said Emerson,[25] although he never gave a sufficiently concise expression to the meaning of the phrase "moral sentiment" for it to be taken up as a class-wide code of conduct.[26] Indeed, the Cultured individual was moral, and his total concept of morality comprised four basic virtues.

To begin with, the Culturist led an *orderly* life. Orderliness signified a profound respect for natural law whenever blind evolution harmonized with the best interests of the class, and for rationally

25. Emerson, "Aspects of Culture," p. 93.
26. See Frederic Ives Carpenter, *Emerson Handbook* (New York, 1953), pp. 194–203.

monitored progress when it did not. For example, the historical place of women in the social structure was viewed by many intellectuals as a part of natural order, to be altered only at great risk to the balance of life.

Second, the Cultured man was *temperate;* moderation in thought and action was a firm principle. This is seen in the attempt to reconcile the Calvinist doctrine of the virtue of industry with the implicit requirement for leisure in which to pursue Culture. One recourse was to discredit excess in both labor and leisure. "Intemperate devotion to work of any kind, like all intemperance, weakens the power of right living," wrote one critic, invoking the authority of Spencer with the vocabulary of Arnold. "Therefore, in the interest of a better and more truly efficient life, let us heed the gospel of relaxation and recreation."[27] In contrast, aimless leisure, such as the English gentleman allegedly pursued, made life itself worthless.[28] On the assumption that time was equivalent to money, it was held that one ought to be dutifully occupied at some clearly beneficial, if not tangibly profitable, endeavor.

Third, in order to exercise moderation, a man had to be *discriminating.* The Cultured individual recognized a kind of moral triumph in any practical victory over vulgar choices. He sought never to place himself in a position in which he would have to choose between the lesser of two evils or the cheaper of two bargains. As a later apologist for the class said, "They knew the complicated ways of self-denial, and had sifted out the essentials. They had been trained in the knowledge of what was worth paying for."[29] As Emerson expressed it, "A strenuous soul hates cheap successes."[30]

Finally, the moral individual was *decent.* As an antonym for vulgarity, decency meant primarily sweetness and good manners and called for the use of the appropriate word and the considerate deed

27. "Spencer in America," *Harper's,* LXVI (January, 1883), 305.
28. "The American Gentleman of Leisure," *Century,* VII (December, 1873), 239.
29. Katherine Fullerton Gerould, "The Plight of the Genteel," *Harper's,* CLII (February, 1926), 315.
30. Emerson, "Aspects of Culture," p. 94.

according to the requirements of a given situation. In other words, decency stood for orderliness in the area of what contemporary critics referred to as "minor morals." Obviously, the term also denoted the opposite of what Arnold called "lubricity."

In the name of decency there was a general retreat, coincidentally in keeping with Emersonian doctrine, from all sensuousness, in favor of the total intellectualization of beauty as an equivalent of truth and goodness. Only toward the enjoyment of music did Emerson once appear to relax his own censoriousness of sheer animal experience: "I think sometimes—could I only have music on my own terms—could I live in a great city, and know where I could go whenever I wished the ablution and inundation of musical waves—that were a bath and a medicine." [31] On the whole, however, Emerson represented the majority of American intellectuals in his anxiety over decency and his distrust of sensuousness. [32]

One of the results of the system of morality built upon the principles of orderliness, temperance, discrimination, and decency was the emergence of a unique concept of the ideal artist. "We occupy ourselves now with the artist as a man," explained one writer.

> His character counts more and more with us in an estimation of his work. We demand that he shall become increasingly like other men, and subject to the same social and economic laws. And this, without question, is a great gain on the side of morality, sanity, and general righteousness. [33]

It was John Ruskin who seems to have specified the relationship of art and life that the American intellectuals had in mind, centering attention on the character of the artist as a Cultured, moral citizen. "You cannot paint or sing yourselves into being good men," he wrote.

31. Emerson, *Works*, III, 65.
32. See Carpenter, *Emerson Handbook*, pp. 201–2.
33. Gorren, "American Society," p. 633.

"You must be good men before you can either paint or sing, and then the colour and the sound will complete in you all that is best." [34]

Although the moral man was the better artist, it was not only his moralness that made him better; it was also his intellectuality. Indeed, intellectual superiority was a prerequisite to genius. "Intellect lies behind genius, which is intellect constructive," according to Emerson.[35] Intuition was an essential element to the presence of genius, he said; but, without the control of the mind, the intellect could be only receptive, not constructive. Arnold advanced the same point of view.[36] This was not to say that only genius was admissible to the conduct of the musical life of America. Even "talent working with joy in the cause of universal truth lifts the possessor to a new power as a benefactor," said Emerson.[37] In any case, the whole Cultured ideal of the artist as a morally upright and intellectually energetic gentleman served to place him at the very center of the Culturists' image of the ideal individual.

34. John Ruskin, *Lectures on Art* (1870), quoted in *Ruskin on Music,* ed. A. M. Wakefield (London, 1894), p. 112. Cf. George Bernard Shaw, "Ruskin on Music" (1894), in *Shaw on Music,* ed. Eric Bentley (New York, 1955), pp. 48–55.
35. Emerson, *Works,* I, 208.
36. Arnold, *Lectures and Essays,* p. 261.
37. Emerson, "Aspects of Culture," p. 94.

Chapter III

The Power of Beauty

IN THE AMERICA of the Cultured generation every good and beneficial activity seemed to have its rightful place; either it was guaranteed by the Constitution or the Bill of Rights, or it fulfilled an obvious moral, ethical, or practical purpose in the daily lives of all citizens. The arts, however, had neither legal nor logical places, either in the rationale or in the pragmatic sphere of democratic existence; and music, calling for the greatest expenditure of time and money for practitioners and institutions and often demanding special knowledge for its appreciation, theoretically seemed least welcome of all. During the colonial and revolutionary eras, when it had functioned as the handmaid of religion and the mirror of patriotism and when popular tavern-music and balladry clearly satisfied the social needs of most of the people, music had required few, if any, apologists. From the beginning of the second generation of the nineteenth century, however, a taste began to develop, chiefly among the growing class soon to become Cultured, for a higher music, representing, as John Sullivan Dwight put it, "beauty as a type and symbol of the highest truth."

An acute awareness of the superior quality of their musical insights, combined with the motivations of Cultured ideals, compelled the new music-lovers to find ways to share the power of the beauty of music with all citizens—in other words, to find the real ontological situs of music in American life *and* in American living. They set upon the problems with the full force of Arnoldian criticism, the "free play of the mind." In theories of the essential nature of music they discovered the one; in definitions of the musical experience they found the other.

Eternal Principles

Explanations of the divine origin and inspiration of music had once been sufficient to answer all pertinent questions, but, in a more scientific age, thoughtful individuals wished to be assured that music was a part of the design of the universe, that it existed not only before and beyond human reason but even irrespective of supernatural power. References to the deity as the direct creator of music were conspicuously and not surprisingly minimal in the magazines the Cultured class read; when they did appear, they were often used in a figurative rather than a literal sense. Instead, the phenomenon of music was traced to its "eternal principle" either via the science of acoustics or through the logic of evolution.

In 1870 Dwight summarized for the readers of the *Atlantic* the application of Hegelian dialectic to the realm of music that Moritz Hauptmann had undertaken in *Die Natur der Harmonik und Metrik* (1853; English ed., 1888). Dwight explained that, from a single pitch—in Goethe's phrase, "a word of God"—and its inherent series of overtones, all melody, harmony, rhythm, and form had evolved— "as beautiful and wonderful as growth of plant or crystal." "Thus logically," wrote Dwight with Emersonian resonance, "as tree from germ, out of the first tone . . . that ever rang, may we deduce the art of music in its infinite varieties, all singing, pleading for and prophesying UNITY, as the grand hope of human mind and heart, the highest word of science and religion" (A-XXVI, 622).

It is as if the next question was, Which tone was the first? In 1875 the *Century* noted that two German geologists had discovered that the notes C, E, G, and F belong to all rushing water. A few years later Eugene Thayer, a Boston organist and composer, offered a detailed and definitive musical analysis of the world-famous symbol of nature in America, Niagara Falls (C-XXI, 583–86). He pointed out that the "tone" of Niagara is a G-major seventh chord, "note for note the dominant chord of our natural scale in music! Here has nature given us a dominant, to last as long as man shall last." Rhythmically, the chief "accent or beat" of the Falls was precisely one per second. "Here is our unit of time—here has the Creator given us a chronometer which shall last as long as man shall walk the earth. It is the clock of God!" The quality of the tone, he continued, is "Divine! There is no other word for a tone made and fashioned by the Infinite God. I repeat, there is no *roar* at all—it is the sublimest music on earth!" Two distant subscribers, one in Wisconsin and the other in Minnesota, expressed their doubts on one or two minor points, but Thayer merely restated his theory briefly, and the discussion came to an end. Thus was music shown to be a link in the Great Chain of Being.

S. Austin Pearce, a teacher of vocal music at Columbia College and critic for the *New York Evening Post,* revived the ancient Greek theory—which had since been brought up by Kepler and Leibniz— of the "music of the spheres" (H-LXIII, 286–88). He stated that the major ninth chord (C, E, G, B-flat, D), which he called "the basis of modern harmony" and "the normal combination from which all other harmonies are formed by modification," was built of intervals whose proportional expressions corresponded to the relative distances from one another of the several planets. Thus modern music, and especially the music of Wagner, was shown to be capable of attuning men's souls with the divine plan of the universe.

Evidence that music was not a capricious invention but a part of Nature was also extracted from studies of the songs of birds.[1] In the

---

1. The theory of the origin of music in human imitation of bird songs is as old as Lucretius, at least (see Warren Dwight Allen, *Philosophies of Music History*

Century alone there appeared, between 1887 and 1898, a disconnected series of ten full-length articles on the subject. Seven of them were signed by Simeon Pease Cheney, a composer, voice-teacher, farmer, and one-time member of a renowned family concert troupe. Another, entitled "The Sportsman's Music," was by William J. Henderson; still another was by Charles Allen, the Boston violin-teacher; the last was by John Burroughs, the eminent naturalist, critic, and poet. Cheney demonstrated that "bird music is akin to our own: the same intervals are used as in the major and minor keys." One of the songs of the robin, which he notated as

reminded him of "the first half of an old melody sung by the spinning-girls fifty years ago, as a substitute for counting, while reeling their yarn":

"Who," he asked musingly, "is the plagiarist?" (C-XXXV, 847–48).

At the very least, theories of the origins of music were probably

[New York, 1962], pp. 53–54). Renewed interest in it in the eighties and nineties might have been stimulated by the Darwin-Spencer debate over the question of the origins of music. In *The Descent of Man* (1871) Darwin propounded the theory that music had not only preceded speech but had been, in fact, the source of speech. In 1857 Spencer, in "The Origin and Function of Music," had reaffirmed the speech theory that had been the basis of the writings of members of the Florentine Camerata, who had originated the *dramma per musica,* as well as Rousseau, Diderot, and Roger North—that music was born of emotively heightened speech. The final, revised version of Spencer's original article appeared in the American *Popular Science Monthly* in 1890. At about the same time a public dispute between Spencer and Darwin took place in the English periodical *Mind.* Another debate over the origins of music, this time between Spencer and Ernest Newman, took place from 1899 to 1902. None of this aroused any specific comments from American writers in the literary magazines. See Peter Kivy, "Herbert Spencer and a Musical Dispute," *Music Review,* XXIII (November, 1962), 317–29.

interesting to Cultured readers as exercises in deductive reasoning, if not as merely entertaining essays in the art of inference. They were too obviously remote from the circumstances of contemporary musical life, however, to have a profound effect on musical thought in general. The connections between bird songs and art songs were simply too tenuous to provide a workable basis for an objective assessment of the latter genre, and that was what was really needed. At best, speculations as to the origin of music were viewed as integral parts of the "organic hypothesis," which thoughtful men were beginning to transfer from the biological world to the world of music.

Darwinism and Spencerism were strongly influencing the writings of eminent European critics like the Belgian, F. J. Fétis, and the Bohemian, August Wilhelm Ambros.[2] Meanwhile, in the United States the more rigorous intellects among the Culturists, who by natural proclivity kept close track of current foreign musical literature while reserving their right to modify its conclusions, were also assimilating the precepts, and even the new vocabulary, of evolutionism. The history of music, in its parts no less than in the whole, was regarded as an organic unity, illustrating the processes of growth and change and of natural selection. The implications of those processes were systematically worked out in a procedure known as historicism—a coherent, analytical, chronological interpretation of events which provided a means of evaluating the present and predicting the future by showing their organic relationships with the past.

For example, Apthorp, though himself a dedicated Wagnerian, proved the transience of Wagnerian music drama on the grounds of the organic nature of music. He showed that Wagner's idea was but an individualistic attempt to revive the experiments of the founders of the *dramma per musica,* the Florentine Camerata, whose theories had been subversive to the organic integrity of music *as music,* and that pure music would ultimately supersede the musicodramatic coalescence advocated by Wagner. As Apthorp put it, it was

2. See Allen, *Philosophies,* pp. 108–9, 261–62.

aesthetically unavoidable that an organic evolution of some sort should go forward in the music of the lyric drama; that it should remain wholly inorganic and amorphous was impossible; for it is contrary to a fundamental law of nature that that which contains within itself the potency and power of organic development should remain for ever inorganic. And that music does contain within itself such potency and power has been abundantly proved.

His "proof" lay in the observable fact that *forms* had evolved, chiefly out of the tonal system. "What we call *form* in music is virtually identical with organism, or organic structure," he wrote. "Under the sway of the . . . law of tonality, musical forms became not merely organic, but essentially vertebrate; music developed a spinal column." The principle of symmetry and contrast, of Aristotelian beginning-middle-end form, was a result of the gravitational effect of tonality. The critic concluded that, "if we may trust the lesson of the past, the evolution of the future will still be one from simpler to more complex and more highly organized forms" (S-VII, 487–96).[3]

Reginald de Koven also applied Darwinian-Spencerian theories to the criticism of opera, but, unlike Apthorp, he believed Wagnerian music to be a sport of nature, incapable of surviving the temporary reputation of its creator or of generating its own offspring. Whereas Apthorp had declared that future composers would be unable to stop at Wagner's achievements, de Koven insisted that they would in fact have to go back to *Lohengrin,* or else turn aside to Verdi's *Falstaff,* in order to find a regenerative stage of the organism of opera (S-XXIII, 81–84). He was also hopeful that somewhere in the scheme of the evolutionary process there was a built-in system of controls over the musical destiny of man. He allowed, reluctantly, that the "power of the Schools" had been broken, that the subjective judgment of "the ear" had supplanted academic rules, thus allowing free play of the essential, organic nature of music. Nevertheless, de Koven cherished

3. Cf. Allen, *Philosophies,* p. 110 ff.

the hope that, "while the human ear may be trained to accept as agreeable, combinations of sound from which, in its untrained state, it would recoil, there must be surely a limit to the possibilities of such aural development, or we should, in time, recur to savage noise and barbaric discord" (S-XXIII, 84).

De Koven's remark reflected the anxiety of many Cultured listeners who had experienced the music of post-Wagnerians like Richard Strauss and were reminded thereby that the materialistic determinism of the theory of evolution could be a threat to the revered, hierarchical, absolute standards of aesthetic value they considered their prime heritage.[4] For the time being, however, explanations of the connections between music and the over-all plan of the cosmos were ways of convincing thoughtful individuals, if not all potential music-lovers, that music was really a part of human existence. Yet critical explorations of music as a form of human experience were more germane to the exigencies of daily musical life than esoteric dissertations on essences, for what concerned the majority of Americans, thoughtful or not, were questions concerning the relationships between musical values and the valuative criteria of everyday living.

Music and Emotion

The proposition that music is the language of the emotions had originated as a tenet of radical romanticism; and the influences of German thought, including the emotion theory of music, by sheer force of volume, not to mention logic, had penetrated American popular philosophy, from systematic academic formulations to everyday use. Nevertheless, it was difficult for the Culturist, with his background in ultraconservative moralism and rural New England Protestantism, to accept this proposition without reservation, and even

---

4. Apthorp, after "two nights' sleep and a day's rumination" upon Strauss's *Don Juan,* concluded that "one cannot believe in such music wearing well," and he was among the more liberal critics. See the *Boston Evening Transcript,* November 2, 1891.

harder for ordinary folk. As one writer who attended Harvard in the mid-eighties recalled, "The habitual attitude . . . of the New Englander was that emotion was a kind of pernicious influence which might 'go off' at any moment and kill some one, or at any rate lead men astray." [5] Therefore, more than a few critics addressed themselves to the difficult task of dispelling American music-lovers' anxieties about the matter.

One of the most fascinating writers on the subject of the relationship of music to emotion, from the perspective of the Cultured generation, was the Reverend Hugh Reginald Haweis, an English clergyman and musician who was probably cited more frequently in American musical literature than any other contemporary foreigner of comparable repute. His relative bibliographical and biographical oblivion belies his real, if mostly superficial, influence on American musical thought during the last generation of the nineteenth century. Haweis' most popular book was *Music and Morals,* which first appeared in 1872 and was reprinted some twenty-four times up to 1934. In a *Harper's* article consisting of excerpts from the book, Haweis explained that music and emotion have in common the characteristics of elation and depression (high and low pitch), velocity, intensity, variety, and form (H-XLIV, 756). Apthorp, reviewing the book a few months later, dismissed the thesis as "nothing more than a rather ingenious conceit, not unamusing to read, but of no philosophical value" (A-XXX, 626). Evidently such judgments did not appreciably diminish the appeal of the book to American and British readers; thousands of them found it amusing to read, and thousands more must have been at least titillated by the title.[6]

5. Walter Raymond Spalding, *Music at Harvard: A Historical Review of Men and Events* (New York, 1935), p. 144.
6. Haweis addressed the Parliament of Religions in the Hall of Columbus on September 20, 1893, during the Columbian Exposition in Chicago. In a homily which is, from the perspective of nearly a century later, "not unamusing to read," he traced the connections among music, emotion, and morals, and why emotion had got a bad name. "Music is the language of emotion," he began. "I suppose you all admit that music has an extraordinary power over your feelings, and therefore music is connected with emotion. Emotion is connected with thought. Some kind of feeling or emotion underlies all thought, which from moment to moment flits through your mind. Therefore music is connected with thought. Thought is

Richard Hoffman, an English pianist who had toured America with Jenny Lind, exhibited twelve pairs of similar musical phrases by different composers and pointed out that in each pair the emotions expressed were identical, even though the compositions represented various times, places, and personalities (C-XLII, 475–76). But the idea that music could convey specific emotions attracted few adherents among the Cultured writers, perhaps because the usual proofs of its validity were empirical and subjective rather than scientific. On the other hand, John Comfort Fillmore, in his study of Indian music published in the *Century* in 1894, established the intrinsic and universal emotionality of modern music with what, to many thoughtful readers, must have been entirely adequate testimony:

> In the absolute supremacy of the imaginative and emotional elements which dominated every moment of the Indians' criticism of my work, I was continually reminded of the outbreak of the German romantic movement about 1830. Here, as with Schumann and Wagner, the all-important matter was the feeling to be expressed (C-XLVII, 623).

If nothing else, the appeal to Wagner was sufficient to corroborate the tacit implications of Fillmore's ostensibly disinterested observation.

Pleasures of the Mind

To the individual who was genuinely dedicated to the creeds of Culture, however, another step was needed to justify art music to

---

connected with action. Most people think before they act—or are supposed to, at any rate, and I must give you the benefit of the doubt. Thought is connected with action, action deals with conduct, and the sphere of conduct is connected with morals. Therefore, ladies and gentlemen, if music is connected with emotion, and emotion is connected with thought, and thought is connected with action, and action is connected with the sphere of conduct, or with morals, things which are connected with the same must be connected with one another, and therefore music must be connected with morals." Emotion is suspect, he declared, because it is "so often misdirected, so often wasted, so often stands for mere gush without sincerity, and has no tendency to pass on into action" (Haweis, *Travel and Talk,* 2 Vols. [New York, 1896], I, 209, 211).

the American people in a sense that was consistent with the concept of the "higher life of the mind"—namely, to show that its apparent emotionality was inherently intellectual in character. This was the definition of the musical experience that best suited the ideals of the Culturists, and once again the example of ancient Greece recommended it. Pure exercise of the intellect was one type of pleasure that Aristotle had connected particularly with music. The noblest use of the art, he taught, is to fill one's leisure with an activity that is altogether good, meaning complete and rational, having form and sweetness, and not being subject to decay.[7]

Early in the Cultured generation Dwight elucidated for thoughtful readers the intellectual nature of music by connecting the best music with the highest, or intellectual, level of human consciousness. Such music, according to Dwight, obeyed its own organic laws without depending on extrinsic relationships like programs, and transcended "music which is shallow, maudlin, commonplace in its expression, attractive to the selfish, sentimental, vulgar mind." "The truest feeling, such as true art, true music breathes and makes appeal to, is of a more intellectual temper," he explained. "Heart quickens brain; then thought reacts on feeling, and carries it up to a sense of perfect order, to a holy love and yearning after unity." Thus the greatest music appealed to the emotions via the intellect, and the conception and perception of forms occupied the greatest composers and the best listeners. The sonata and the fugue were the sublimest of forms, said Dwight, the fugue being "in music what the spiral law of growth is in the plant, . . . the perfect type of unity in variety." Furthermore, the intellectual force of music could be brought to bear upon the listener not just through "theoretic study as such." "By mere familiar intimacy with such forms, such music in the concrete, . . . we become possessed with them, informed with their own spirit, our instincts get attuned into a sympathy with universal law and unity" (A-XXVI, 619–25).

There were, of course, easier ways to relate the higher and lower

7. Aristotle *Politics* 8.

levels of human experience. The one most frequently employed relied upon English empiricism, or associationist psychology. "What is the best thing to do with the mind when listening to music?" wrote a Contributor in the *Atlantic* in 1886.

> "Do nothing with it," some one may reply; "let it take care of itself." But this implies a mistaken idea as to its ways. It seldom does, in point of fact, take care of itself. It is bound to follow the successive suggestions either of certain outside impressions, or of certain inner impressions which also had originally an external source. One may as well choose a little among these.

The choices included imaginary visual panoramas or narratives; or "the music may but breathe an ethereal essence of human life universal, too elusive for any individual incarnation" (A-LVIII, 137–39).

Similarly, George William Curtis held that the pleasures of music were essentially intellectual. Music, he wrote,

> is partly reminiscence—tender association, vague regret, and reverie. The pleasure which the ear—that is to say, the mind through the ear—derives from a single musical sound is akin to that which it gains from color through the eye. But the combination of color, as of sound, is a suggestion of association. Its source is native, not foreign. Fine music does not inspire great thoughts so much as deep emotion (H-XLIV, 458).

The analogy of painting with music was obvious to men familiar with romantic theories of synesthesia. "It is singular," wrote Henry Krehbiel,

> that so many persons who would not admit that they had seen a painting if the vision were so fleeting as to leave the im-

pression only of a mass of colors more or less harmoniously combined, are yet willing to permit a musical composition to pass before their senses like a sort of audible phantasmagoria.

The intellectual activity which music requires is the exercise of the memory, and, lacking this effort, the listener deprives himself of "the pleasure which it is the province of memory to give," he said. "A great deal of music is direct in its influence upon the emotions, but it is chiefly by association of ideas that we recognize its expressiveness or significance" (H-LXXX, 530–36). Obviously, Wagnerian music drama could be easily explained and justified in this way; a music-lover who could identify all the *Leitmotiven* in *Tristan* was trans-mogrified into a Perfect Wagnerite!

The pseudoscientism of associationist theory, combined with the idealism of the transcendentalist aesthetic, served the entire Cultured generation for purposes of abstract argument, music education, and criticism. In 1895 Philip H. Goepp, the Philadelphia organist and writer on music, reasserted the primacy of the symphonic idiom, re-iterated the principle of the coalescence of intellect and emotion in the musical experience, and reviewed the mental operation the sonata required of a listener: "The first object is to grasp the themes, fixing the principal melody in the mind as literally the text or motto of the whole, then awaiting the appearance of the second melody," and so on. Like Dwight, and like Waldo Selden Pratt five years later, Goepp denied the efficacy of programs and programmatic titles and restated the proposition that the object of a symphony "is the communication of a sentiment such as that under which great deeds are done and genuine greatness is achieved, which does not depend for its force on its definability" (A-LXXV, 43–45).

The Mandate for Meliorism

Having established that music was an organic manifestation of cosmic beauty which was apprehensible by the intellect, it remained to be shown how the power of beauty could directly affect the lives of ordinary Americans. Dwight, in 1870, maintained that we needed "this beautiful corrective of our crudities" and that exposure to great music would foster

> a culture moulding us insensibly, a sort of atmospheric culture, weighing gently upon each and all, like wholesome air, expanding the chest, warming the heart, putting the nerves in tune, disposing to unconscious courtesy and kindness, prompting each to fill his place cheerfully and unobtrusively, forgetting self in the harmonious whole, weaving a sympathetic bond, making us all feel like happy, trustful children, free and not afraid.

"The finer the kind of music heard or made together," he concluded, "the better the society" (A-XXVI, 328–29).

At the turn of the century Pratt stated the same ideas:

> In our commercial and materialistic age, we sorely need influences to develop otherwise neglected sides of real life, such as the hunger for the beautiful, the passionate momentum of the eager heart, the reaching up after the invisible and the ideal, the capacity for burning zeal and holy reverence. The function of music and the other fine arts is to help us toward these great experiences (A-LXXXVI, 830).

During the thirty years between Dwight's and Pratt's articles the same basic precepts were repeated over and over, with more or less emphasis and eloquence according to the context in which they were presented, for the Platonic doctrine of the ethical value of music, revived during the middle decades of the century, appealed more widely than any other proposition relating music to American life. The anonymous critic in the Culture and Progress department of the *Century,* for example, wrote that "music, if it means anything, means vital culture—an enlarging and elevating influence for brain and soul" (C-IV, 122). Sidney Lanier was committed to the same general line of thought. Music, he said, is capable of expressing "wise expansions and large tolerances and heavenly satisfactions" which could "stream into the soul of him that hath ears to hear" (C-XIX, 904).

There were still more pragmatic benefits to be derived from the application of music to the problems of daily living. Curtis, for instance, held that beautiful music could exert a positive influence on the lives of the masses, refining their crudities, as Dwight said. Cheap "music for the millions," [8] he believed, was "one of the most refining and civilizing agencies" (H-LXX, 808). The *Century's* critic was convinced that the meliorative benefits of music were specific:

> When one sees the vast silent crowds that drink in the harmonies of Bergmann's and Thomas's orchestras, it is pleasant to think that many in that assembly might, without such opportunities, be sitting in desolate moodiness in narrow city apartments, and slowly laying up the seeds of a disordered brain (C-X, 254).

One of the few writers in the literary magazines who rejected the Platonic view of the function of music in life was Josiah Gilbert Holland, who was skeptical on religious grounds. There was sufficient evidence at hand to suggest that the Muse was not to be trusted with the souls of men. "Does not music purify those who devote their lives to it?" he asked. "Not at all. . . . There is no more reformatory or saving power in music than in the lowest of menial pursuits" (C-XVI, 433). Samuel Osgood, an Episcopal minister who substituted for Curtis in the Editor's Easy Chair for a few months in 1873, was of a similar mind. "We spend time and money on [music] as for no other

---

8. The phrase probably came from the English singing-teacher and musical journalist Joseph Mainzer, via William Henry Fry. See Percy A. Scholes, *The Mirror of Music, 1844–1944*, 2 Vols. (London, 1947), I, 3–10; William Treat Upton, *William Henry Fry, American Journalist and Composer-Critic* (New York, 1954), p. 145.

art," he wrote, "yet it has not ennobled daily life and invigorated and exalted our culture according to its promise" (H-XLVII, 774).

About the only critic who fully embraced the formalist aesthetic of Eduard Hanslick, the famous Viennese critic and champion of Brahms, was Richard Grant White, who, in two articles for the *Atlantic,* summarily dismissed as invalid nearly every notion the Cultured class cherished about music. For fifteen years, he claimed in 1878, he had insisted

> that music is entirely without rational significance or moral power; that the creations of this divine art, while they have an exquisite fitness to certain conditions of feeling (in those who have a certain physical constitution), have rarely any definable meaning; and above all that a fine appreciation of even the noblest music is not an indication of mental ele- vation, or of moral purity, or of delicacy of feeling, or even (except in music) of refinement of taste.

He asserted that, despite the testimony to be found in the works of such literary heroes of the romantic era as Shakespeare, Ruskin, Bulwer, Disraeli, Mme de Staël, and Byron, it was a "fundamental musico-logical fact" that music cannot possibly possess moral prop- erties or ethical powers (A-XLII, 488–93). He took special pains to discredit the Aristotelian doctrine of the purgative power of music and then turned upon the Scottish Realists the very analogy that Thomas Reid, the leader of that school of philosophy, often used: "No one will pretend that the pleasure derived from the form and color or the perfume of a rose is other than sensuous, or has any other than a physical origin." Yet he admitted that music can imbue the listener with a sense of happiness and, "as all happiness gives elevation to man's character and dignifies his life, music has thus indirectly a moral value" (A-XLII, 760).

Arguments like White's evidently failed to sway the majority of Cultured music-lovers from their convictions, however, for though the doctrine of ethos tended to be degrading to music insofar as it equated art with propaganda, it was nevertheless consistent with Arnoldian classicism. Moreover, it allowed certain mid-century ideas as to the social utility of music to survive,[9] satisfying the equalitarianism of the public-school music educationists as well as the altruism of the guardians of Culture; it reconciled ancient musical values with modern democratic circumstances. Only the connection between music and morality, in all its further ramifications, remained to be examined in order to determine the logical as well as the existential integrity of beautiful music as a power in American life.

9. See James H. Stone, "Mid-Nineteenth-Century American Beliefs in the Social Values of Music," *Musical Quarterly*, XLIII (January, 1957), 38–49.

Chapter IV

Music and Morals

RARELY DID A CRITIC for the Cultured class seriously ascribe to music the qualities of morality or immorality as an intrinsic factor. William Dean Howells was merely restating his life-long belief that music ought to occupy a functional place in society when he wrote, in 1889:

> The law of right rests even upon the fabric of sound that comes and goes in a breath; it cannot be defied without shame and ruin. All arts decay when they begin to exist for themselves alone, or merely for the pleasure they can give, since truth beyond and beside them must be their incentive (H-LXXVIII, 820).

Extrinsic relationships established the moral quality—or absence of it —in music.

Morally Questionable Music

Opera was indicted for immorality more readily than any other medium, and the guilt was ascribed on the grounds of association with the theater. "From the dawn of the drama until the present time, the stage has been associated with unworthy lives, impure connections, the most degrading jealousies, the bitterest rivalries, and the most disgusting selfishness," wrote Josiah Gilbert Holland (C-XVI, 433). To a certain extent also, the stigma of opera was a consequence of its traditional support by the wealthy leisure class, and it was often subjected to moral proscriptions on the ground that its cost was inordinately high. It could become moral in proportion to any decrease in its cost to operagoers or, to put it another way, proportionately as its function as a commodity for conspicuous consumption by the Barbarians was diminished. Music "should be more of a brave inspiration than an indolent luxury," said Samuel Osgood from his temporary occupancy of *Harper's* Easy Chair in October, 1873. "The modern opera," he continued,

> is morally and intellectually a monstrosity, and Wagner . . . is probably right in his onslaught upon it, and in his plea for wedding the divine art of song to good sense and manhood, instead of leaving it to the foolish doggerel of the pattern librettos and the harlotry and ruffianism of the pattern heroes and heroines (H-XLVII, 774).

On the contrary, needless to say, Wagnerian opera and music drama, with all their murder and mayhem, adultery and incest, were frequently the subjects of moralistic disquisitions (see Chapter VIII).

The music of the opera was extremely offensive to many Culturists when it was introduced into the worship services of the churches, for its alleged sensuousness was deemed entirely inappropriate—*unseemly* —in such a setting. "People with retentive ears, who sedulously attend church, the opera, and the concert, have a right to dissent from listening on Sunday to the same melodies the week has associated with warbling Manricos and Lucrezias," wrote an anonymous Contributor to the *Atlantic.* Furthermore, he added, "in nine cases out of ten, the maceration and disharmonization of these same melodies by the 'arranger'

introduce a side-question of artistic morality" (A-LI, 282). Richard
Grant White was not as acerbic in his analysis of the problem: "There
has been much outcry amongst those who wear their beards of severe
and formal cut because of the transfer of opera music to the church
choir," he wrote in 1878. "But rarely is there any good reason for this
protest, except on the ground of association" (A-XLII, 757). In any
case, operatic melodies and medleys and the "realistic sentimentalism"
of the church music of certain unnamed French composers (A-XXX,
124) seemed to violate the laws of orderliness and decent sobriety
that were preconditions for the Culturists' religious experiences, the
historical precedents of their own idols, Bach and Handel, Haydn
and Mozart, notwithstanding.

Puritanical rejection of the theater and of all music associated with
it, and the attendant repression of lyric and comic types of musical
drama, had created voids in American life that were readily filled by
imported forms of amusement such as Italian opera and French
opéra bouffe, according to Howells. The impact of the latter upon
the American scene, beginning in 1867 with Offenbach's *La Grande-
Duchesse de Gérolstein* and followed within a year by the same composer's infamous parody *La Belle Hélène,* forcibly raised anew the
issue of the connection between music and morality; for, in addition to
calling up a latent suspicion of French ideas and tastes for idle luxury,
the genre was obviously marked with the stain of lubricity. While the
public responded to the invasion with enthusiastic pleasure, Cultured
observers strove to view the alien intruder with studied objectivity.
Howells, reflecting on the above-mentioned operas, found that, although the music itself was not essentially immoral, the combined
effect of the music, the libretto, and the performance of the talented
star, Mlle Tostée, was one of coarseness and immodesty (A-XXIII,
637). Matilda Despard allowed that even the old Christy Minstrels
were better, or at least less harmful, than "the odious trash of Offenbach, the shameless *opéra bouffe,* which has so vitiated musical taste,
so blunted the sense of purity and modesty in its audiences" (H-LVII,
120).

William Foster Apthorp went so far as to assert that the music of

Offenbach's operas was "often to the full as suggestive of 'the thing unclean' as is the text" and that Offenbach had "most conclusively proved the falsity of the old saying, that 'music is the only art that cannot be made to serve the Devil.' " He regained his Cultured disinterestedness before concluding his remarks, however, and—being a competent critic of drama as well as of music—pointed out that

> free and easy impudence and flippancy are yet better than hypocrisy, and we think that with all its more than doubtful points, *Opéra Bouffe* is better than those so-called "moral sensation dramas" which infest our stage, and which instead of making sin and crime a vehicle for a wholesome moral, desecrate the moral of the fable by using it as a mere pretext for wading through sickening tales of crime and misery, and bringing upon the stage such moral and social garbage as only belongs in a low police court (A-XXIX, 509–10).

In 1874, in response to the torrent of virtuous indignation which Offenbach's *La Périchole* and similar works had elicited from the daily press, Apthorp reiterated that of all the forms of tainted literature and art, including "a large class of French fiction," *opéra bouffe* was by far the least injurious. "Opéra Bouffe," he said soberly, "at most offends the sense of decency" (A-XXXIII, 759).

Even the righteous but loyal John Sullivan Dwight arose to the defense of music's sullied reputation:

> Music may run into frivolity, may be coupled with immodesty, and with sheer atheism, that makes a jest of honesty, believing in no good, as in the *opéra bouffe* of Offenbach; but music in itself has no such tendency. It can be gay, light-hearted, droll, and set the soul free from its mortal clogs a while, . . . but never did it wear filthy channels for itself (A-XXVI, 618).

Relief for troubled moral and aesthetic sensibilities arrived from England in 1879, when Gilbert and Sullivan's good ship *H.M.S.*

Pinafore began to call at American ports. The *Century* claimed that
it was "the best light musical comedy written in our language since
the 'Beggar's Opera'—not excepting Sheridan's 'Duenna,' or Moore's
'M.P.' " It displayed, the Home and Society columnist reported,

> all the good qualities of the best French *opéra bouffes*—with
> none of the bad—none of the blemishes which so often dis-
> figure even the finest French humor. . . . Its humor, its
> satire, its moral—all these are as clean, as honest, as healthy,
> as the most rigid respectability could desire (C-XVII, 904).

George William Curtis called it "a prolonged good-natured laugh set
to music." "With the Easy Chair's compliments to the future discoverer
of this page," he continued, "it would respectfully say that *H.M.S.
Pinafore* is a very much more respectable entertainment than the
opéra bouffe of Offenbach which amused the town a few winters ago"
(H-LVIII, 779). It was also more respectable than the *Black Crook*,
he said (H-LVIII, 932); and it soon stimulated a Gilbert and Sullivan
craze on both the professional and the amateur stage. Frederick Nast
hailed the "new era in the history of music in this country" which the
new English opera had introduced, for now "thousands of the best
people" could with clear consciences allow their wives and daughters
to accompany them to that kind of amusement (H-LXII, 810). Yet
popular antagonism against music in the theater was still so intense
that even *Pinafore* in its relative purity was assailed by some persons
—chiefly from the pulpits—as "utter frivolity" (H-LVIII, 932; H-
LIX, 947).

Opera and the comic theater were not the only harborers of morally
questionable music. At the turn of the century Richard Strauss and
Tchaikovsky were at or near the top of the popularity polls among
symphony-concert patrons, and it was possibly to their music that
Waldo Selden Pratt referred as "certain styles . . . that are now

much in vogue," which tend to exercise a "debilitating and even immoral influence" on listeners. These "deadly forms of delight," he said, possess the power to "instill a peculiarly insidious miasmatic poison of sensuality, or of luxurious indolence, or of downright pessimism" in unsuspecting individuals (A-LXXXVI, 832).

Total Perfection

At some remove from the obvious connections between music and morality in its merely sensuous aspect, there were other factors concerning personal attributes and conduct of or among musicians that were grouped under the heading of morality. Specifically, morally acceptable music was recognizable as the product of a morally admirable man working in an equally virtuous environment; even an "immoral" performer could degrade the art. Pratt's dictum was but a platitude by the time he phrased it in 1900: "As a rule, a composer's style corresponds with fascinating precision to the atmosphere of thought in which he lived, and to the innate quality of his personality" (A-LXXXVI, 831). Dwight had written practically the same thing at the very beginning of the Cultured generation: "Music is an expression of character, of the moods, the spirit, the meaning of the man that makes it. His words can only tell the meaning of his thoughts; his actions, the meaning of his present purpose; his music tells the meaning of *him*" (A-XXVI, 615). Consequently, writers on music were constrained to deal with the lives of musicians and their national backgrounds as much as with their artistic products, if not more so. The doctrine of racism, which was a part of Arnold's concept of Culture, gained momentum toward the close of the century and prevailed well into the following decade, accompanying the rise of full-blown American musical nationalism. "To deny music the racial expression we find so significant in the human face is to withhold from art what nature has given to the flowers, to deprive melody of the color of language," wrote Redfern Mason in 1913, echoing the Darwinian convictions of the Cultured generation.[1]

Arnoldian "total perfection" was at the core of the Culturists' ideal of the moral musician. It was to be attained by living a life of the broadest possible intellectual and experiential scope, though any deviation from a central course between excesses was a step toward a kind of immorality. However much a man might be absorbed in music, Dwight insisted, he "need not be a moral weakling or a fool" (A-XXVI, 616). The ideal musician, to the Cultured class, was a Cultured gentleman who possessed a "disinterested" education and led an orderly, temperate, discriminate, decent life; he was not only the "intellect constructive" but also a moral intellectual. The professional was criticized if he seemed to be excessively preoccupied with music to the exclusion of other matters of the mind. As Horace Elisha Scudder pointed out, "There is a certain thinness about the life of a musician who is only or chiefly an artist" (A-LI, 542).

Above all, the ideal musician had to satisfy the standards of the time-money crasis. He was considered inferior if he did not have steady work and at least a modest income, for, according to Protestant ethics reinforced by Spencerian sociology, if a man were any good he would be "worth something."[2] Seemingly, little allowance was made in the Culturists' concept of genius for undisciplined inspiration or for any conduct of life that might be considered to reflect a merely intuitional approach to artistic creativity. In addition, "mere" virtuosity or "empty display" in a performer was an equivalent of insincerity, which was a mark of "gentility," and that was a deplorable trait. Finally, a musician was considered to be susceptible to immorality if

1. Redfern Mason, "Nationalism in Music," *Atlantic,* CXI (March, 1913), 394–99. As early as 1877 the Englishman Francis Galton, encouraged by Herbert Spencer, had experimented with the use of multiple-exposure techniques to contrive "typical" portraits of faces allegedly representative of specific races or nationalities. See John T. Stoddard, "Composite Photography," *Century,* XXXIII (March, 1887), 750–57.

2. The history of the socioeconomic status of the musician in nineteenth-century America has been discussed by Abram Loft in "Musician's Guild and Union: A Consideration of the Evolution of the Protective Organization among Musicians" (Ph.D. diss., Columbia University, 1950), esp. pp. 294–319.

he was in a position to court fame, since fame was capable of begetting vanity, vanity of jealousies, jealousies of enmities, and enmities of un-Christian behavior.

Felix Mendelssohn-Bartholdy, whose musical and literary images permeated and dominated American musical life throughout the entire second half of the nineteenth century, was recognized as a living denial of all these faults in a musician. While he was alive, American readers were kept apprised of the highlights of his career, not only in the music magazines but also in the general daily and weekly press. Following his death, on November 4, 1847, a flood of eulogies began to appear in America. These, as well as the ensuing translations, summaries, and condensations of his biographies, letters, and memoirs, contributed to the construction of a composite image of the transcendent ideal of a genius and a truly gentle man.

The early eulogists, even more than the later biographers, stressed the composer's wealth, which had guaranteed him immunity from many of the tribulations a young musician was expected to have to undergo and which later signified both his continuing success and his right to it. Emerson's charge that "art is a jealous mistress, and, if a man have a genius for . . . music, . . . he makes a bad husband and an ill provider"[3] was not applicable to Mendelssohn. On the contrary, as William B. Bradbury wrote to the *New York Tribune* on the day of the composer's interment: "He has left a young and accomplished wife and four beautiful children to mourn his loss; but *not* as is too often the case with men of talent, without pecuniary support: Mendelssohn was rich."[4]

The Mendelssohn family's wealth enabled him to acquire extraordinary educational advantages, and its social position allowed personal associations and leisure habits through which he embraced an unusually wide variety of interests and accomplishments. As a result, he possessed a humanistic culture and a breadth of intellect equaled by few musicians anywhere, which appealed profoundly to thoughtful

3. Ralph Waldo Emerson, *The Works of Ralph Waldo Emerson*, 5 Vols. (New York, n.d.), III, 76.
4. *New York Tribune*, December 13, 1847.

Americans. Mendelssohn was doubly admirable: not only was he rich—he was smart!

The most impressive evidence of the scope of Mendelssohn's interests and background, and of his character, was found in his letters; they showed the "everyday side of his genius" (A-LXIII, 270; see Plate 1). W. L. Gage recommended the two-volume American edition of the *Letters . . . 1833 to 1847,* therefore, as "books which our young men, our young women, our pastors, our whole thoughtful and aspiring community, ought to read and circulate" (A-XV, 127). The letters to Moscheles contained affirmations of his opposition to the grandiloquent pianism of fashionable virtuosos like Franz Hünten and his pupil Henri Herz, as well as to the contemporary vogue of program music. His early admirers had already termed him "original" in the sense that he had produced unique musical utterances without employing the hollow gestures of the showmen or the extramusical references of the "upstart school" of Berlioz and Liszt. His dedication to the sheer power of structural and lyrical beauty in music appeared to have been deliberate and steadfast.

Even more important than his economic security, his intellectual superiority, and his musical purity was his moral integrity. It was observed that, owing to his inherent strength of character, he was neither selfish nor lazy, despite his wealth.[5] Moreover, few men could boast a life so energetic, a career so successful, and a fame so widespread, yet remain wholly untainted by darkened episodes. "There is nothing to forgive, nothing to be sorry for," one critic exclaimed (A-XXXI, 420). No writer on Mendelssohn in America pretended that he had been unfamiliar with adversity, but few denied that he had been aptly named—Felix—and that he had continually displayed charity and equanimity in his dealings with others. Apthorp's judgment was typical:

> His whole life, as performer, conductor, and man, was one unintermittent struggle to promote the welfare of all that was

5. *Literary World,* January 22, 1848.

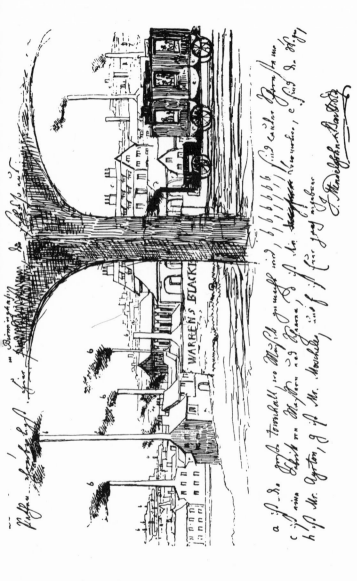

PLATE 1. Cultured readers admired Mendelssohn's interest in the broader aspects of human experience, evidenced in the sketches with which he frequently illuminated his letters. Readers could no doubt identify with him also because of his sensitivity to the quality of his environment, as reflected in this pen drawing of Birmingham, England, in which the ubiquitous belching chimneys (*lauter Schornsteine*) of the factories are most conspicuous. Reprinted in Apthorp's article "Mendelssohn's Letters to Moscheles" (S-III, 142).

purest and most without reproach in music. No man ever had a higher ideal of what an artist should be, and few have lived up to that ideal with such inexorable conscientiousness (S-III, 332).

In Mendelssohn, great art and a noble life were reconciled as in no other single individual. He was a conspicuously Cultured, Christian gentleman.

Mendelssohn's musical image was equally pure and spotless. Much of his piano music, especially the *Songs without Words,* and some of his orchestral work, especially the *Midsummer Night's Dream* music, provided an important staple in American concert life from the urban centers of the east coast to the remote frontiers of Arizona and Montana. *Elijah,* however, was perhaps the best known of Mendelssohn's works among American musicians and music-lovers. Oratorio was recognized as the preeminently respectable musical genre, partly because it employed large numbers of citizen-musicians, partly because it was ostensibly religious in character, and partly because oratorio performances were often devoted to the benefit of charities. Thus the early and persistent popularity of *Elijah* in America perhaps may be ascribed to the fact that the association of the music of Mendelssohn with the exercise of the democratic opportunity and the implicit discharge of a Christian duty was sufficient to outweigh all other apologies for the art of music.

When combined, Mendelssohn's literary and musical images strengthened the Platonic view of the nature and function of music that dominated nineteenth-century American attitudes toward art. It was assumed that so perfect a man as he would naturally produce the noblest music conceivable, and it in turn would elevate and purify the souls of all Americans. He was an ideal for all aspiring American musicians to emulate, and the Cultured class desired all American musicians to resemble him.

The Qualities of Manliness

Not the least of Mendelssohn's attributes, in the view of thoughtful Americans, was his manliness. Since so much of America's musical life was patronized and conducted by women, especially in the parlor where the average man encountered it, music was popularly regarded as a woman's affair; male musicians were effeminized by implication. Therefore, critics and apologists were careful to call attention to notable manifestations of the opposite tendency when they were present.

Manliness was discernible in objective terms of physical appearance; a decent musician would *look* like other men, in dress and bearing. In 1884 the reviewer of the "Paris Classical Concerts" observed that the pianist Francis Planté was "slight, pale, and gentleman-like, looking on the whole not unlike a certain good type of American, and with nothing of the lion about him except the superfine manner in which he poised his fingers upon the keyboard." No doubt the Cultured American could readily visualize himself in the audience at the Conservatoire: "There are a few women of fashion in the boxes, but the majority of the hearers are men—men not of elegance, but of distinction" (A-LIII, 743, 752). Charles Santley, a renowned English baritone, was judged by one critic to be uninspiring as a singer, but to have at least "a chaste, manly style" (C-III, 502). Paderewski was credited by William Mason for his "broad and calm, manly and dignified" interpretations of Beethoven (C-XLIII, 723).

The qualities of manliness might also be located in the image a musician presented as a productive member of society; a decent musician would *live* like other citizens. Hans von Bülow, who toured in America three times between 1870 and 1890, personified the ideal that Americans cherished of the musician whose existence was integral with daily life on an economic basis. As the piano pedagogue Bernard Boekelman said, Bülow

resented the idea that musicians should be treated differently from other men. He wished music to be a manly calling. He

would not have it degraded into a matter of patronage. . . .
To build music up into the rank and standing of an independent profession was the dream and struggle of Bülow's life.
Every musician who values his own manhood owes to him an
opportunity of self-respect heretofore unheard of (C-LII,
466).

The Role of Women

Self-respect on the grounds of manliness could also be nourished by clarifying the distinctions between the roles of the sexes in
music. For example, Edith Brower explained the absence of women
among the recognized musical geniuses of the world by arguing that
"woman is less idealistic than man," that "man, not woman, is the
emotional being *par excellence*," and that, since music is an idealiza-
tion of emotion, men, not women, logically have the capacity for
greatness in music. The "musical idea," she concluded, is *masculine*
(A-LXXIII, 332–39). On the other hand, Rupert Hughes maintained
that women are more emotional than men but that "the evolution of
music has made it so complex that it demands . . . a special aptitude
for invention, which has been rare among women," and that therefore
men are the better composers, while women are the better performers
(C-LV, 768).

Most orchestra players, in fact, were men; though arguments like
Hughes's seemed reasonable, women in general were reluctant to
devote themselves to media other than the voice or the piano. Sidney
Lanier suggested, in 1880, that women's roles in performance could
be expanded to a mutually profitable degree.

Let our young ladies . . . address themselves to the violin,
the flute, the oboe, the harp, the clarionet, the bassoon, the
kettle-drum. It is more than possible that upon some of these
instruments the superior daintiness of the female tissue might
finally make the woman a more successful player than the
man (C-XIX, 902).

Whether Lanier's encouragement had any direct, immediate effect is uncertain, but within a decade or so there were several amateur all-female orchestras in existence, such as the Fadette Ladies' Orchestra of Boston, consisting of fourteen women under the direction of Carrie B. Nichols.[6]

A woman's place was in the home, however, and there music might serve a moral use as an element of beauty to soothe the pangs inflicted upon her husband by the market place, as well as to distract her from the frustration of her own lot. The Reverend Hugh Reginald Haweis wrote that

> many a woman, though capable of so much, is frequently called upon in the best years of her life to do but little, but at all times society imposes upon her a strict reticence as to her real feelings. What is she to do with the weary hours, with the days full of the intolerable sunshine, and the nights full of the pitiless stars? . . . To women—and how many thousands are there in our placid modern drawing-rooms!— who feel like this, music comes with a power of relief and a gentle grace of ministration little short of supernatural (H-XLIV, 760).

There was good reason to guard against the indiscriminate encouragement of womanly music-making in the American parlor, according to Holland, for the time and money spent on the musical education of young ladies with such a purpose in view was frequently extravagant, and often futile, and in those instances immoral. Too often, he lamented,

> under the tuition of her teacher, the universal American girl learns her dozen pieces so as to play them fairly, and never goes beyond them. These she plays until they are worn out to her own ear, and the ears of her friends; gradually she

---

6. *Boston Evening Transcript*, March 20, 1893.

loses her power to play these well; and then she drops the
piano altogether, especially if she is married. The money paid
for her accomplishment, and the precious time she has ex-
pended upon it, are a dead loss.

The whole system, Holland implied, was evil.

A method of teaching which universally produces the result
of dependence upon the teacher, stands self-condemned. What
would be thought of a teacher of mathematics who, under
fair conditions, could not teach his pupils to reason for themselves? (C-X, 110; see also A-LIX, 569–70).

To many readers of the literary magazines, morality had a simpler
and more sensational definition, and Jenny Lind was described as the
perfect example of a morally upright female musician. She was
remembered for the "moral worth of her character, even by those who
were mainly concerned with her artistic work"; her abdication of her
position as leading prima donna of the operatic stage was applauded
as evidence of her "love of home" and "craving for domestic peace"
—both desirable and presumably traditional Swedish and American
virtues (C-XLV, 207–8). She had, another critic reminded his readers,
unusual intellectual culture and "a character of unaffected goodness,
kindness, and high moral principle," qualities that were "struggling
to find expression in our own American artists and composers." She
was said to possess "dignity and innocence" and "chastity" and appealed to "emotions that not only are most natural, but are most
sedulously cultivated, in American women." Finally, she was the
personification of Arnold's Cultured individual: Jenny Lind was "full
of sweetness and light—of *kindly* light. Her message was optimistic. . . . The 'enthusiasm of humanity' pervaded it" (C-LIV, 554,
559).

The Qualities of Genius

There was only one way that a musician who could not satisfy all the canons of gentlemanliness might achieve fame, though it was all but inaccessible to an American: by acclamation as an eccentric luminary. The *genuine* eccentric luminary, as opposed to the merely unconventional-looking "artiste" with "loose locks and disordered appearance" (H-LX, 831), had a public history as well as a half-obscure private history, both real and true enough to invite serious examination and speculation. His quaint idiosyncrasies in the area of "minor morals" were the very badges of his eminence; his major departures from morality were usually overlooked. Liszt, said by William Mason to have possessed an "intellectual-emotional" temperament (C-XLIII, 722),[7] exhibited positive musical qualities that amply compensated for the flaws in his personality. "His caprices are sometimes tyrannical," reported the *Century,* "but those who are permitted to listen to his matchless play, feel amply repaid for all the whims of the great artist" (C-II, 211). Beethoven, Handel, Schumann, Schubert, and Chopin each displayed the marks of the genus, but Dwight explained that the stigmas were but proof that the men were ahead of their times. "*Their* souls were strung up to heaven's concert pitch; it was the age, the world around them, that was false and gave out an uncertain and bewildering sound" (A-XXVI, 618). Emily Royall said of Berlioz that "his genius was unique, his character heroic, his life a tragedy" (H-LX, 411).[8] Verdi's "peculiar habits" were noted, and Félicien David and even Jean-Jacques Rousseau were presented with similar frankness as romantic heroes with colorful

---

7. Arnold T. Schwab suggests that this comment is Huneker's. See Schwab, *James Gibbons Huneker* (Stanford, 1963), p. 63.

8. In 1879 Apthorp published a book of excerpts from Berlioz' prose writings in which he sought, through his selections, to show "what the man was, rather than what he did," pending the judgment of the future as to the greatness of his music. See A-XLI, 32–42; A-XLV, 699–702; A-XLVIII, 746–51; A-LXIII, 846–50; A-LXXII, 560.

personalities and picturesque careers (see C-XXXI, 414; H-LIV, 15–18; H-LIV, 206–9; H-LVIII, 229–34). At a time when the anti-anarchist hysteria brought on by the Haymarket Riot of 1886 compelled editors to expunge the very word *dynamite* from stories and articles, no one recalled the political escapades of the youthful Berlioz or Wagner. On the contrary, the spectacle of a figure like Liszt or Berlioz or Wagner, glorified by ever-expanding companies of dedicated followers after long and bitter struggles with societal or professional persecution, seemed to hold a special fascination for the Culturists, perhaps because it embodied the triumph of an individual over a hostile environment—the survival of the fittest.

An American could hardly dare to aspire to this status, for eccentricities in an American were liable to be construed as bad manners, bad character, or bad citizenship. Degeneracy was excusable only in the life of a European. Thus the problem of the public status of the artist in America was paradoxical. If a musician fitted integrally into his artistic and social milieu, as he was expected to, then there was no more to be said about him than about any other ordinary man; he had no flair, no flash, and he stirred no giddy homage. He could transcend his circumstances only through his music, which had to meet rigid standards of excellence. Even when his music warranted praise, it redounded on him only as an "intellect constructive." No critic in the literary magazines ever attempted to "discover" or contrive an American counterpart to Liszt, Berlioz, or Wagner. Dudley Buck, John Knowles Paine, William Wallace Gilchrist, and Edward MacDowell were respectable skillful artisans who gradually earned their reputations by occasionally producing works of recognizable intrinsic merit.

It was extremely difficult for an American composer to join the ranks of Emerson's "representative men." The closest America came to the possession of such a figure was in Theodore Thomas, who combined the strongest qualities of the Cultured musician with some of the badges of eccentric luminescence. In the face of continual criticism, widespread misunderstanding, and numerous personal and professional misfortunes, he carried forward a methodical educational theory, employing music and a musical discipline often surpassing European models, with the express purpose of improving American musical tastes. He was an uncommon, universal man, a true servant of the people. He had a function in society, and he was evidently always busy, and usually successful, at it. What is more, he could show at least some profit; he had "won his prosperity without stooping for it" (C-IX, 458); he had conducted his career with decency and integrity; he was a moral gentleman. Unfortunately he was not a composer, and, in view of the disinclination of music historians to see the art in its full scope as a social act, he counts hardly for anything in textbooks.

Chapter V

The Progress of Taste

THERE WAS NO DOUBT in anyone's mind that the United States had made material advances at an astounding rate during its short history; that was a matter of international envy. It was also obvious to the Cultured class, which paid close attention to such things, that great strides had been made aesthetically, too, and in music most of all; and they sought to make that a matter of national pride. In 1881 Frederick Nast asserted that, although the fine arts and the drama had made noticeable progress throughout the United States during the preceding generation, "in neither of these has the advance been so great as in music" (H-LXII, 804). Nearly thirty years later, in 1907, the critic and essayist Hamilton Wright Mabie reiterated the point: "In no art has there been so rapid and so wide a growth of intelligent interest during the last fifty years" as in the art of music.[1] Extravagant as such statements may seem, there was abundant evidence to prove that they were true, and writers on music for the literary magazines documented them by contrasting the present with the past, especially "before the war"; by reporting and analyzing musical condi-

1. Hamilton Wright Mabie, "Art," *Atlantic,* C (November, 1907), 633.

tions on the western frontier; and by comparing American with European conditions in musical taste and activity.

Upward, Unbound

There appeared to be a groundswell of demand by concert-goers for music of better and better quality, as well as a continual change in interests with respect to media. John Rose Green Hassard observed in 1875 that

> no manager would venture now to fill a concert programme with such rubbish as we used to applaud five or six years ago —polkas for the cornet, operatic pot-pourris, and worthless marches—and though it is still prudent, even for Theodore Thomas, to add a little music for beginners to his summer selections, the quality of these trifles is always at least respectable, and their number is fast diminishing (C-IX, 462).

The gradual advance in taste had already been seen in an increased interest in programs of chamber music (C-IV, 122). Matilda Despard perceived that up to 1878 New York audiences had moved, step by step,

> through quaint old English operettas, English versions of Italian and German operas, pure Italian and German compositions of Rossini, Bellini, Verdi, Spohr, Weber, and Mendelssohn, up to the present high development of taste for and appreciation of Meyerbeer [!], Gounod, Schumann, and colossal Richard Wagner, at last—giant destroyer of ancient opera traditions (H-LVII, 115).

The trend continued, and George William Curtis predicted in 1882 that the coming May Festival under Theodore Thomas in New York would reveal "the growth of the taste for music other than the opera." "There is a general consciousness," he wrote, "of the beginning of a new musical epoch. The phrase, 'music of the future,' which was so long ridiculed as the affectation of musical aesthetes, has acquired a distinct significance" (H-LXIV, 308). Cultured critics expected change, desired improvement, and discovered both.

By Cultured standards, the basic aesthetic motivations of American audiences were improving, also. "Our New York public," wrote the Culture and Progress columnist for the *Century* in 1872, "can count an ever larger class of cultivated people who love music simply, purely, and for its own sake. The fact is full of promise" (C-IV, 122; see Plate 2). There were skeptics, of course, who doubted the sincerity of the affection and the reliability of the promise, but one of Boston's oldest and most highly respected musicians, Benjamin Lang, answered their objections in 1894:

> It is a well-known fact that many persons who today show much interest in music confessedly cared nothing about it some years ago. The question naturally arises, Is this departure genuine? To say that it is not, and to suggest fashion as the probable cause, is to match shallowness with shallowness.

Widening interest in Wagnerian music drama, with its alliance of music and "the romantic in literature," supplied incontrovertible evidence of the authenticity of the "departure." After all, he pointed out, "journeys to and from Baireuth for the hearing of a single opera . . . are experiences not persistently endured for fashion's sake" (A-LXXIII, 208–9).

Moreover, there were ample indications that a taste for good music was emerging in countless individuals with little or no background or experience in music, and it was clear to many observers that Thomas' programs had either caused or encouraged that tendency. Thomas' work, said the Culture and Progress columnist in 1873, had "opened to the multitude a treasury which was closed before to all

PLATE 2. *Matinee at the Academy of Music.* Rehearsals of the New York Philharmonic Society were open to the public, ostensibly for the benefit of serious music-lovers who wished to hear a given program more than once. Early in the 1870s tickets were fifty cents for the first and second weekly rehearsals and one dollar for the third, compared with two dollars for the regular evening concerts. The result was recorded in this cartoon by the New York painter and illustrator, Thomas Worth (C-III, 512).

except a few highly educated connoisseurs." The columnist, reporting on Thomas' performance of the Ninth Symphony in New York in the spring of that year, found "cheering evidence of progress" in the fact that "two or three thousand people, representing all classes, the accomplished musician, and the tyro who has hardly got beyond the scales, listened to it with a delight that was almost rapturous" (C-VI, 372).

The increase in the number of teachers, composers, and performers, especially singers, was keeping pace with other aspects of musical maturation. "The progress which the American people show in every branch of music is remarkable," wrote one critic in 1883, "and not less astonishing is the great number of young people having beautiful voices" (C-XXVII, 159; see also C-XXII, 125). More importantly, the scope and depth of musical literacy was advancing among the people, and ready proof was to be found, for example, in the growing number of civic choirs, as well as in the noticeable improvement in the quality of their performances. Curtis took pride in pointing out in 1887 that American audiences included many persons who were capable of following performances with a score and were themselves admirable performers, whose skill was "known only to the domestic circle" and who represented "a great mass of musical knowledge, taste, ability and training" (H-LXXIV, 977). More objective evidence of the high level of musical literacy among the Cultured class is present in the numerous musical illustrations that accompanied many of the critical and historical articles in the quality magazines.

The American musical imagination was improving, too, and Cultured critics were sensitive to derogatory remarks about it. In the *Century* in 1887 George H. Wilson, a leading American vocal pedagogue and choral conductor, took offense at Charles Barnard's implication that trivial works like G. F. Root's cantata *The Flower Queen* represented the current level either of American audiences' tastes or of American composers' aspirations.

The reminiscences and historical sketches by Curtis, Richard Grant White's four-part series on opera in New York, beginning with the March, 1882, issue of the *Century,* and other retrospective surveys dated the beginning of America's growth toward musical maturity at around 1825, the year Manuel Garcia introduced Italian opera to New York.[2] John Sullivan Dwight set it in the forties, when the Brook Farmers studied Beethoven sonatas and the masses of Mozart and Haydn and walked to town to hear more "great music . . . in full affinity with the best thoughts stirring in fresh, earnest souls" played at the Academy of Music (A-XXVI, 323). Americans of the mid-century generation had heard Jenny Lind, Alboni, Thalberg, Ole Bull, Vieuxtemps, Wieniawski, Artot, "and other, slighter figures" (H-LVIII, 777), and the fund of experiences and traditions of the prewar period was made to serve as a basis for present Cultured growth toward an even more perfect future. Quasi-historical studies were indulged in, not for their own sake, but to isolate and elucidate the promises the past held for the future in the name of progress. As late as 1914, Arthur Farwell, himself an offspring of the Cultured generation, wrote, "Prophecy, not history, is the most truly important concern of music in America." [3]

There were also strictly material evidences of musical progress. When Jenny Lind toured America at mid-century few auditoriums were large enough to accommodate the audiences she attracted, but by the end of the century some of the finest public halls in the world had been built. More and more of the Barbarians were beginning to see their duty and do their part, especially during the prosperous seventies. In Cincinnati, the first of Thomas' great festivals, in 1875, inspired generous philanthropy. One man gave $50,000 "for music in the park *in perpetuo,"* and another citizen gave $125,000 toward a music hall. "The men of wealth vie with one another in munificence toward all objects that elevate the social, intellectual, and asethetic tone of the people" (C-X, 510). It required very little effort in the next decade to build a Metropolitan Opera House or a National Conservatory of Music.

---

2. See Curtis' articles in H-XLII, 295–96; H-XLVIII, 291–93; H-LXI, 307–8; H-LXXXIII, 633–34. See also H-LXIII, 306–7; H-LXIX, 388–404.
3. *The Art of Music* (New York, 1914), IV, *Music in America,* ed. Arthur Farwell and W. Dermot Darby, vii.

Even the topics of writings about music, other than the historical essays and reminiscences, may be interpreted as indices to the scope of progress. William Foster Apthorp's article "Orchestral Conducting and Conductors" (S-XVII, 384–92), the author himself said, was demanded by a growing popular interest in the subject, as evidenced by an exceptionally large amount of newspaper publicity devoted to certain notable conductors. ("Printer's ink is a pretty sure gauge of popular interest in any question," he remarked.) Moreover, he continued,

> were this particular interest an isolated fact, a mere passing fashion or fad, unconnected with the progress of the Art of Music itself, it would have little significance. But this is not so; it is to be recognized as a direct outcome of the modern artistic spirit, a sign of the times, and is hence worth studying.

Cultured individuals despised mere fashions and fads.

The German Element

Every thoughtful observer realized, and often acknowledged, that the principal stimulus to musical progress in America had long been "the large German element," which had superseded the "melodious Italian traditions" in the development of American musical taste (H-LXXIV, 979). As far back as the early forties, when a concert was an event, "professional" church choirs were rare, and piano-playing was an almost undeveloped art, "the resident musicians were nearly all English or Anglo-American, but already German talent and influence were beginning to share the honors and the profits" (H-LVII, 115). The influx of Germans at the end of the same decade reinforced the trend, especially through the Germania Orchestra. "The very unprecedented popularity of the organization at this time," wrote Joseph Bunting, referring to the season of 1852–53,

certainly exercised a powerful influence over the taste of the
public. Negro minstrelsy declined. Music at the theaters became almost passable; dancing music and even street bands
improved, particularly in the character of their selections,
because the people demanded better food than the diet of
previous years (C-XI, 105).

The Germans provided the example of amateur neighborhood choral
societies, and groups like the Sylvania Vocal Society, a suburban New
York chorus, were the result. "There is no element of national character which we so much need," said Dwight, "and there is no class of
citizens whom we should be more glad to adopt and own than those
who set us such examples" (A-XXVI, 329).

George P. Upton was lavish in his tribute to immigrant German
musicians:

They form the overwhelming majority of military band and
orchestral players in the United States. . . . Their music
constitutes the principal part of every programme. Their
instrumental artists, notably violinists and pianists, are the
principal interpreters of the higher music. To their conductors the American public largely owes whatever of musical
taste and culture its possesses. It has been acquired under the
tuition of such eminent leaders as Anschutz, Eisfeld, Bergmann, Thomas, Mosenthal, Zerrahn, Kotzschmar, Hendschel
[sic], Gericke, Damrosch, Seidl, Van der Stucken, Balatka,
Singer, and many others. Amid many discouragements they
have always remained true to the highest ideals (S-XIV, 73).

Curtis was more eloquent, but no less earnest:

Some future poet will say that of all of the good fairies who
came to the birth of the free nation, none was more generous
than Teutonia, who brought the refining, elevating, human-
izing gift of music (H-LXIII, 305).

The impact of German traditions upon American musical life was notably visible in the West. The presence of a great number of German-born people in Cincinnati contributed measurably to the successes of Thomas' festivals there, while in Chicago, wrote Curtis, "upon the shore of Lake Michigan, so large is the German element of the population that Beethoven and Mozart are household words" (H-LII, 610).

Inasmuch as the leading literary magazines found most of their readers in the urban centers of the Northeast, their reportorial contents were oriented chiefly toward local persons, places, and events. Relatively little attention was paid to happenings elsewhere, so references to the musical life of the West might tend by their scarcity to attract the student's attention disproportionately to their significance. Nevertheless, it is clear that even if interest in the musical life of Cincinnati and Chicago was partly due to an interest in Thomas' career and to concern for the possible effects of his midwestern successes upon music in New York and Boston, a considerable amount of it was also due to a growing national pride in the evidence that the sense of the power of beauty was moving westward with the frontier.

The influences of Thomas and of lesser German immigrant musicians were often cited as the principal stimuli to musical growth in the West—to the Mississippi, and beyond; but there were unique psychological and sociological factors at work as well. "The progress of Western culture has been distinguished by the characteristic haste and impetuosity of that rapid region," noted a writer in 1875, "so that it has reached in two years the result which the East hardly accomplished in six" (C-IX, 463). Josiah Gilbert Holland considered Cincinnati a more musical city than New York and claimed that the festival there in 1875 had been, perhaps, "the greatest musical achievement of which our new country can boast—greater than New York has ever known—great beyond New York's present possibilities" (C-X, 510). Indeed, it sometimes seemed that the West would outreach the East in such achievements; for, although Boston was still recognized as the guardian of New England culture, Baltimore, the scene of the first triumph of the Germania Orchestra, had long since ceased to thrive musically. The course of American musical life was invincibly onward and upward; its destiny was preordained.

Signs of Growth

Ignorance of the effects of progress upon American musical life could be embarrassing to a European performer seeking to win additional fame in the United States. Critics were wary of outworn virtuosos seeking to grant the boon of their fading light to a benighted land, as Grisi, Tamburini, and Lablache had done in the fifties and early sixties. Critics expected mature, seasoned artists in the prime of their careers, equal to the exertions of the competitive musical market place America had become after the war. When singers like Enrico Tamberlik arrived, or when Mario returned, they were given notice they could not fool American audiences. They were viewed as "operatic reliques" who could arouse no more than "a little stir of sympathetic curiosity" (C-VIII, 246).

In 1882, after conquering all the chief cities in Europe as an opera diva, the great coloratura singer Adelina Patti returned to New York, where she had made her debut thirty-one years earlier, and reintroduced herself with a concert of simple ballads such as might have appealed to audiences in the fifties. Cultured Americans were chagrined, and Curtis felt constrained to apologize for her from the Easy Chair: "She knew that the Philharmonic Concerts at that time [1851] . . . were not the delight of the great public. She knew also that Jenny Lind sang only in concerts, in supposed deference to the great 'serious' public sentiment of the country, which was not friendly to the theatre." She had not suspected, he explained, that the country she had revisited was "an America which had half out-grown the Italian opera." It was, indeed, a cultivated, intelligent, musically developed America, "accustomed to hear the greatest works of the greatest masters performed in a manner which would not discredit the Akademie in Berlin, the Gewandhaus in Leipsic, the Conservatoire in Paris" (H-LXIV, 467–68).

Possibly the most gratifying signs of progress, to thoughtful men, were found in the contrasts that were apparent even to the casual critic between American and European conditions. The slightest evidence that European civilization was, as many Americans suspected, decaying was readily convertible into proof that American civilization was vital. Whether at any time American conservatories actually were superior, Boston programs more sublimely classical, New York concert life more various, than those in Berlin, Paris, or London was of minor importance if it momentarily *seemed* that such was the case and that, in its musical life, a youthful American civilization was gradually but incontrovertibly surpassing its aging parent.

Hassard claimed that symphonic music was appreciated more genuinely in the United States than in any other country except Germany (C-IX, 462). In addition, American audiences were capable of recognizing and securing the best talent from abroad. Whereas formerly the greatest stars had come to America only after they had passed the peaks of their careers in Europe, the *Century's* Culture and Progress editor observed that, by 1872, "many a light of the artistic world, in the zenith of his power and fame, finds the temptations of Yankee managers strong enough to draw him from the choicest blandishments of Old World capitals" (C-V, 129–30).

Testimony in behalf of the United States supplied gratuitously by European musicians was particularly reassuring. In 1881 Sir Julius Benedict, who came to America with Jenny Lind and stayed to teach, averred that America possessed extraordinary musical resources, since "New York, Boston, Philadelphia, Chicago, and Cincinnati can boast of operatic establishments equal, or, in many cases, superior to those of Paris, London, Milan, Berlin, or Vienna, not to speak of the recent gigantic musical festivals of Philadelphia and Boston" (C-XXII, 132).

It was also satisfying merely to identify the areas in which American musical life equaled that of Europe. Rupert Hughes wrote in 1898 that the three countries that were then "working along the best lines of modern music" were Germany, France, and—America!" "Its tendencies are towards the best things," he said (C-LV, 770). In 1878 *Harper's* Easy Chair expressed the confident opinion that the

Philharmonic under Thomas was playing as well as the orchestras at the Sing-Akademie in Berlin and the Conservatoire in Paris; many concerts in New York, said Curtis, could afford comparison with the best in Europe. More and more European artists were appearing in America, and in 1881 Curtis thought it would soon be unnecessary to go to Europe to hear the finest music. In the spring of 1888 he said that the recent musical season in New York had been more interesting than in any other great city in the world.

In his short series of detailed articles on Parisian theaters, Apthorp described some musical conditions in France by drawing comparisons with corresponding circumstances in the United States. He explained that the famous orchestras of Edouard Colonne and Charles Lamoureux were to be ranked "about with the New York and Boston symphony orchestras, perhaps a little below the latter" (S-XI, 496). He deprecated the programs of the two Parisian orchestras for their conservative character and especially for their unmistakable deference to popular taste. "You only semi-occasionally," he complained, "see an instance of that purely art-for-art's sake spirit which has long been conspicuous in musical doings in New York, and perhaps still more so in Boston." "Mozart, Haydn, Beethoven, Schubert, Weber, and Mendelssohn are played continually," he wrote, whereas "very little by Raff, Dvořák, Goldmark, or Grieg has been given in Paris; only one symphony by Brahms (the No. 2, in D) has ever been played there." Wagner was the only foreign composer who was popular then (S-XI, 634).[4] Finally, Apthorp contrasted Parisian with American stages:

> I doubt whether any theatre in Paris has its stage completely lighted by electricity alone; certainly such a perfect system of electric lighting as is to be found at the new Tremont

4. All of these composers were well known to American audiences and were found in Thomas' programs (see Theodore Thomas, *A Musical Autobiography*, ed. George P. Upton, 2 Vols. [Chicago, 1905], II, 359–71). Brahms's Second Symphony was first performed in this country by Thomas in 1878, the year after it was composed.

Theatre in Boston is utterly unknown there. The very description of it, given to a noted Paris stage-manager by an American, was received with evident incredulity. It takes half as many men again to shift scenery as it does in our new theatres (S-XI, 632).

American ingenuity also enabled the Metropolitan Opera House to surpass Wagner's own *Festspielhaus* in the contrivance of effective stage machinery (C-LIX, 63–76). But then, in the purely technological sphere, Yankees simply could not be equaled by anyone.

The Progress of Disenchantment

After 1880, claims of the beneficence of progress were made with gradually diminishing frequency and emphasis. Although advances continued to be made—for example, permanent orchestras were established in Boston and Chicago—little or no notice of them was recorded by writers in the literary magazines. In fact, Henry Krehbiel observed in 1887 that the people of America, "taken as a whole," did not always seek out the best art and that, in that sense, the taste of the musical public was in reality quite low (C-XXXV, 317). In a similar vein, Edvard Grieg uttered the familiar despairing cry of the romantic artist trapped in the democratic environment and sounded an early note of the twentieth-century disenchantment with the ideals of the Cultured class that soon was to permeate the entire art life of the United States:

> It is rarely the happiest inspirations of a creative spirit that win the hearts of the many. In that respect the musical intelligence of the so-called cultivated society leaves much to be desired. . . . Everywhere it is cheap art which has a monopoly of appeal to the general intelligence (C-XLVII, 447).

To the Culturally faithless, the dilemma was inescapable and unresolvable; the future was bleak, and even the past looked dreary.

"After the war," Henry C. Lahee perceived from the superior vantage point of 1902,

> the conditions changed. Many musical societies were formed, but with the increase of wealth and culture there became a wider difference between the advanced and the elementary grades of knowledge. Thus while a high class of music was cultivated amongst the few, the masses of people did not advance—in fact they appear to have retrograded.[5]

If that was true, it was not for lack of deliberate constructive effort on the part of the Cultured class.

5. Henry C. Lahee, "A Century of Choral Singing in New England," *New England Magazine,* n.s. XXVI (1902), 111.

Chapter VI

Meliorism through Music

THE PRINCIPAL DUTY of the Cultured class being the improvement of American society, and the chief utility of music being, according to the Platonic aesthetic to which that class subscribed, the building of good citizens, it was incumbent upon Cultured music-lovers to extend the benefits of the art to all persons and to insure that those benefits would be intelligently seized. "Consider . . . the simplest, *prima facie* claim of music; consider its civilizing agency, so far as it may become part of the popular, the public education," wrote John Sullivan Dwight in 1870. "We need this beautiful corrective of our crudities" (A-XXVI, 326). The ambitions of the musical meliorists were supported by the assumptions that the highest musical experience was an exercise of the intellect and that music itself was a kind of symbolic language, consisting of a variety of dialects ranging from vulgar to refined and employing a vocabulary that could be systematically imparted to benighted or deprived individuals.

The Education of Audiences

The musical education of adults was the most pressing concern, and the best classroom for that purpose was the concert hall. Within it the individual could learn a sense of the power of beauty at his own pace and evolve into a music-lover to the extent of his natural capacity. The public concert was a self-regulating institution: neophytes were afforded continuous experiences that would cumulatively result in broader knowledge and understanding, and at the same time pleasure was afforded to those among the audiences already sufficiently cultivated to appreciate them fully. The example of European concert life spurred the efforts of the Culture-guardians. "The popular concerts of Vienna are perhaps the most effectual in training the musical apprehensions of the people: time, form, rhythm, are unconsciously borne in upon them," wrote the New York author Mary Alice Seymour from abroad (H-LXIV, 826).

The concept of the concert hall as a classroom gained momentum after the war, though it had been implicit in the work of the Germania Orchestra at mid-century. William Foster Apthorp noted in 1872 that, although the symphony concerts of the Harvard Musical Association had originally been organized, in 1865, for the benefit of the musically educated few, they had quickly become "a most important agent in the higher education of the musical many" (A-XXIX, 118; see also A-XXXII, 757). The Oratorio and Symphony societies of New York, founded by Leopold Damrosch in 1874 and 1878, respectively, Gericke's Boston Symphony Orchestra, and schools such as the Peabody Conservatory also contributed measurably to the elevation of the tastes of large numbers of individuals through their concerts.

Individual performers, too, were given credit for their efforts. The Culture and Progress editor reported after the close of the season of 1870–71 that, "while music is depressed in New York, it is some satisfaction to know that our best artists are not altogether silent, but, like missionaries of culture, are carrying the song and symphony in triumph through the provinces" (C-I, 685). Richard Grant White, in his series on the history of opera in New York, made a point of mentioning whether a given singer or impresario had striven to improve musical taste.

The mammoth festivals in Boston and New York around 1870 and 1880 were milestones in the progress of musical taste in America. But the Jubilees of 1869 and 1872, especially, exhibited certain unfortunate evils:

> expense of time, money, and pains, excitement, confusion, interruption of ordinary and more legitimate business, the unfair prominence given to clever and energetic but not artistically significant people, and the unpleasant air of charlatanry or vulgarity which indirectly and unfairly comes thereby to attach to musical enterprises in general (C-IV, 504).

Gigantism was, in Apthorp's estimation, their worst feature:

> Great harm is done by creating in the general public an unnatural and perverted appetite for what is merely big, rather than for what is great and good, a craving after quantity rather than an appreciation of quality. Even though a large mass of the public probably heard fine specimens of classic music for the first time on coming to the Jubilee, the performance of the music was, from the nature of things, so vaguely imperfect and ineffective that little if any real good can be hoped from their making its acquaintance in such a manner (A-XXX, 378).

George William Curtis, however, praised Patrick Gilmore's mammoth Jubilee of 1872 precisely because its size demonstrated the democratic orientation of American musical life, and the *Century* allowed that the element of size was "favorable, if not essential, to grandeur of effect" (C-IV, 503). Nor did the meliorative effects of the large festivals, however slight, escape the notice of concerned observers. The *Century's* Culture and Progress columnist approvingly quoted Gilmore: The participants, Gilmore admitted, had come down from the country to hear the more sensational parts of the program, "but when they went back they took with them the score of 'He, watching over Israel' " (C-IV, 504). A decade later, following Leopold Damrosch's New York festival, Curtis pointed out that "the popular interest awakened by such an enterprise, and the education that attends the admirable rendering of admirable music, are in themselves incentives to such festivals, and vindications of their usefulness" (H-LXV, 308).

It was generally agreed among thoughtful musicians and critics that the concert-hall education of the people should be carried out according to some rational plan of programing that would lead upward from music of almost wholly sensuous appeal to music representative of the higher life of the mind—the "classics." Apthorp advocated just such a logical "principle of aesthetic education," as opposed to merely *"amusing* entertainments." He maintained that the conductor should not pander to the extreme demands of either the supersophisticated listener or the totally inexperienced one.

> Instruction cannot and must not be forced down the public throat; it must be conveyed in the most fascinating and gradual form possible. . . . It is certainly not to be done by an abrupt introduction to the higher classic music, much less by the poorer and more trashy compositions of sterling composers, such as the march from Gounod's *Queen of Sheba,* the good in which is only to be appreciated by musicians, and the bad in which is beneath the notice of anybody (A-XXXIII, 383).

Even in presenting unfamiliar works to experienced audiences, the conductor should skillfully "conciliate his public, and, if possible . . . impress them favorably with the music he is trying to introduce . . . by first playing to them such things of the new school as they are pretty sure to like" (A-XXXI, 248). As Dwight said, "the programme ought to be an art-work in itself" (A-XXVI, 327).

Steadily throughout the seventies and eighties, Theodore Thomas sought to carry out just such a plan to advance the people's interest and discrimination with respect to good music, in New York, Boston, and Chicago. His intention was that his programs reflect not only the strict classical school, like those of the Philharmonic concerts at the Academy of Music, but also the modern, or Berlioz-Liszt-Wagner, school. Furthermore, each program, as well as each season as a whole, was to have a cumulative effect toward the education and elevation of taste.[1]

The *Atlantic's* staff critic, however, complained that Thomas' programing was often merely "miscellaneous." In seeking to appeal to a wide variety of tastes, Thomas frequently appealed to none, said Apthorp. "We have yet to see a programme of Mr. Thomas's that bears the stamp of any artistic *raison d'être* whatever," he wrote in the fall of 1873.

> His chief object seems to be to present as many novelties as possible. We find Wagner, Liszt, Berlioz, Volkmann, Hornemann, and others thrown together pell-mell into a programme, with perhaps a movement from a Beethoven symphony, a Strauss waltz, a Meyerbeer march, and some Franz or Mozart songs, and a harp solo by Godefroid (A-XXXII, 757).[2]

Not only did Apthorp object to Thomas' programing; he also found fault with the conductor's interpretations. He castigated

1. See C-III, 633; C-VI, 372; C-VIII, 245–46; C-IX, 458–66; C-X, 510–11; C-XVII, 148–49; H-LVII, 121, 935; H-LXII, 804, 809, 817; H-LXV, 307; H-LXX, 807; H-LXXXIII, 309; H-XCVI, 473–76.

2. To cite a specific example, the concert presented by Thomas in Boston on December 7, 1872, consisted of Beethoven's *Egmont* Overture; [Alexander?] Ritter's Introduction and Scherzo; a Schumann *Fantasiestück;* Hans Seelig's *Gnömen Reigen;* the Schubert-Liszt *Soirée de Vienne;* selections from act 1 of *Lohengrin;* Hornemann's "Fairy" Overture, *Aladdin;* two songs by Robert Franz; violin solos by Heinrich Ernst and Miska Hauser; a Strauss waltz; *Serenade* by Rossini; and *Saltarello* by Gounod, in that order. See Theodore Thomas, *A Musical Autobiography,* ed. George P. Upton, 2 Vols. (Chicago, 1905), II, 151. See also *ibid.,* pp. 15–20; A-XXX, 377; A-XXXIII, 381; A-XXXV, 753; A-XXXIX, 122; C-IX, 460–62.

Thomas for his use of grotesque dynamic effects and for tempos that were too fast or too slow. The critic admitted that the superior skill, control, and ensemble of Thomas' orchestra had taught Bostonians to expect better performances from their own local organization—and it undoubtedly helped to create the conditions of taste and enthusiasm that ultimately brought forth the Boston Symphony Orchestra in 1881—but he insisted that the conductor's interpretive style belonged to "a bad school" and was by its very brilliancy calculated to vitiate the public taste and to weaken the hold of the classics upon the Boston musical public.

In view of what the Culture-guardians were trying to achieve, Apthorp's accusations may seem unduly stringent, though the critic merely may have felt that Thomas played down just to Boston audiences. Yet H. B. Fuller, in his account for the *Atlantic* of the conductor's career in Chicago to 1897, enumerated some of the same strictures, so we may be sure that the Boston critic was not alone in his judgments. From the scope and intensity of the controversy that Thomas' educational plan elicited—it even raged in the daily press now and then (see A-XXXV, 122)—we may also infer that, as classrooms, his concert halls were not dull. In any case, questions of procedure were crucial, for Cultured music-lovers felt weighing heavily upon them the responsibility to defend American audiences from the debilitating effects of bad music and to allow the ethical power of good music to exert its full force.

Pleasure for the Populace

The arbiters of Cultured taste were determined to see that force was brought to bear upon citizens at all economic and social levels, but especially upon those at the lower end of the spectrum, whom the struggle for existence had impoverished economically as well as Culturally. "The man less fortunately situated needs recreation and stimulus even more than the other," wrote Louisa T. Cragin in 1875.

Warmth, light, companionship, he must have. The gin-palace offers them, ruining body and soul, while it affects to comfort both. Tear down the rum-shop, turn the trades-union into a choral society, bring good music with attractive surroundings before him, educate his children to take part in grand old folk-songs, glees, and madrigals, and in a generation a strange revolution would be wrought.

The Wordsworthian idyl of the happy toiler still lured the Culturist:

When the genius of song crowns the gospel of work, there will be fewer strikes, the grimy faces will be less haggard; under the unconscious influence of beauty, harmony, and rhythm, labor will be more cheerfully, more faithfully performed (H-LI, 739, 741).

European precedents were inspiring to the musical meliorists. A writer for the *Atlantic* noticed that in Paris, in 1884, at the Théâtre du Châtelet and the Théâtre du Château d'Eau, huge audiences "of all classes of society" attended the concerts. "The large proportion of poor people in them all is a very interesting and touching element," he wrote. "Hundreds of men who cannot afford to pay for a seat come in before the great work of the programme—most often one of Beethoven's symphonies—and stand through it, many of them through the entire performance," to be "transported into the higher regions of thought, feeling and enjoyment. This is a priceless gift to have bestowed upon one's fellow-citizens" (A-LIII, 742, 748).

During the late eighties and early nineties the altruism of the Culturists was indulged by several choral societies, including Chicago's Apollo Club and Boston's Cecilia, which regularly presented special low-priced performances reserved for "wage-workers." [3] Thomas had

3. The Cecilia defined "wage-workers" as persons earning fifteen dollars or less per week and sold its cheap (twenty-five cents) tickets to them through their employers. The latter frequently expropriated the boon for their own families and friends, to the dismay and embarrassment of the society. Moreover, some sensitive wage-workers took offense at the patently condescending air of the Cultured Cecilians. See the *Boston Evening Transcript*, December 7, 12, and 14, 1895.

intended to climax his career as a concert-hall educator with his colossal World's Fair scheme of 1892–93, stressing opportunity and appeal for the workingman, but that was terminated prematurely.[4] Nevertheless, George P. Upton's satisfaction with the results of all such experiments was unrestrained, for they clearly suggested "new possibilities for music in its application to some of the problems of the labor question." They could lead to a new phase in American musical life

> in which the wage-workers themselves will make the music, and where they themselves will experience in their too barren lives the uplifting influences of inner contact with the ideal, the orderly, and the celestial—all of which music is. . . . Why should not the musical society be a humanitarian practice-ground in which the great goal of effort is brotherhood, sympathy, and mutual helpfulness? (S-XIV, 82).

That proposition was destined to remain among the more durable Cultured ideas about music; indeed, it has not yet been entirely discarded by music educators.

Hopes for the Future

The success of the systematic use of the concert hall to foster an increase in adult interest in music was rewarding to contemplate.[5]

4. In fact, the plan came to an end a few weeks after Upton's description of it appeared in *Scribner's* in July, 1893. Thomas had been asked to resign as music director of the fair on May 17. He finally did resign on August 12. The whole sordid story is told by Charles Edward Russell in *The American Orchestra and Theodore Thomas* (New York, 1927), pp. 205–36.

5. In their anxiety to expand the audience for good music as quickly and as much as possible, most of the critics for the thoughtful class overlooked—or perhaps were ignorant of—one purely technical obstacle to the fully effective employment of the concert hall as classroom. Only Apthorp, prompted perhaps by his study of Berlioz' writings, observed that orchestras in America, which rarely numbered more than fifty or sixty players, were considered too small in proportion to the auditoriums in which they had to perform, such as the Boston Music Hall,

Yet it was not enough simply to accumulate listeners; they ought to be *intelligent* listeners. As B. J. Lang, one of the most highly respected teachers and conductors in Boston, pointed out in 1894: one who is entirely ignorant of music as an art may be musical and perceptive; but if his intellectual apperception of the musical experience is hindered by ignorance, his love of music is false and not genuine. "The listener who comprehends in one of Beethoven's toneworks nothing but the music is dangerously like the reciter who carries only the words of a poem, or one who sees nothing in a picture but its color" (A-LXXIII, 208). The little didactic treatises that appeared in the literary monthlies, such as Apthorp's "Musicians and Music Lovers" and William J. Henderson's letter "To Persons Desiring to Cultivate a Taste in Music," reached but a limited readership. The obligation to educate the entire potential audience challenged the Cultured imagination. Forward-looking individuals dreamed of the possible blessings of the phonograph as an educational tool: "There is a good time coming for the poor man of good taste," predicted one writer (C-XLVI, 153). A Contributor to the *Atlantic*'s Club proposed that free open-air music schools be established in public parks in the summer. "By the use of the stereopticon, electric light, scroll-played musical instruments, and combined ordinary voices . . . may be taught musical notation, thematic analysis of musical works, and the history of music" (A-LXXVII, 138).

The entire potential audience at any given moment included the children who would compose the audience of the future, and that element also challenged the musical meliorists. "If we are to become a musical people, it must be through the instruction of the masses in our public schools," wrote the eminent Boston school music-teacher H. E. Holt (C-XXII, 629; see also C-XXVIII, 951; C-XXXVII, 319). Conditions in Europe were cited to show that Americans were still behind in this matter. Gounod's remark, concerning a performance of his Mass in Germany, must have spurred on the advocates

---

which seated fifteen hundred persons. The effects of both classical and romantic orchestral works were unavoidably distorted, the one by the oversize rooms, the other by the undersize orchestras (A-XXXVIII, 759–63; A-XXXIX, 123).

of school music education: "A single rehearsal [of the chorus] was sufficient—thanks to the generality of musical education which is found in Germany only" (C-XLIII, 393). Every conceivably relevant argument was invoked to further the cause. The study of music was recommended to the *Century*'s readers for their children on purely practical grounds, such as might appeal to businessmen:

> All our life long we are addressing ourselves to others, frequently in cases where it makes a considerable difference to ourselves whether we commend our cause or not. Hence a pleasant voice is greatly to be desired, and can be acquired by almost everyone if right methods of speaking and singing are formed in childhood (C-XXVI, 196).

Progress was slow in this area of Cultured endeavor, to be sure. As late as 1886 the federal commissioner of education reported that less than two hundred fifty school systems were teaching music as a recognized subject. "We may yet awake fully to the immense help of both music and drawing in our elementary education," wrote an observer in 1890 (A-LXV, 719).

Nevertheless, there were many encouraging signs, and the outlook was generally optimistic. "The next generation," predicted Louisa T. Cragin, will "reap the harvest this generation is so wisely sowing" (H-LI, 739). Apthorp concurred:

> The next generation will be upon us soon, and let our leaders look to it that they be in fit condition to preach the evangel of Bach and Beethoven to these coming youngsters, who *do* know their right hand from their left. The generation of "musical infants" is passing away (A-XXXV, 124).

There was no question in the minds of the Culturists but that all musical activity in the public schools was properly to be conducted as a preparation for adult musical life, and not as an end in itself. That notion had been bequeathed them by the preceding generation. "When the study of singing was first introduced into the public schools of Boston, the most utopian anticipations were indulged in with regard to the degree and value of the musical culture that would then become the acquisition of every child," recalled William L. Tomlins, the Chicago educator. "Two advantages, in particular, were counted upon: That fluent singing by note would become common, and that a foundation would be laid for a genuine appreciation of good music" (C-XXVI, 195). Unfortunately, no one, Cultured or not, was able to make clear the legitimate connections between the one sphere and the other or between the tastes and abilities of children and those that could be expected from adults. While on the one hand the Culture-guardians were striving to establish orchestras and opera companies, for which patrons, not performers, were required in great numbers, on the other hand they were vigorously debating the best methods of teaching the fundamentals of musical performance to every juvenile American. For the next two generations, music educators were doomed to punish themselves with the accusation that they were continually, and inexplicably, falling short of their lofty goals.

There was a wide range of opinion concerning basic aims and procedures. A full comprehension of musical notation was considered essential by those to whom it seemed reasonable that an educated music-lover should be able to read the language. "The better trained the audience, the better oratory they will demand and receive," said Louisa T. Cragin. The principles of literary education should be followed in a child's musical education, she maintained, "till, unconsciously, the page of music is as expressive and intelligible to him as a page of printing" (H-LI, 740). Julius Eichberg, the conductor, composer, eminent violin-teacher, and superintendent of music in the Boston public schools, published a series of music textbooks early in the seventies which Apthorp considered excellent because "the simplest rudiments, not only of vocal culture and solmization, but also of harmony and the general theory of music" were set down in a clear and systematic form (A-XXXI, 117). "In some schools," wrote

an anonymous columnist in 1900, "the musical instruction is treated
more intellectually than in others, more importance being given to
sight-reading, and to the necessary fundamental mastery of the scale,
and less to the working-up of show-songs for purposes of exhibition"
(S-XXVIII, 250).

Other observers, like the reviewer of Charles E. Whiting's series
of six music textbooks published around 1890, were "glad of anything
which emphasizes the importance of thorough training in vocal music
in our public schools" (A-LXV, 719). Henry Krehbiel, too, who
believed that "a more general, more zealous, wiser cultivation of
choral music is the greatest of the socio-educational needs of the
United States," encouraged any educational method that would further
the attainment of that end (C-XXXV, 318).

The effective teaching of basic musicianship, however, often was
accompanied by insufficient attention to elementary vocal pedagogy.
Emilie Curtis, possibly a Boston music-teacher, complained that
current ideas concerning the second matter had led to a characteristic
sound among American schoolchildren that was simply hideous.
Tomlins had explained, nearly ten years earlier, that school music-
teachers were often chosen for their knowledge of notation and sight-
reading rather than for their understanding of the physiology of the
child's voice and that, consequently, "the exercise of singing as
commonly conducted in the public schools is . . . positively harmful
to the voice and destructive to future ability to sing artistically"
(C-XXVI, 195). He also outlined his concept of voice culture and
suggested remedies for the commonest vocal faults.

Thomas ignited the long heated discussion of problems in public-
school music, which took place mostly in the *Century,* with his assessment of "Musical Possibilities in America" in March, 1881, in which
he expressed his extreme dissatisfaction with existing practices. He
not only objected to the ways in which the voice was usually treated
but called the "movable *do"* system of sight-singing "a make-shift,
invented by amateurs," and strongly advocated the Continental system
of solmization. "Pupils should learn something about absolute pitch
of tones, instead of merely their relative pitch," he insisted.

The first public response to his article came from Tomlins, who pointed out that even the best music students in the schools were not able to sing accurately any but the simplest music. In August, Holt explained that it was not the "relative pitch system" itself that was the cause of the failure but "the ignorance of those who have it in charge as to the fundamental principles of teaching singing without instruments" (C-XXII, 628). Two months later, J. Spencer Curwen wrote from England in defense of the movable *do,* or "Tonic Sol-fa," system that his father had developed there, beginning in 1844. The discussion continued elsewhere for several years until Theodore F. Seward, the leading promoter of the English system in America, reviewed the history of the Curwen movement and recommended not only the teaching system but the notational form as well. Finally, Krehbiel lent the weight of his prestige to the cause of the movable *do* on the grounds that it was, as its originator had intended it to be, better suited to the study of vocal music than the competing system, which instrumentalists preferred.

Only a few Cultured critics strongly opposed the idea of teaching music, with a view to elevating taste, through performance. Tomlins had asserted that, whereas in the study of the English language and literature, the progression from simplicity to complexity led all the way to Shakespeare and Milton, in music even the most talented pupil was held to a very low level of repertoire; but he blamed the methods rather than the objectives.

On the other hand, White, who was largely self-taught as a composer and performer, saw in himself an instance of the evolution of a natural type, born, not educated, to music. He extended his experience into a generalization: "Among the mistaken notions that have long prevailed in regard to music," he wrote in 1878, "is the one that a taste for it may be planted and cultivated in almost any young person, and that some skill in musical execution may be attained by almost any one who will begin early enough and practice long enough" (A-XLII, 749). Mrs. John Lillie, a New York writer, also disapproved of American educators' emphasis upon performance, invoking the example of England to support her argument. There, she wrote in 1880, "music is invariably taught every pupil in every school-room, and the result is that instead of cultivating taste, it desecrates fine sound, and the young student who drones through Beethoven and Mozart as a duty, never learns to appreciate either" (H-LX, 841). She suggested that "unmusical" children might better be taught to listen intelligently rather than to perform badly.

Ten years later Krehbiel reiterated essentially the same conclusion, and still another decade later the European example was summoned to reinforce it, this time by an anonymous correspondent to *Scribner's,* who pointed out that, in Germany,

> musical rudiments are imparted incidentally, which may be the first step in the future development of the art as an accomplishment or a profession. These, however, must of necessity be too insufficient to count. It is what girls and boys get into their souls by music that counts. Germany is, of modern countries, that in which this is best understood. There music is handled as a form of spiritual gymnastics" (S-XXVIII, 251).

It was often the grand rhetoric of such propositions that made the Cultured writers' disagreements so readable.

Education for Musical Leadership

There was one principle the majority of Culturists tacitly agreed upon, however, and that was the sanctity of the individual's ultimate right to make his own judgments, even in matters of musical taste—so long, of course, as the over-all range of choices embraced the higher levels of value. The education of taste was not meant to lead to the equalization of taste among all citizens, for that would have conflicted with natural law. "Society," Apthorp wrote with Spencerian assurance, "rapidly falls into distinct musical classes, and he who cannot keep up with the foremost must take his chance in the rear." Moreover, he went on, the establishment of an elite guard is essential to the cultural health of the country. "Where the most highly cultivated nucleus exists," he wrote, "there will be the highest general cultivation. Nothing is more fatal to general culture than that intellectual and aesthetic communism which would have the foremost wait until those who lag behind shall have caught up with him" (A-XXXV, 122–23). The highest type of music, as Dwight said, appeals to the highest type of individual. The "bond of union" supplied by chamber music, for instance, "only reaches the few; coarser, meaner, more prosaic natures are not drawn to it" (A-XXVI, 329). What is more, as Waldo Selden Pratt pointed out, in musical taste as in other areas of life, "the educated man or woman should be a leader in fostering the good and refusing the bad" (A-LXXXVI, 830). The success of the concert hall as classroom, and the sometimes doubtful promises of public-school music education, eventually made the inclusion of music in formal higher education another important goal of the Culturists.

Most universities, however, excluded the fine arts from their official curricula, and the few that allowed any room for them at all included only theoretical and historical studies. Of the twenty representative institutions chosen for comparison by Charles F. Thwing in 1877, only six announced instruction in any of the arts, and only two, Vassar and Harvard, offered any credit in music. Harvard devoted eighteen hours per week to the arts, including four courses in music under John Knowles Paine.[6]

Furthermore, among those that included music in their curricula, most considered their province to be the training not of performers, teachers, or even listeners but of composers; and, given the assumption that genius is a constant quality among all the arts, a conventional classical education was deemed equally suitable to the stimulation of

---

6. Charles F. Thwing, "College Instruction," *Century,* XIV (September, 1877), 710–11. Even as late as 1936, Edward J. Dent was called on to "defend the dignity of Music as a subject of university study" in his acceptance of the first honorary Doctor of Music degree conferred by Harvard University. See Edward J. Dent, "The Historical Approach to Music," *Musical Quarterly,* XXIII (January, 1937), 1.

the creative imagination, regardless of the medium of expression. "The studies that nourish the soul," said Charles Eliot Norton in 1890,

> that afford permanent resources of delight and recreation, that maintain ideals of conduct, and develop those sympathies upon which the progress and welfare of society depend, are the studies that quicken and nourish the imagination and are vivified and moralized by it.[7]

That same year, Yale University established its Department of Music, with Gustav Stoeckel as director and Battel Professor of Music. In his inaugural address, Stoeckel explained that the aim of the department was to foster native American "tone poets." Materialistic motives were expressly abjured in behalf of the students. "Simple, unvarnished truth . . . eternal truth—the aim of all research in science and all attempts in art, must forever be the beacon light to the earnest musical student," he proclaimed. The practical and technical aspects of composition and performance were barely mentioned, but it was stressed that "a composer needs all the available knowledge which science and philosophy can give." [8]

Judging solely from the evidence of the literary magazines, Pratt was among the first to suggest a different, or at least an additional, approach to the subject at the college level. "It is clear that our time has begun to demand a higher educational treatment of music," he wrote in 1900, "simply because music affects social life widely and profoundly." He recommended that the college course in music "should address itself explicitly and largely to the needs of those who feel themselves shut out from the experiences of musicians, who do not expect to become musicians, and who even seem to lack special musical aptitude." Music should be taught, he said, like literature and science—not as a professional discipline but as an intellectual pursuit

7. Charles Eliot Norton, "Harvard University in 1890," *Harper's*, LXXXI (September, 1890), 590.

8. "University Topics," *New Englander and Yale Review*, LII (May, 1890), 466–79.

with a potential appeal to all intelligent persons. Therefore, a recital
or concert series must be furnished so that studies will not be entirely
abstract. Above all, a teacher of music to the general college student
should have special qualifications:

> First, he must be analytic in method, with the mastery of defi-
> nition and classification that follows. Second, he must have a
> broad historic sense, since nothing in musical progress is lumi-
> nous or correct in perspective except in its historic relations.
> Third, he must have a sure hold on the bearings of all the fine
> arts, music included, upon the fundamental features of human
> life (A-LXXXVI, 826–32).

Significantly, Pratt's essay was entitled "New Ideas in Music Education," though within a decade the ideas began to spread; the first
edition of his own music-history textbook for college students appeared in 1907.[9]

Meanwhile, the expansion of interest and activity in music among
Americans of all classes and ages had resulted in steadily increasing
opportunities for performers and for teachers of performance
(H-LXXIV, 977), and the conservatories efficiently met that need
(A-XXXI, 376; A-XL, 128; A-LXXX, 539–40). The Oberlin
Conservatory was established in 1865, followed two years later by
the Boston and Cincinnati conservatories, the Academy of Music in
Chicago (later called the Chicago Musical College), and Eben
Tourjée's New England Conservatory, and in 1868 by the Peabody
Conservatory.[10] By 1875, it was reported, the New England Con-
servatory had enrolled thousands of full-time and part-time pupils,
and they in turn had helped to raise standards of performance and
appreciation everywhere (H-LI, 743).

9. See Warren Dwight Allen, *Philosophies of Music History* (New York,
1962), p. 130.
10. The Oberlin Conservatory opened under private sponsorship, but in 1867
became a part of Oberlin College, where a Chair of Sacred Music had been
founded in 1835.

The desirability of a "national" conservatory over independent private-studio education in music was repeatedly expressed in the literary magazines. Mendelssohn's Leipzig Conservatory, featuring class instruction in performance, was an especially appealing model, for it seemed to embody democratic principles, mainly economy. Mendelssohn himself ("no higher musical authority seems possible") was quoted concerning its other virtues: "It produces industry and spurs on to emulation; it is a preservative against one-sidedness of education and taste, a tendency against which every artist, even in the student years, should be upon his guard" (H-LI, 742). The idea was partly implemented in the National College of Music, established in Boston in 1872 by Thomas Ryan of the Mendelssohn Quintette Club. Apthorp, who was a member of the piano faculty, described the institution:

> The teachers in each department look to some one definite head for guidance in the management of their various classes. The head teacher in each department has been brought up in the same school of playing or singing as the other teachers under his direction, many of whom have for some years been his own pupils and coworkers, so that a pupil may begin at the lowest grade in any department and successively pass on to higher and higher grades, without being forced to adopt a new system at each successive step (A-XXXI, 376).

One month after the school was opened, the great Boston fire occurred, forcing many students to withdraw, and the school collapsed in financial ruin at the end of its first year.[11]

After earlier attempts to establish a similar institution in New York, which failed despite the encouragement of men like Thomas (C-XXI, 780) and the organist and voice-teacher Gottlieb Federlein (C-XXVII, 158–59), a National Conservatory of Music was organ-

11. See Thomas Ryan, *Recollections of an Old Musician* (New York, 1899), pp. 172–73.

ized in 1885 through the "energy and liberality" of Mrs. F. B. Thurber, the wife of a prosperous wholesale grocer.[12] Parke Godwin, a leading New York newspaperman, was elected president; August Belmont, the New York banker, diplomat, and former stockholder in the Academy of Music, was named vice-president. Emma Fursch-Madi, the famous French soprano, was chosen as director of the conservatory, and Jacques Bouhy, an eminent Belgian baritone, was named professor of opera. Instruction was free to selected applicants in all branches of music that related to the production of opera, and an American opera company was immediately established, under the musical direction of Theodore Thomas, in order to eventually provide graduates with a means of using their talent and training professionally (C-XXXI, 477–78). The opera company failed during the first season (see pp. 138–39), but the conservatory continued, making news again in 1892 when Anton Dvořák became its director for a few years. Obviously, education was considered a better investment than American opera.

The very existence of the National Conservatory in 1886 was remarkable, but Cultured Americans took it as another indication that their aims and methods were consistent with the tendencies of cosmic forces. "Accustomed to their own quick ways of doing everything, in business or art, they are less surprised than others at the rapidity of their own triumphs," remarked the *Century* (C-XXXI, 478). Even by 1881, pointed out Frederick Nast, America had developed countless "composers, conductors, organists, and critics among our own people, whose influence for good can not be overestimated; who have taught thousands what good music is, and have elevated the taste of the entire public who care for music at all" (H-LXII, 804). Conditions were auspicious in the two media that were still more basic to American musical life—the voice and the piano. In 1888 an *Atlantic* Contributor predicted that "it will not be long before every facility

12. See Mrs. Thurber's letter to the *New York World* describing the origins of the conservatory and the opera company, reprinted in the *Boston Evening Transcript,* January 7, 1887. See also Nicolas Slonimsky, "The Plush Era in American Concert Life," in *One Hundred Years of Music in America,* ed. Paul Henry Lang (New York, 1961), pp. 112–15.

for the acquirement of the art of singing will be attainable at home"
(A-LXII, 715)—though an almost hysterical debate over principles
of adult vocal pedagogy raged, mainly in the *Atlantic,* during the late
eighties and early nineties. The tradition of the piano in America was
equally encouraging—and evidently much less controversial; though
most American pianists had deserted the concert hall in favor of the
studio because of the insecurity of the former (H-LXII, 814), a
result was that at the very end of the century, as far as the advanced
study of the piano was concerned, the United States offered fully as
many opportunities as Europe (C-LX, 864).

By the turn of the century, music education of all types had become a big business, susceptible to the laws of supply and demand
and capable of fiscal manipulation like any other industry. Thus
music may be said to have found an integral place in American life
by the inherent power of the educational organism, but in reality it
was vivified principally by the rhetoric of thoughtful disputation. As
a writer for the *Atlantic* observed in 1908, "the musical activity of
this country may be generally attributed to an altruistic purpose on
the part of a minority to teach the great majority to find pleasure and
comfort in the divine art." [13] That was undoubtedly one of the most
complimentary tributes that could have been paid to the Cultured
class.

13. William E. Walter, "The Industry of Music-Making," *Atlantic,* CI (January, 1908), 96.

Chapter VII

Cosmopolitan Nationalism

PERSUASION AND EDUCATION could be used to demonstrate the integrity of music with American life on purely logical grounds, but a surer proof would have been the discovery of a national musical identity—a matrix of ideas and institutions, and a musical language—that would not only complement the national character which was evolving but that the world would instantly recognize as American. Everyone knew the basic characteristics of the "average" American citizen; self-awareness was a national obsession, and reporters eagerly solicited analyses of American strengths and weaknesses by every quotable visitor from abroad.[1] The difficulty lay in determining the organic connections between personality and musicality.

The Predicament of
American Musicality

Anton Dvořák, who came to America to head the National Conservatory in 1893, told the thoughtful readers of *Harper's*

1. See, for example, Allan Nevins, *America through British Eyes* (New York, 1948), pp. 348–94.

nothing they did not already know when he wrote that "the two American traits which most impress the foreign observer . . . are the unbounded patriotism and capacity for enthusiasm [he also called it "push"] of most Americans" (H-XC, 429). He believed that those attributes could be made to serve as the bases for an American "school" of composition; but he could not show precisely how the development might occur, other than through subscription to the gospel of work and through faith in the mysterious laws of evolution. Indeed, Dvořák was especially attractive to American musicians and music-lovers because his own life had been "a story of manifest destiny, of signal triumph over obstacle and discouraging environment"; he had won his way to the exalted position he occupied "by an exercise of traits of mind and character that have always been peculiarly the admiration of American manhood," said Henry Krehbiel (C-XLIV, 657).

There seemed to be weaknesses in the American character that had to be overcome, too; and here the connections between life and art were sometimes easier to perceive. Dvořák found fault with his American students for their reckless determination to reach all goals by the quickest possible means, but George William Curtis had already recognized the lack of self-discipline among his musical countrymen. Commenting to a friend on the superior playing of an orchestra composed mainly of Germans, Curtis explained sarcastically: "We cannot practise to the necessary degree. Those people have all fiddled on two notes for twelve hours together. But no American would submit to do that. Something must be allowed to the spirit of liberty" (H-LXXVI, 961).

Furthermore, some observers felt that Americans, as a people, lacked a natural affinity for beauty of any kind, including music. To be sure, the indices of progress showed that Americans definitely possessed educable susceptibilities, as Theodore Thomas frequently pointed out, but evidently no innate desires were present. A Contributor to the *Atlantic*'s Club, for instance, noted in 1878 that "what may be called the necessity of art, the natural hunger and thirst for the beautiful, the *desiderium pulchri,* is not born in us" (A-XLII,

769). "Americans are not so fond of music as are the people of [Germany and France]," wrote another Contributor about a decade later; "music is not one of their matters of course" (A-LIX, 568). It was primarily a matter of racial capacities, and Europe again supplied the examples: "As a national characteristic, to be song and music lovers belongs to the Irish and German races rather than to the Saxon," said Louisa T. Cragin. "It is rare to find a German or an Irish girl without an ear for music" (H-LI, 739). Music, George P. Upton claimed, "is the one thing always near to the German's heart. It is his by tradition and by the strong forces of heredity" (S-XIV, 73).

The presence of those musically blessed races in America might have helped make it a musical nation, as Cragin pointed out: "We Americans are a conglomerate race, made up of the best of every people under the sun, so transfused that the origin of even a single family can scarcely be traced without an element of Celtic or Teutonic race discovering itself" (H-LI, 739). However, some critics insisted that the process of conglomeration was not sufficiently advanced for the full force of it to have any noticeable effect upon American music. "The chief hindrance to the development of a national school of music," wrote Frederick Nast in 1881, "lies in the diverse character of our population. American composers may flourish, but American music can not be expected until the present discordant elements are merged into a homogeneous people" (H-LXII, 818; see also A-XXXV, 122).[2] Henry T. Finck also asserted that the emergence of a genuine American school of music was a prospect of the future and that it would be, "like the perfect American woman, a mixture of all that is best in European types, transformed by our

2. Henry Krehbiel enumerated those elements in 1889, stressing the implications they held for the future homogeneity of music in America when "the inherited predilections of the reflective German, the mercurial Frenchman, the stolid Englishman, the warm-hearted Irishman, the impulsive Italian, will have all exerted their influence upon the popular taste," and "the American composer will be the truest representative of a universal art because he will be the truest cosmopolitan as a citizen" (see "The Evolution of American Music," *New York Tribune*, reprinted in the *Boston Evening Transcript*, September 28, 1889).

climate into something resembling the spirit of American literature" (C-LIII, 449).

Meanwhile, every circumstance from which evidence of an innate musical Americanness could be extracted was proudly examined. The anonymous author of the *Century*'s Culture and Progress department perceived an American type among voices:

> The French is elegant, weak, unsubstantial, over-refined [any good Culturist would have suspected as much]; the German, strong and hard; the Italian, rich, sensuous, and passionate. The American has more of the bird-like quality, more purity and freshness than any of these. It is equal to any in flexibility; it rather surpasses the Italian in sweetness, though it lacks both richness and strength. It is the voice in which youth should carol its joys, and maiden modesty sing its love; not the voice of tragedy, of spiritual exaltation, or of fiery passions.

The best example of this somewhat Whitmanesque ideal, a "pure American soprano—clear, fresh, true, and sympathetic," was Clara Louise Kellogg, one of the first wholly American-trained, native opera singers, who had achieved the status of an international star, incidentally, "by sheer hard work and Yankee pluck" (C-I, 686). There was too little such evidence, however, to permit any reasonable person to infer that an American musical sovereignty based on natural propensities rather than inculcated tastes was anything but a dream for the future.

The temporary lack of a national musical identity was no more a hindrance to musical activity than it was to the continued growth of national pride, for there was other work to be done. The laws of evolution, which transcended national boundaries, dictated that Americans should look to Europe in order to gain a sense of perspective by which the development of a genuinely American music and musical life could be abetted. There was no apparent alternative to the necessity to build orchestras, opera companies, choral societies, schools of music, music libraries, concert halls, opera houses, and all the rest of the institutions that had evolved in the natural course of events over there. Nor was there anything for American composers to do but to carry on from the point in history to which centuries of European tradition had led them.

First, an American composer was obliged to learn all that European composers had learned, and to do so within the formalized academic system he had inherited. Second, since contemporary practices in Europe were to be considered causes that would ultimately have effects to be reckoned with even by Americans, a composer was required to take a clear stand with respect to current stylistic trends, including musical nationalism. Conservatories in Munich or Leipzig, or even in Boston, New York, Cincinnati, and Baltimore, could satisfy the first need, and little comment seemed to be necessary. The second was not a matter for strictly academic concern, however, for it had implications that reached to the very roots of everyday life and thought. It was a "live issue," a fit subject for the "free play of the mind." The very idea of a real American musical speech warranted careful scrutiny.

The Search for a National Musical Costume

As the Cultured critics saw it, there were, judging from European precedents, two possible bases on which a national school of music might be constructed—one historical, the other ethnic. Germany, Italy, and France had arrived at unmistakable musical dialects through long, complicated processes of historical evolution from simplicity to complexity within the confines of their respective cultural or racial, if not national, boundaries. When, along the way, folk music had been drawn upon, its features had been thoroughly sublimated for use in the higher music. On the other hand, composers in the Slavic and Scandinavian countries had challenged the slower organic process in using the harmonic vocabularies and the developmental forms of their larger neighbors to clothe, in exotically revealing fashions, the unique melodies and rhythms of their own peasantry.

No critic for the Cultured class could bring himself to recommend that American composers draw upon the historical legacy of their own country, for none could be found that was truly viable. Richard Grant White, opening his public quarrel with the music historian Frédéric Louis Ritter in the *Century* in 1884, explained that he had once been asked to write a history of music in America but that he had declined because there was no American music to write about. The New England psalm-book makers and singing-school teachers seemed to him

> about as much in place in the history of musical art as a critical discussion of the whooping of Indians would be . . . not because their labors were simple and unpretentious, but because they were the development of no germ, and themselves produced no fruit, except some chorus material (C-XXVII, 948).

Just what was desired in the way of a historical tradition was stated more explicitly by John Sullivan Dwight in 1882 in his study of seventeenth- and eighteenth-century American music, significantly entitled "Our Dark Age in Music." During the entire era, he said, there had existed only Puritan psalmody, "a very dull and sanctimonious music," and "a very shallow, frivolous and popular reaction" to the ritual music, worthless as a foundation for a higher musical life. "And here we are," he concluded,

> well into the nineteenth century, and nothing yet but psalmody! Nothing that properly can count in the history of music here *as art*. The distinctively New England, homespun psalmtune contains no germs of musical progress, nothing which by

thematic development of genial contrapuntal treatment could lead up, like the German choral, which was *kern-melodisch,* into higher and larger forms of art—the oratorio, motet, passion, sacred cantata, and Te Deum (A-L, 822–23).

Of course, there were certain other, more recent, varieties of indigenous music which might have spawned an American national school of composition. Curtis had once expressed a genuine fondness for the music of Stephen Foster. "The air is full of his melodies," he had eulogized a few weeks after the composer's death. "Their simple pathos touches every heart. They are our national music" (H-XXVIII, 567). Gradually, however, Foster's name faded from the ledgers of the Culturists' accounts, for as the market for a higher type of music grew more active, the arbiters of taste became more and more impatient with the less noble types. In 1881 Nast superciliously dismissed all "plantation melodies and minstrel ballads" as products of "the lowest strata of society" (H-LXII, 818). Cankerous commercialism had rendered the genre sterile.

Louis Moreau Gottschalk had made an indelible impression upon his own generation, and it lasted well into the next decade, but it was primarily a personal, visual, and aural one. William Foster Apthorp, judging the *Célèbre Tarantelle de Bravura* to be the best of the posthumous works he had seen as of 1875, nevertheless concluded that the work could be fully appreciated only by persons who had seen and heard Gottschalk perform and who could call to mind "the maddening fascination of his playing." The music itself, nondeveloping and perhaps nondevelopable, was adjudged to embody little more than "a certain indescribable charm and vivacity of style"; for when put into "the retort of criticism on high art principles," very little real musical value was to be detected in it (A-XXXV, 380–81). Great performers, and the music they concocted for their own purposes, were sufficient unto themselves, but intrinsically valueless compositions were congenitally impotent.

The Civil War produced lyrical effusions of such profound and sustained popular force that concerts of soldiers' songs were occasionally presented during the ensuing decade or two. Brander Matthews, writing in the *Century*'s series on the war in 1887, suggested that the time was ripe "for the musician who shall richly develop, with sustained and sonorous dignity, the few simple airs which represent and recall to the people of these United States the emotions . . . of the four long years of bitter strife," but no one appeared to heed him. It is no wonder, of course; for no matter how one looked at the musics of the American past, whether recent or remote, it was demonstrably certain that they had all been evolutionary anomalies; they had not prevailed by virtue of their own organic power, so they must have been unfit for survival. Furthermore, America was coming of age, and Cultured observers were pleased to see her errant, childish tastes supplanted by the traditions of her parent civilization in Europe. Even men like George F. Bristow, William Henry Fry, and Anthony Philip Heinrich, the sincerest of Americanists, were entirely ignored.

The Problem of a
Folk Tradition

The same circumstances that left the American composer without any usable fund of historical tradition deprived him also of an ethnic or folk tradition. As we have already seen, racism dictated that the folk songs of, say, German or Irish immigrants could never become truly American but were immutably Teutonic or Celtic. Similarly, evolutionism proved that the songs of the Negro and the Indian were not American but primitive. No one was American merely because he resided on American soil. Nevertheless, by the early nineties there were a few thoughtful persons who were willing to arbitrarily choose a body of folk music and try to develop a national musical language out of it, thus forgoing the assurances of natural processes and boldly facing the obvious risks of artificial selection. Dvořák suggested how it might be done.

When Dvořák's new "Americanistic" works, including the *New*

PLATE 3a. *The Voodoo Dance.*

PLATE 3b. *The Bamboula.* These etchings were made by Edward W. Kemble for George Washington Cable's article on Creole music (C-XXXI, 517–32; 807–28). Henry F. B. Gilbert, one of the leaders of the nationalist movement among early twentieth-century American composers, drew inspiration from Kemble's drawings and Cable's descriptions, as well as from the musical illustrations by Krehbiel and others, and used a title of Cable's for his symphonic poem, *The Dance in Place Congo* (1906), which he later transformed into a ballet-pantomime (1918).

World Symphony, were heard in New York and Boston early in the concert season of 1893–94, certain critics hastened to assure their readers of the seriousness of the composer's motives and intentions. "In Dvořák's attempts," wrote Charles Dudley Warner, "he has not in any way departed from the highest musical traditions." Warner went on to quote Krehbiel: " 'He has shown that there are the same latent possibilities in the folk-songs which have grown up in America as in the folk-songs of other peoples' " (H-LXXXVIII, 803). Krehbiel's judgment was liberal, though by no means radical, for he was a Cultured gentleman himself. His own interest in Negro music had been evidenced in 1886 by his arrangements of slave songs and dances for George Washington Cable's two-part essay on Creole music in the *Century* (*see* Plates 3a and 3b), but he had predicted a few years later that the emergence of an American musical nationalism along the lines established by Scandinavian and Slavic composers, though inevitable, would require a generation or more of time.[3]

Reaction among Cultured musicians and critics to Dvořák's "attempts" was by no means unanimously favorable, however. Apthorp's attitude was typical; confirmed as he was in his evolutionist point of view, he was constitutionally opposed to the nationalist movement, especially the use of Negro or Indian music. As early as 1874 he had taken his stand in a review of a posthumous publication of Gottschalk's *Rayons d'Azur* polka:

> As Chopin was the most perfect exponent of the Polish element in music, so was Gottschalk the great interpreter of the Hispano-Ethiopian element, and by as much as the Polish esthetic spirit is higher and more developed than the Negro, by so much was Chopin higher than Gottschalk (A-XXXIII, 256).

Apthorp was against any retrogressive tendency in music. In 1880 he rejected the suggestion by the French composer Louis-Albert

3. See *ibid.*

Bourgault-Ducoudray that Greek and Oriental melodies might serve as a source of melodic inspiration for Western composers. "Our tonal system is not the result of a merely empirical selection," the critic explained, "but is a natural musical development. To seek inspiration from the old modes is, in almost every case, to go backwards" (A-XLVI, 412).

Apthorp's review of Dvořák's *New World* Symphony, which appeared in the *Boston Evening Transcript* on January 1, 1894, contained his most succinct enunciation of his view of nationalism:

> To our mind, the great bane of the present Slavic and Scandi-navian schools is and has been the attempt to make civilized music by civilized methods out of essentially barbaric material. The result has in general been a mere apotheosis of ugliness, distorted forms, and barbarous expression. We gladly admit exceptions; but this seems to us to be the general rule.

Predictably, he reacted to Edward MacDowell's *Indian Suite* in the same way, in the *Transcript* on February 3, 1896, adding that "most barbarous tunes, of no-matter-what origin, have so much in common that it takes an expert to recognize anything very specific in their musical character"; so the whole notion of an American music based on Negro or Indian melodies was fallacious.

Critics like Apthorp perceived that it would ultimately be the ineffable essence of folk song, rather than the imitable surface of it, that would infuse American music with its Americanness. Francis Korbay, the Hungarian composer and godson of Liszt, who taught voice and piano in New York from 1871 until 1894, identified the principle:

> National music [i.e., folk music], the source of all cosmopoli-tan music, is in the same measure attached to language and poetry as race characteristics, fine arts, and sciences depend upon climatic, geographical, and political conditions. Thus it

is a nation's language which generates its musical rhythm; its poetry which creates its melody; and its temperament, the spirit of its dignity, tenderness, mirth, sadness, or flightiness, whichever may express the respective people's national character (H-LXXXII, 564).

Not for nearly fifty years would American composers and critics begin to repudiate conscious Americanisms and awaken to a full comprehension of the Cultured point of view.[4]

Until after the turn of the century, the quest for an American musical costume patterned after ostensibly indigenous models was merely a fad which posed no serious threat to Cultural ideals. Most of the articles in the literary magazines concerning folk music, such as Theodore Bacon's "Some Breton Folk Songs" or Lafcadio Hearn's ". . . Japanese Folk Songs," and even the epochal ones like T. W. Higginson's "Negro Spirituals," which appeared in the *Atlantic* in 1867 (the same year the famous Allen-Ware-Garrison *Slave Songs of the United States* was published), as well as Cable's study of Creole music, reflected either a kind of sociological or anthropological curiosity or a literary or linguistic fascination and had little or no connection with current ideas about the art of music.[5] Furthermore, there was considerable credence given as late as 1899 to the assertion that the education of the Negro in the South was "gradually abolishing a species of folk-song as interesting as it is unique" (C-LVIII, 577). The popular conviction that all folklore was by definition ephemeral and exotic even prompted the declaration that "the commercial spirit of the age, and our conventional mode of existence,

4. See Aaron Copland, *Music and Imagination* (New York, 1952), pp. 92–94; Virgil Thompson, *Music Reviewed, 1940–54* (New York, 1967), pp. 168–69.

5. Higginson, a noted clergyman, abolitionist, and military commander of the first "slave regiment," was primarily interested in the texts rather than the music of the spirituals, because of their documentary value. "Now that [the Negroes'] patience has had its perfect work," he wrote, "history cannot afford to lose this portion of its record. There is no parallel instance of an oppressed race thus sustained by the religious sentiment alone. These songs are but the vocal expression of the simplicity of their faith and the sublimity of their long resignation" (A-XIX, 694).

have so far effaced original types of character and romantic phases of life that the folk-song seems already a thing of the past." [6]

Purely Practical Matters

The stirrings of the ethnic nationalists in search of a usable tradition, like the frustrating researches of the historians, were stimulating to American musical life; they compelled Cultured critics to clarify and reaffirm some of the fundamental tenets of their creed. Meanwhile, there were other issues equally fundamental to a national musical identity that had to be dealt with.

It was evident that support of American musical life by the government was absolutely necessary. Nast and Curtis were somewhat encouraged by the recognition which Mrs. F. B. Thurber's National Conservatory of Music received in the form of state and federal charters. If it were true that citizens would tend to reflect the attitudes of constituted authority, then the charters were effective means of indicating a sort of legal relationship of music and life. The example of Europe, however, pointed to the need for subsidy, and Dvořák was among those who urged it:

> The great American republic alone, in its national govern-
> ment as well as in the several governments of the States, suf-
> fers art and music to go without encouragement. Trades and
> commerce are protected, funds are voted away for the un-
> employed, schools and colleges are endowed, but music must
> go unaided, and be content if she can get the support of a few
> private individuals like Mrs. Jeannette M. Thurber and Mr.
> H. L. Higginson (H-XC, 430; see also H-LX, 843).

If music were a line item in the national budget, then its security in the national mode of existence would be absolutely unquestionable.

6. Emma Bell Miles, "Some Real American Music," *Harper's*, CIX (June, 1904), 118.

Copyright laws and immigration practices also needed revision, and men like Curtis and Josiah Gilbert Holland worked hard to bring it about; but even the Culturists seemed unable to isolate the real problems, much less to persuade Congress to deal with them disinterestedly. Foreign composers' works could not be copyrighted in this country, so their authors and composers could not receive their due royalties. A conscientious *Century* columnist recommended in 1879 that

> if "H.M.S. Pinafore" is played anywhere by American amateurs, let the authors benefit by it. No honest man will use the labor of others without reward. Messrs. Gilbert and Sullivan . . . have no legal right to demand payment; and the moral right on our part therefore to pay them . . . is but the stronger.

A fee of from five to twenty-five dollars was suggested (C-XVII, 906). One or more scrupulous publishers sent honoraria to Gilbert in 1886, but the Englishman took this gesture as a sign of condescension, and Curtis subsequently scolded the composer from the Easy Chair.

One effort to revise the copyright law, a bill introduced by Representative Treloar of Missouri in 1896 (H.R. 5976), requiring that all music sold in the United States, all works by Americans sold abroad, and all works by foreign composers sold here be engraved and printed in this country, was ostensibly designed to protect American composers as well as printers and engravers. John Knowles Paine, Horatio Parker, and Edward MacDowell opposed the bill, however, Paine claiming that American composers were "beginning to find European recognition a very important factor in the development of native music in a young country" and that publication of an American's composition in England or Germany was more likely to assure world-wide acceptance than American publication alone. Parker did not see how, "in a question of copyright pure and simple, the interests of laborers or mechanics can in honesty be considered at all" (C-LII, 474–76). The bill died in committee.

The protection of American "artisans," including musicians, was the aim of the authors of the Contract Labor Act of 1887, but it nearly prohibited the entrance of Arthur Nikisch into America to become conductor of the Boston Symphony Orchestra in 1889,[7] and it almost prevented Johann Strauss and his orchestra from visiting America in 1890 (H-LXXXI, 147). Thoughtful critics despised the perversion of values such laws reflected. Unfortunately, while they sometimes marshaled the forces of reason in extremely impressive array, they needed the power of numbers; lacking votes, they could accomplish little in the way of concrete benefits.

In the long run, the best function of the Cultured critics was to practice a consistently disinterested review of American music and musicians. Apthorp avoided "puffing" native composers or performers on purely patriotic grounds; he bestowed appreciation and encouragement only when it was clearly justified by the presence of intrinsic merit and used nationality only occasionally as an explanation for inadequacy. He was restrained but evidently sincere in his praise for certain of Dudley Buck's compositions; but he castigated him several times for his tendency toward sentimentality and for his "redundantly sensuous" harmonies, and he credited the composer but little for his "good musical commonplaces, such as appeal directly to the generality of hearers" (A-XXXIV, 759). With his *Forty-sixth Psalm* of 1874, however, Buck had, according to Apthorp, "earned the right to be treated fairly and on a level, without being shielded behind considerations of nationality or inexperience" (A-XXXIV, 251). Furthermore, though the questionable musicopoetic theories of the librettist Sidney Lanier had weakened Buck's *Centennial Meditation of Columbia*,[8] the composer was said to be, "above all things, a musician [who] never allows the dramatic possibilities of his text to lure him away from a musically self-dependent and consistent form" (A-XXXVIII, 123; see also A-XXXIX, 123), and that was

---

7. See "American Music for Americans," *Boston Evening Transcript,* July 22, 1889.

8. For the background to the commissioning of the cantata for the Centennial in Philadelphia, see Albert H. Smyth, *Bayard Taylor* (Boston, 1896), pp. 240–41.

unquestionably the highest praise any composer could earn from Apthorp.

Paine's First Symphony (1876) was the recipient of comparable accolades from Apthorp, who had already called his oratorio *St. Peter* (1873) "the first great work of America in the domain of music" (A-XXXII, 251).[9] Of the symphony, the critic observed that the development technique in it was "purely organic" and that the form displayed "perfect equilibrium" (A-XXXVII, 633). John Fiske was equally impressed by Paine's classicism, and he emphasized that the composer had won admiration from a skeptical audience on the sheer strength of his innate ability and not by imitating others. "Whatever anxiety or lack of entire faith any one may have felt beforehand must have been removed by the very first phrase, which . . . proclaims at once the technical skill and boldness of design that belong only to masters of symphonic writing." Almost apologetically, he added that "some feeling of local as well as national pride is . . . more than pardonable" (A-XXXVII, 763).

Paradoxically, the "innate ability" of Paine and Buck could be discerned only by the light of criteria evolved in Europe; no other illumination was available. Thus Edith Brower could cite Mac-Dowell's pre-eminence as an American composer and discover its basis in his respect for traditional forms and procedures, his capacity for original invention, his "melodial instinct," and his effective management of discords, "the main essential that makes for modernity in music" (A-LXXVII, 394–402). Finck held, for approximately the same reasons, that MacDowell seemed "destined to place America musically on a level with Europe" (C-LIII, 453), and William Mason went so far as to assert that "the principal American composers of to-day [1900] are the peers of any who are now living" (C-LX, 864). The inherited criteria could be used to prove that a youthful

9. Living by his conviction that critics should avoid "snap-judgment" (A-XXXVIII, 379), Apthorp discussed Paine's oratorio twice (A-XXXI, 119; A-XXXI, 506–8) before he handed down his final opinion, several months after the *première*. The second article was inspired by a "not altogether favorable" review of Paine's oratorio and Buck's cantata by W. S. B. Mathews. See the *Nation*, February 13, 1873, pp. 116–17.

American musical culture was surpassing its aging parent and ac-
quiring its own unique identity.

The Essence of
Musical Americanism

There were, to be sure, not many particulars in which the
youth was surpassing its parent to the extent that it could in-
disputably claim maturity and independence. But, according to
Thomas, at least in the field of vocal pedagogy Europeans were no
longer meeting the needs of Americans. "No teacher in a foreign
country can rightly understand how to prepare pupils for practical
work here," he insisted. "Though the taste for singing was awakened
by Italian opera, and though the Italian method of using the voice
commends itself to us, the educated American is not satisfied with
the Italian repertory, and soon outgrows it" (C-XXI, 779–80). In
1894 one Jean Forsyth, a young woman from Owasso [Owosso],
Michigan, recounted her experiences as "A Singing-Student in
London" for *Harper's*. She had gone abroad, at a considerable
financial sacrifice on the part of her brother, to study under a
"famous" teacher, whom she depicted as somewhat phony, with
ridiculous affectations and absurd methods, whose genuine knowledge
was limited to what he could give out in the first two lessons. The
songs she learned were either too high class for Owosso, or they were
"silly English ballads." Nevertheless, the Cultured Miss Forsyth
lamented, the more gullible among her home-town acquaintances
would assuredly give her credit for having studied with a great
master, even though *she* knew she had wasted her brother's money.

Accusations like Thomas' and Forsyth's no doubt pleased the
numerous American music-lovers of the type who supported Treloar's
bill and the Contract Labor Act and who frequently annoyed the
Culturists with their chauvinism. "There are some [Americans],"
wrote Curtis in 1879,

who evidently think that the only escape from flunkyism to Europe is vigilantly to withstand the furriners. . . . [But] the prejudice which discredits foreign excellence, which resents deference to foreign judgment, or the adoption of foreign measures and inventions which are proved to be good, is nothing but the Chinese wall (H-LIX, 621).

Besides, as Apthorp had pointed out, Germany's own greatness as a musical nation had been partly the result of foreign (French, Dutch, and Italian) influences over a period of several centuries (A-XXXV, 122). Rupert Hughes expressed a similar opinion in behalf of American composers in 1898: "It has . . . taken men whole centuries to learn music," he wrote.

They do not yet seem able to write it well in isolated communities without the benefits of association with old and new masters, and a chance for the publishing of ambitious work to a competent audience. America, through pilgrimages to Europe, is only now giving hope of a national school of music" (C-LV, 768).

As we have seen, American critics and musicians cultivated a rigorous independence of opinion and taste insofar as possible, despite the obvious necessity for reliance upon standards that had originated in Europe. They knew that unimaginative eclecticism and total servility to foreign dominance might interfere with the growth of the American musical identity that the laws of evolution seemed to promise them. If they would not submit dumbly to ultramarine forces, neither could they justify any attempt to sever all ties, to short-cut progress, to leap into the midst of destiny. All evidence led to the conclusion that American civilization was a kind of biological descendant of European civilization. Therefore, the beginnings having already been accomplished in Europe, there could be no thought of beginning again in America, Turner's frontier hypothesis notwithstanding. The natural polarity of opposing forces, of dependence and independence, could not be artificially resolved. Temporarily, the only reasonable recourse was to regard the question of a "national school" with cosmopolitan detachment. After all, as Finck pointed out to the *Century*'s readers, "Cosmopolitanism is the essence of American life!"

Chapter VIII

Opera for America

GIVEN THE PREMISE that music can have a formative influence on the lives of intelligent listeners, it is no wonder that opera was considered "the highest form of musical composition" (A-LIX, 568). Its ennobling, civilizing power was a concomitant of its fundamental formal and aesthetic complexity. Since it was a combination of theater and music—specifically, of drama, scene design, costumery, pantomime, dance, and solo and ensemble music for voices and for instruments—it seemed logical to expect that opera ought to draw a larger audience than any single medium. And if various media naturally appealed to different types of individuals and to different levels of appreciation, then opera ought to be expected to draw together in one experience a greater cross-section of social classes than any single medium.

The complexity of opera also meant that there was a great deal that could be said about it; consequently, it was the most frequent subject for a "free play of the mind" in the literary magazines. Theories of opera, its Florentine origins, national characteristics, languages, singers and singing, musical styles and interpretation, and economic factors were discussed repeatedly, and often at a length that seems rather inordinate until we realize that all that most Americans could do with respect to opera was to read about it.

A Matter of Faith

Not all critics or readers agreed on the efficacy of opera, to be sure. Arthur Sedgwick, in a chronicle of "New York Theatres" for the *Atlantic* in 1879, excluded it from his remarks on the grounds that "it has really no connection with the regular theatrical life of New York, as it is an imported luxury" (A-XLIII, 457). William Dean Howells had expressed the same opinion twelve years before, although more than two decades later he allowed that Italian opera was, after all, more "at home" in New York than in its native land.[1] Even the fundamental idea of opera—sung drama—was assailed in the literary magazines with varying degrees of eloquence. Mary Tucker Magill's satire for *Harper's*, "A Georgian at the Opera," dealt amusingly with the absurdity of singing everything ("it is agin nachure"), the unrealistic complexities of the typical libretto, and the stylized gestures of the singers, concluding that, if one were to *study* long enough, one might learn to appreciate opera, but it hardly seemed worth the trouble. In 1896 William F. Biddle called opera before "the Court of Reason" in the *Atlantic*. Advancing a literal interpretation of the Aristotelian doctrine that art is imitation, he showed that, since the accompaniment of dramatic action by music is inconsistent with natural human action, then "serious grand opera or music-drama is an artistic blunder; . . . it is approaching recognition as such; and . . . even in the state of the world's thought about art it is almost an anachronism." Some of the more obvious conventions of opera were also the butts of numerous jokes and cartoons (see Plate 4).

Cultured opera-lovers, who had to share the world with less discriminating, more pragmatic inhabitants, were sensitive to such ridi-

1. William Dean Howells, The Easy Chair, *Harper's*, CVIII (May, 1904), 964–68.

I. THE HEROIC TENOR.

II. THE LYRIC TENOR.

III. THE PRIMA DONNA.

IV. THE AMATEUR.

PLATE 4. *High C, and How They Take It.* Drawings by Henry Mayer (C-LIX, 158–59).

cule of their favorite medium and patiently refuted the sophisms of the infidels. "The opera is a world beyond the realm of common sense," explained Curtis (H-LIX, 139). "The true operagoer leaves his mind and conscience at home. . . . When you have granted the first point, that human intercourse shall take place by singing instead of talking, everything is conceded and the word improbable ceases to have any meaning" (H-LXIII, 305). Opera-loving was basically a matter of faith.

The Cultured class and its spokesmen may not have changed the minds of many doubters with their polemics, but they did keep their own ideas in a continual state of ferment. One result was a reinforcement of the conviction that America's musical destiny was linked with opera. As William Foster Apthorp put it, "An established opera is the point at which are concentrated the musical executive forces of a community," and "in almost every capital in the world the opera is the standard of executive excellence" (A-XXXII, 634). Another result was the implication that opera had an ever-increasing popular following. "It is not to be denied that the conditions in our country are unlike the conditions of France or Germany. . . . But neither can it be denied that when a fair opera comes for a while to an American town, most of us go. Parquet and gallery are jammed with people" (A-LIX, 568).

The Singers

The illusion that operatic opportunity existed in the United States was both engendered and nourished by the commitment of the many European opera-singers and impresarios who came to the United States in ever-increasing numbers throughout the nineteenth century, confident that there was sufficient interest and money to assure them success and prosperity. Their activities were followed with close attention, especially during the seventies and eighties, by American critics, who first stringently re-evaluated the reputations they brought with them. Pauline Lucca, Ilma di Murska, Hermine Ruders-

dorff, Amalie Materna, Etelka Gerster, Emma Albani, Lillian Nordica
—these and many other visitors were continually under the watchful,
sometimes almost suspicious, eye of the daily press, and monthly or
seasonal reviews of their careers appeared in the monthly magazines.

Singers dominated American musical life to such an extent that
anyone could judge a new one on purely comparative criteria. In the
seventies, comparison with Jenny Lind was itself a complimentary
gesture toward a singer and was used sparingly by men like George
William Curtis, whose precious recollections of the Swedish Nightingale's song were still vivid. Christine Nilsson was likened to her by
Curtis, and Euphrosyne Parepa-Rosa, who also won "flowers of rhetoric" from Howells after the Peace Jubilee of 1869, was compared to
her by Edward King (C-VII, 735). The third stanza of King's poem
to the younger singer began:

> Like to that splendid Swede who swayed the souls
> Of prince and peasant, dids't thou live and sing;
> So long as Time's firm hand the years outrolls,
> The memories of ye twain shall bloom in spring.[2]

Technical and personal criteria were also employed. Theodore
Wachtel, a German tenor famous for his high C, made his first tour
of the United States in 1871, during which the *Century*'s critic observed that his great personal popularity, especially among German-
Americans, was incommensurate with his qualifications as a singer.
The critic then enumerated Wachtel's strengths and weaknesses in
close detail that would put a sportswriter to shame. On the other hand,

2. Nilsson also inspired at least one poet, John Fraser, who invoked the
analogy of the nightingale (C-VII, 557):
> Winter has come, the birds have fled,
> Their leaves the red-lipped roses shed;
> But in thy liquid throat, Christine,
> Perpetual Summer lurks unseen;
> And sleeps therein, in shine or hail,
> The perfect-throated nightingale;
> While on thy lips the roses lie,
> That live when all their sisters die.

the English baritone Charles Santley was "recognized immediately as
a musician of fine culture. . . . But this rigid musical excellence
filled the ear without touching the feelings, and Mr. Santley created no
enthusiasm" (C-III, 502). Nilsson was recognized as having certain
vocal limitations but was hailed by both Curtis and Apthorp as the
greatest singing actress of the day.

Whereas the private lives of European singers, like that of the
sensational Austrian soprano Pauline Lucca, were usually ignored,
critics frequently tried to say the best they could about the character
and citizenship of American singers like Annie Louise Carey, Clara
Louise Kellogg, and Adelaide Phillips. "Miss Phillips's career illus-
trates a phase of artistic life which we are tempted to consider as
peculiarly American," wrote the *Century's* critic in 1872.

> Commencing her life-work, as many of our readers will re-
> member, in early youth, almost childhood [Jenny Lind helped
> her begin formal study in 1850, when she was 17], Miss Phil-
> lips has gone steadily onward, in face of more than usual em-
> barrassment, bravely, honorably, kindly, and generously win-
> ning her way to her present high position both in professional
> and private life, untouched by any shadow of reproach, un-
> spoiled by praise, and careless of the smaller devices which
> are conventionally supposed essential to artistic recognition
> and applause (C-IV, 253).

The Repertoire

The Cultured critic was no less meticulous in his treatment of
operatic repertoire than he was in his analysis of singers. Being anxious
for American musical Culture to arrive at its millennium, thoughtful
persons were eager to hear not only the finest singers but the newest
operas, as soon as there was sufficient reason to believe they represented steps in the forward, upward direction required by progress.
Furthermore, being conscious of Darwinian principles of classification,
the abler critics continually viewed and reviewed the old as well as

the new operas in terms of their organic relationships with all discernible historical antecedents and contemporary varieties. Ambroise Thomas's *Mignon,* composed in 1866 and first performed in New York in November, 1871, was said by Curtis to be representative of the "modern French manner," by which he meant "the instrumentation and the singing are . . . a setting for the drama" (H-XLV, 134). The *Century*'s critic held a different view of French style, and of *Mignon*'s essential nature:

> It is a gracious rather than a great work, built rather than evolved by the latest French method. . . . The concerted music is of the eclectic order, employing all the modern expedients to enhance its effect, but lacking breadth and color, and failing in the intenser situations to rise to the height of dramatic expression (C-III, 378).

Apthorp agreed with the latter judgment, devoting nearly four columns to a detailed analysis and likening the style to that of Meyerbeer.

A "Meyerbeer opera" belonged to a special category, a sport of nature in the organic history of opera, incapable of generating improvements on itself. Apthorp's analysis was representative of the majority of opinions: "There is so much of artifice, so little of real art, so much that is transparently factitious, so little that is convincingly spontaneous and great in it!" It was, he said, full of "effect," of "seeming" (A-XXXIII, 511). He was also disappointed in Verdi's *Aida,* presented for the first time in Boston by the Strakosch troupe in 1874: "Strange as it may appear, the heretofore reckless and devil-may-care Verdi has written what is to all intents and purposes a Meyerbeer opera" (A-XXXIII, 509).

The categorization of operas according to the national tradition embodied was seldom mentioned, since the critical vocabulary was misleading in this connection. Theoretically, French operas included those by Meyerbeer, Halévy, Grétry, Gounod, and Thomas; Italian opera consisted of all works by Bellini, Rossini, and Spontini, and some by Verdi; English opera comprised operettas and comic operas, such as *The Doctor of Alcantara,* by the Boston composer and teacher Julius Eichberg. Until the late seventies, German operas in the standard repertoire were those by Weber and Mozart and the early works of Wagner, though in the early eighties the term "German opera" became synonymous with Wagnerian opera and music drama alone, in the minds of many persons. Indeed, the subject of Wagnerism grew to such importance in American musical life between 1870 and 1900 that it deserves a separate chapter in this study.

To the layman, however, national designations indicated not the tradition embodied, nor even the allegiance of the composer, but the language in which a work was to be sung at a given performance. This was determined by the nationality of the majority of the singers in a company, for multilingual singers were unusual in those days. As Apthorp reminded his readers, previewing the season of "Italian opera" to come in the spring of 1873 in Boston,

> The Italian element in its composition stands rather in the background, the best of the singers being German, American, and French, and the best of the operas being the work of German and French composers. The singing, however, is done in the Italian language (with a pleasing variety of accents), which fact may give some coloring of appropriateness to the name, which otherwise does not mean much (A-XXXI, 374).

The term "Italian opera" signified far more to the Cultured class than either language or nationality, however. It stood for a constellation of circumstances which were but ramifications of the demonstrable fact that certain Italian composers had taken an evolutionary course leading away from the original Florentine idea of opera as *dramma per musica* and had made nondeveloping, lyrical melody the dominant stylistic element. In short, "Italian opera" denoted any work featuring the beautiful voices of a few stars, who were engaged at great expense, with a resultant lowering of quality in the areas of supporting singers, chorus, orchestra, ballet, and *mise en scène*. These characteristics could, of course, be imposed forcibly upon numerous operas by composers of other nationalities, in any language, but they were most frequently associated with the works of the Italians. Understandably, in view of their belief in the superiority of opera as a union of drama and music, thoughtful people viewed the perpetuation of the Italian tradition with a jaundiced eye. The Easy Chair had always doubted it would ever become "a permanent fact among us" (H-VIII, 695–96). The Culturists were disinclined to encourage Americans to burden their musical lives with a species which was not only at an evolutionary dead end but which embodied so many conditions that were inimical to the precepts of Culture.

The Star System

The dominance of Italian opera was not without its positive benefits, of course. "Americans, and especially New Yorkers, have grown up with Italian opera, which for more than half a century has kept the field," wrote an observer in 1883. "Fondness for beautiful voices and appreciation of refined execution in singing have been greatly developed by this education" (C-XXVII, 158). By the same token, as Apthorp noted, when a great singing actress like Nilsson appeared in Italian opera, she made the dramatic vacuity of the genre all the more evident (A-XXIX, 118). Cultured persons were as susceptible to the allurements of beautiful voices as any frail mortals, but they demanded that artistic integrity be the basis of all musical expression.

The expense of the star system reflected a confusion of aesthetic values with market values, which was also distressing to the Culturists. All sorts of factors affected the economic structure of Italian opera, of course, such as the greater expense of maintaining an impermanent, itinerant company as compared with a permanent, resident company. But in any case, competing entrepreneurs would bid against one another for the most popular stars. "The enthusiasm for a favorite singer is so overpowering, and her audiences so sure," wrote Curtis, "that every manager fears to lose his chance by the high offer of his rivals, so that the singers demand the most extravagant sums, and they are allowed" (H-LII, 142). Other considerations aside, any chance of making Italian opera a workable part of American musical life was obstructed by the implications of the obvious fact that someone was always willing to pay the asking price for a prima donna—if it were high enough. "When one singer asks five thousand dollars for a single appearance in Italian opera [the reference is to Adelina Patti, no doubt], the nature of Italian opera as a fabulous luxury is clearly demonstrated," wrote Curtis in 1884 (H-LXIX, 962). Ostentation was a form of gentility, and gentility was an attribute of false Culture.

The speculative nature of the star system compelled most managers to sacrifice some, if not all, of the less obvious aspects of their productions to those which would have the most appeal in an advertisement. The Italian opera season presented by Max Maretzek's company in New York in the autumn of 1872 was not entirely satisfactory to thoughtful operagoers for that reason. "It was felt that the management depended too confidently on its prime donne. Its tenors and baritones were weak in voice and uninspiring in action" (C-V, 393). Apthorp was hardly sympathetic with the disappointed patrons of the same troupe in Boston the following season:

> If we want operatic performances with good chorus and orchestra and respectable *mise-en-scène* we must either pay exorbitant prices or else give up the world-renowned stars. And inversely, . . . if we insist upon turning up our noses at any company that does not boast two or three stars of the first magnitude, we must be content with execrable performances (A-XXXIII, 127).

Whenever an impresario managed to present a performance in which the diva did not completely rule the stage, the Cultured critics were quick to applaud. The *Century's* Culture and Progress columnist congratulated the Parepa-Rosa English Opera Company on "general soundness and symmetry of all essential elements" (C-IV, 253). The productions of Col. James H. Mapleson's opera company won Curtis' approval in 1881 on the basis of "the symmetry of the whole." "No part is slighted," he said (H-LXII, 306). Curtis had predicted two years earlier that Mapleson's balanced productions would make Italian opera both permanent and profitable in New York. He was unable to foresee from that point the rise of the Metropolitan Opera Association, a monument to the natural fact that the appeal of a prima donna was addictive and that the rich people who subsidized opera regarded it not as a strictly musical form but as a social vehicle, a form of what Thorstein Veblen was soon (1899) to call "conspicuous leisure."

The resistance of the rich box-holder class toward all efforts to meliorate its motives for patronage was no less annoying than the ways that class had of showing its disdain for the lofty ideals of the Culturists. For example, they infuriated the Culturists by talking in their boxes during performances, except when interrupted by some favorite aria or some "fashionable" singer, and the basic conflict of aesthetic and social interests prompted sometimes immoderate expressions of opinion on the matter. No spokesman for the Cultured class was more persistent in attempting to reform the Barbarians than Curtis. Once or twice each season he scolded the benefactors who were "not yet fully emancipated from the manners of the gulch and mines and rude frontiers in which probably the family money was made." He was even defiant:

> Some [of the box holders] are reported to have said that they supplied the money for the maintenance of operas, and they should certainly talk in their boxes if they chose. To this ultimatum the parquet can only offer its own. If the boxes chatter, the parquet will hiss. If for that reason the parquet is closed to lovers of music, the opera itself will disappear (H-LXXXII, 638).

The boxes were eventually quieted temporarily not, ostensibly, by the Cultured occupants of the three-dollar seats in the parquet but by the board of directors.[3]

Temporary Triumphs: German and "American" Opera

The ultimate futility of Curtis' effort was symptomatic of one change that was taking place in American operatic life. When opera had been in the province of free enterprise among independent entrepreneurs, the opinions of the Cultured critics seemed to matter a little; at least they sounded relevant. But with the rise of the Metropolitan, wealth and social power completely overrode the might of Cultured criticism and rendered impotent all competition from conscientious men like Mapleson, with his symmetrical presentations. In 1896 *Scribner's* chastised the anonymous author of a letter to the *New York Evening Post* who had complained of the box talk of the plutocrats: "It is very certain that these magnificent music-dramas are only made possible for him by the more ornate portion of the community." Curtis was gone from the scene by this time, and opera-lovers among the remnant were beginning to accept the consignment of their favorite medium to that aesthetic and social limbo it would thenceforth occupy in the United States. Meanwhile, the core of the Cultured class had only two transitory consolations for its losses: the seven-year reign of German opera at the Metropolitan and the brief, mercurial sojourn of "American" opera.

The sudden change of course at the Metropolitan was neither disappointing nor unexplainable to the Culturists, who were already convinced of the essential rightness of Wagnerism. Apthorp had long held that, although as music the Italian genre was still acceptable for certain types of entertainment, as opera it was definitely dated and its value as an art form was no longer arguable on either evolutionary

3. See Irving Kolodin, *The Metropolitan Opera, 1883–1966*, rev. ed. (New York, 1967), p. 53.

or aesthetic grounds. Some observers were convinced that the great singers trained in the "old Italian school" were dying out and that the genre could no longer be performed as it was supposed to be. Curtis agreed and added that the Metropolitan Opera House was too large for the delicate nuances of the *bel canto* tradition to be fully appreciated. "Or, indeed," he went on,

> is it not at all upon the stage, but wholly in front? Is it the mere fickleness of favor, the artists not being in the least degree changed, and only the public a little sated? . . . Are the very foundations of things shaken, and is the taste for Italian opera changing, even declining? (H-LXVIII, 642).

Curtis welcomed the competition between Mapleson and the Metropolitan that began in 1884, viewing it as a "Contest of Nightingales," Italian on the one hand and German on the other, confident that the fittest would survive. Mapleson soon abandoned the field, and the victor became a German house; the outcome of the struggle reassured the Cultured class. Curtis was rudely disenchanted of his cherished confidence in the machinery of progress, however, when in 1891 Italian opera returned to the Metropolitan, bringing French opera along. He responded with scathing sarcasm:

> The axiom . . . that men are queer, has been strongly confirmed recently by a decision of the authorities of the Metropolitan Opera-house in New York. That important body, producing the figures, has announced in effect that as it is clear from the accounts that the presentation of German opera is more profitable than that of Italian and French opera combined, it is evident that the public desires to hear Italian and French opera, and therefore for the present the German opera will be discontinued. . . . It is a striking illustration of the superiority of man to money, and in the mad struggle for a mere material advantage, this devotion to pure art, condemning the expense, is a noble tribute to the unselfishness of human nature (H-LXXXII, 797).

The brief and ignominious history of the American Opera Company under Theodore Thomas began at the Academy of Music in January, 1886, one month after Mapleson's Italian company had collapsed in the same house. The concept of an American opera company was possibly Thomas' to begin with. In 1873 he published in the *New York Evening Post* what John Sullivan Dwight called a "strange, long, and may we not say windy document" in which he outlined the scheme—Dwight termed it a "Great Bayreuth-ian Project" —which evidently was the basis of the American Opera Company and the National Conservatory eventually "founded" by Mrs. F. B. Thurber, who seems to have been involved almost from the beginning.[4] Preliminary planning was actually under way in 1873; the target date was 1875 or 1876. The American Opera Company, Limited, was established in 1878, but it remained merely a paper operation for another seven years.

The general aim of the original plan was the permanent support of "opera sung by Americans." More specifically, according to the company's prospectus of 1878, the objective was to present grand opera in English sung by "the most competent artists," a chorus "composed entirely of young and fresh [American] voices," with a ballet corps of Americans, American-made costumes and properties, scenery designed and painted by American artists, accompanied by "the unrivalled Thomas Orchestra," all under the direction of Thomas. "In a word," the prospectus announced, "the object of the American Opera Company is to present ensemble opera, giving no single feature undue prominence to the injury of others, and distinctly discouraging the pernicious star system, long since discountenanced in continental Europe."[5] The second year, as the National Opera Company of New Jersey, it was established on an ingenious business plan independent of the Conservatory, which was intended to assure that

4. See *Dwight's Journal of Music,* September 6, 1873. Concerning Mrs. Thurber's conservatory, see pp. 101–2 above. The complete story of this long and complicated episode in American musical life has not yet been written.

5. Quoted in Theodore Thomas, *A Musical Autobiography,* ed. George P. Upton, 2 Vols. (Chicago, 1905), I, 186–87.

the company would both represent and serve the nation at large rather than a single city.[6]

As far as the critics were concerned, Thomas' company was decidedly a success. The unique "symmetry" of the company's performances was their most impressive aspect. A columnist for the *Century* explained the effect in May, 1886:

> This close knitting together of all the parts—something much more than we usually mean when we speak of the *ensemble* —was the characteristic note of the representations which Thomas began at the New York Academy of Music last January. He plays operas as he would play a symphony. To him it is a symphony of voices and instruments.

That same month, Curtis reminded his readers with pride that the manifest destiny of American operatic life was coming to pass. "The opera that began with Malibran, and which has charmed generations, ended, and the German and American opera, vigorous and triumphant, sits supreme upon the double throne of the two houses, surrounded by loyal taste, wealth, and fashion." He viewed the company as "another warble of American independence" and "the latest proof that Jonathan has come of age" (H-LXXII, 969–70). Evolution was true!

Furthermore, an *Atlantic* Contributor exclaimed, the company is

> a final answer to some minor objections which I shall merely name: that the quality of American voices is too shallow for good music; that nothing operatic can be sung in English on account of our unmusical tongue; and that to understand what people are talking about in grand opera will never do in the world.

6. *Boston Evening Transcript,* June 29, 1886.

It was truly "republican opera" (A-LIX, 571). The question of opera in English had been a major issue in American musical life since before mid-century and remained so, well beyond 1900, despite the work of impresarios like Carl Rosa, Clara Louise Kellogg, Emma Juch, Emma Abbott, Henry Russell, Jr., and even Henry Savage, founder of the Castle Square Opera Company in Boston in 1895, who produced opera in English at the Metropolitan in 1900–1901.[7] In July, 1910, for example, David Bispham felt compelled to remind the *Century's* readers "Why We Should Sing in English." The arguments against singing in English were pretty much the same from year to year and were frequently couched in telling rhetoric, if not always sound logic. A writer for the *Atlantic* maintained that

> the libretto of an opera in the original tongue of the composer is apt to be greatly subordinated to the music, and viewed as verse is usually but a weak and meaningless affair. . . . But when the Italian or German is still further diluted into an English version, it becomes as the *vin ordinaire* of the cheap French cabaret, which has been watered to the standard of street railway stock; nothing is left but the color and the twang (A-LXVIII, 574).

The majority of the Culture-guardians, however, were unalterably in favor of opera in the vernacular, and the new company was a vindication of their convictions.

It was not merely a *succès d'estime,* either. The warm response of the general public to American opera was indeed satisfying to Cultured observers. It was "a good thing to see the top galleries filled with people who were evidently enjoying themselves, and for very little money" (A-LIX, 571). Unfortunately, happy galleries and parquets could not guarantee the financial prosperity of "symmetrical" opera; only great stars possessed the centripetal force to draw money

7. Edward Hipsher, *American Opera and Its Composers* (Philadelphia, 1927), chap. 5. See also W. L. Hubbard, ed., *The American History and Encyclopedia of Music: History of American Music* (Toledo, 1910), pp. 246–50.

from the Barbarians. The company lasted two seasons and collapsed in utter ruin in Toronto, Canada, on June 18, 1887. The demise was politely ignored by the literary magazines, and the dream of a "republican opera" faded quickly and disappeared forever.

If Cultured opera-lovers felt any sense of loss, their grief was assuaged by the presence in their musical lives of a genre which, though it lacked certain of the economic and educational features of Thomas' conception, nevertheless appeared to be "symmetrical" by its very definition and which healthily occupied their thoughts: Wagnerian music drama.

Chapter IX

Wagnerism in America

THE MUSIC AND THE THEORIES of Richard Wagner dominated American musical life from about 1870 until the end of the century, producing ideas and attitudes about music that coincided with the tenets of Culture at all important points. In that it had a musical as well as a literary manifestation, and in that those aspects were essentially separate but entirely complementary, Wagnerism was similar to Mendelssohnism in America, but there were two fundamental differences. First, the emphasis of the latter was upon the man himself, whereas Wagnerism was concentrated on music and musical theory, including aesthetics. Second, Mendelssohn represented a classic, transcendent ideal from the past; Wagner was a symbol of the present and a guide to the future.

Musical Wagnerism

Active interest in Wagner's music began about 1852, when the Germania Orchestra under Carl Bergmann began playing excerpts from *Tannhäuser* on its tours throughout the country. It was further stimulated by the arrival of still more immigrant musicians who had played Wagner's works in Europe or had at least had firsthand knowledge of Wagner's undertakings there and by the visits of men like Hans von Bülow, whose life and career had been closely connected with Wagner's. The process of acquainting Americans with Wagner's stage works was begun by Bergmann with *Tannhäuser* in New York, in 1859, and continued for thirty years until the American *première* of *Das Rheingold* in 1889 and a concert version of *Parsifal* in 1891 at the Metropolitan under Anton Seidl.

By the early seventies the desire to hear all of Wagner's works was high among the ambitions of Cultured music-lovers. *Lohengrin,* which had received its first performance under Liszt at Weimar in 1850, was first performed in America at the Stadt Theater in New York on April 3, 1871. The *Century's* critic was exhilarated by the performance but embarrassed for America. "What shall we say of American enthusiasm for art, and enterprise in its cultivation, when a work like this has had to wait twenty years to be heard at all on this side of the Atlantic, and at last is only heard in the Bowery?" (C-II, 216). He might well have taken some pride in the fact that the work had not yet been performed in London or Paris.

Seidl's career climaxed the history of musical Wagnerism in America. When he arrived in 1885, he was looked upon, Henry Krehbiel said, "as a repository of Wagnerian tradition—a prophet, priest, and paladin" (S-XXIII, 758). Not only had he been Wagner's musical secretary for six years; he had also been a member of the composer's household, perhaps in a way unsuspected—or perhaps only politely ignored—by American Culturists.[1] The Culturists accepted his coming as a matter of course, being by then such self-confident Wagnerians that they did not consider the possibility that Seidl might have been an exile from the Wagner circle or that his move might have been a step down. "It was much to his advantage," wrote Krehbiel,

1. See Arthur Farwell, "America's Gain from a Bayreuth Romance," *Musical Quarterly,* XXX (October, 1944), 448–57.

that he came among an impressionable people with the prestige of a Wagnerian oracle and archon, and much to the advantage of the cult to which he was devoted that he made that people "experience" the lyric dramas of his master in the same sense that a good Methodist "experiences" religion, rather than to "like" them (S-XXIII, 758).

It was Theodore Thomas, however, who above all others provided the strongest thread of continuity in musical Wagnerism from the beginning of his career as an orchestra conductor in 1862 to its close in 1905. He opened his very first concert as director of the Brooklyn Philharmonic Society on May 13, 1862, with the first American performance of the *Fliegende Holländer* Overture. He conducted the first performance in this country of the *Die Meistersinger* Overture with the New York Symphony on October 20, 1866. He programed overtures and other excerpts with increasing frequency, until, on September 19, 1871, he presented the first of his so-called "Wagner nights," which, the following season, became a weekly feature of the Central Park Garden Concerts (see H-XLIX, 131). It was a rather tentative experiment, for Wagner usually shared the program with others, like Weber, Beethoven, and Mendelssohn; but a year later, on September 17, 1872, Thomas presented the first all-Wagner concert in America and subsequently performed similar programs on his numerous tours through the country.[2] There were already enough Wagnerians in America for Thomas to successfully organize a "Wagner Verein," after that epochal concert in 1872, to raise money to provide the orchestra members with tickets to the first Bayreuth Festival, still four years away.

Wagner, along with Beethoven, became the pillar of his programs, he said later, though Mendelssohn was also present with conspicuous frequency.[3] Wagner was the highlight of the Chicago, Cincinnati, and New York festivals of 1882 and of the Pittsburgh and San

2. See Theodore Thomas, *A Musical Autobiography*, ed. George P. Upton, 2 Vols. (Chicago, 1905), II, 117, 119; Edwin T. Rice, "Thomas and Central Park Garden," *Musical Quarterly*, XXVI (April, 1940), 143–52.
3. Thomas, *Autobiography*, II, 15.

Francisco festivals of 1883, giving, as Curtis said, "a full revelation of
the character and charm of the modern music" (H-LXX, 807). The
1882 festivals in turn aroused intense interest in the impending *première* of *Parsifal* at Bayreuth (H-LXV, 798). Afterward, in the
autumn of 1882, Thomas conducted excerpts from the *Bühnenfestspiel,* while the memories of the preceding July were still in the
minds of American Wagnerians. In 1884 he took a Wagner festival
on tour for three months, and this, together with the work of Leopold Damrosch in behalf of Wagner, helped to ensure the beginning
of German opera at the Metropolitan in the following season. Thereafter Thomas considered his missionary work virtually complete,
though he continued to include Wagnerian repertoire in his programs.

Thomas would have been an important figure in nineteenth-century
American musical history even if Wagner had never existed. As it
was, no other individual did more to give focus to Americans' ideas
about the composer. One reason was that, as we have seen, Thomas
himself was a man the Cultured critics reported on with both pleasure
and respect. More than that, however, it was a coincidence of a music
like Wagner's with a conductor like Thomas that assured the appeal
of both to American audiences. "There can be no question," wrote
an observer in 1875,

> that in the rendering of the new school of music, the gorgeous
> tone-pictures of Liszt and Berlioz and Wagner, Thomas stands
> entirely alone. No one in this country has yet approached him
> either in the distinct interpretation of their obscure and diffi-
> cult phrases or the rich and majestic delivery of their swelling
> harmonies (C-IX, 466).

To be sure, critics for the Cultured class were glad for any opportunity for American audiences to become familiar with the music of the
master, but their studies of Wagner's theories, as well as their impa-
tience with the tenacity of the Italian opera tradition in America, kept

in their minds the fact that concert performances of excerpts from operas and music dramas left much to be desired. Thomas played the introduction and final scene from *Tristan* in Boston in December, 1871, and William Foster Apthorp was interested in the novelties but was rather harsh in his observation that the selections were, "in spite of their great beauty, hardly suited to the concert-room" (A-XXIX, 248). George William Curtis agreed, on the grounds that "mere orchestration is little in the Wagnerian theory" (H-XLIX, 131), though ten years later he found no fault whatsoever with the lack of scenery and action at the Wagner Festival in New York, for Materna, Winkelmann, and Scaria, avatars of Bayreuthian Wagnerism, were present (H-LXIX, 307).

When full stagings of Wagner's works were given, during the sixties and seventies, they were often "Italianized"; that is, the singers would step downstage center and address their more lyrical lines to the audience. Sometimes this was a result of singers' and directors' inability or disinclination to understand or appreciate Wagner's insistence upon verism in acting and staging. When Adolf Neuendorff presented *Die Walküre* at the Wagner Festival in Boston in 1877, Apthorp dismissed the event curtly: "As the Walküre was given . . . on a false principle—that is, as an opera, not as a drama—it would be idle to criticise the performance" (A-XL, 128). *Tannhäuser* was bowdlerized by Neuendorff during the same season for perhaps a different reason, less obvious and more amusing to us than to that morally more fastidious generation: The Venusberg scene was done by two singers on a bare stage, without a *corps de ballet.*[4] On the other hand, when stylistically correct standards were approached, the effect was quickly recognized. Maurice Strakosch's production of *Lohengrin* in 1874 was enthusiastically approved by the *Century*'s critic (C-VIII, 246), though the demanding Apthorp still found fault with "a want of comprehension of Wagner's peculiar dramatic style by singers bred in a thoroughly Italian school of singing and operatic acting" (A-XXXV, 378).

4. See the *Nation,* April 3, 1877; C-XXIV, 622.

Regardless of either the quality or the correctness of performances of Wagner's works, however, the number and intensity of the reactions they elicited proved that, whether or not music in general had found a place in American life, Wagner's in particular appealed to a broader American audience than any other. Thomas' prime motivation throughout his career had been the certainty that Wagner's music represented the modern spirit, excited its hearers—especially the younger generation—and interested the less musical. Mariana Van Rensselaer, whose usual field was art criticism, reported from Bayreuth after the *Parsifal première* of 1882 that "the people are thrilled by and respond to his music as they do to that of no other man. . . . The young generation thinks and feels and sees with Wagner by instinct and not by effort" (H-LXVI, 541). The music of the future had become the music of the present. An *Atlantic* Contributor expressed himself similarly in 1887: "No one can tell how hard Wagner has hit the eternal nail on the head; but he has surely hit the nail of the present completely" (A-LIX, 571).

Literary Wagnerism

Wagnerism in America not only pleased peoples' ears—it stimulated their minds. The relative infrequency of adequate full-scale performances encouraged the discussion of Wagnerian theories, and a few fundamental ideas came to be so frequently expounded that the most important issues were soon clouded, requiring still further discussion. Many Americans were simply incapable of coping unaided with the difficulties Wagner's music presented to the listener experienced only in the traditional classicism of Mendelssohn, the banalities of Liszt or Raff, or the superficial trivialities of Italian opera; and nothing in their music education could have prepared them for Wagner's "endless melody" or his brassy instrumentation, not to mention the notion of a *Gesamtkunstwerk*. On the other hand, the way Josiah Gilbert Holland looked at it in 1876, the musical innocence—or ignorance—of Americans was an advantage. "[Wagner's] victory was the easier, perhaps, in that our people were less settled than those of the old world in the conventional forms of musical expression. In other words, they had less to unlearn than those who knew more" (C-XIII, 125). Or, as *The Critic* editorialized in its issue of May 3, 1884, "We have no past in art to make us conservative." Still, there was a great deal to learn, and the successful explication or elucidation of Wagnerian theories and practices was a challenge that Cultured critics met with eagerness and energy. Indeed, since it was conceivable that one could become a dedicated Wagnerian without necessarily experiencing any of the actual music, the task of Cultural guardianship was made easier. Theories that could be explained through logical discourse were likely to be much more readily seized and more confidently held by aspirants toward Culture than the ephemeral, sensuous sound of the music itself.

The principle of the *Leitmotiv,* for example, could be grasped by a sufficient number of Cultured readers to make intricate satires on it appealing to editors of the literary magazines. One such satire, which appeared in *Harper's* in 1896, was "Bluebeard: Lecture Recital on a Posthumous Music-Drama by Richard Wagner," by Kate Douglas Wiggin, author of *Rebecca of Sunnybrook Farm.* The "Lecture Recital" is dedicated, "with apologies," to Walter Damrosch, who conducted the first performance of *Parsifal* in the United States in 1896 and led the Metropolitan through its great "German" seasons of 1900–1902, and to Henry Krehbiel, dogmatic critic of the *New York Tribune* and author of the adulatory *Studies in the Wagnerian Drama* (1891).

Wiggin managed to touch most of the bases in the game of Wagnerism. To begin with, an imaginary manuscript has been discovered beneath a certain bedstead in Wagner's house, over which a brilliant halo has persistently hovered. "It is not strange that Wagner should choose to immortalize the story of Bluebeard," Wiggin continues,

> for the beautiful and inspiring myth has been used in all ages and in all countries. It differs slightly in the various versions.

In some the shade of the villain's beard is robin's-egg, and in others indigo; in some the fatal key is blood-stained instead of broken; and the number of wives varies according to the customs of the locality where the myth appears. In monogamous countries the number slain is generally six (the number used by Wagner), but in bigamous and polygamous countries the interesting victims rise (they were always "hung high," you remember) to the number of one hundred and seventeen.

Numerous *"motivos"* are illustrated, including the "Blaubart Motivo," played "with sombre grandeur leading upward to vague desire"; the "Immerwieder-heirathen Motivo (Desire-for-a-new-wife Motive)"; the "Brüder-hoch-zu-Ross Motivo (Brothers-on-a-high-horse Motive)"; and the "Fatima, oder Die Siebente-Frau Motivo":

This Fatima, or seventh-wife motive, seems to be written in a curiously low key, if we conceive it to be the index to the character of a soprano heroine; but let us look further. *What are these two principal personages* in the music-drama *to be to each other?*

If *enemies,* the phrase would have been written thus:

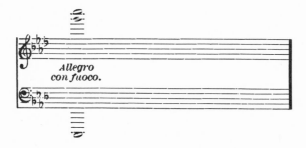

If *acquaintances,* thus:

If *friends,* thus:

If *lovers,* thus:

the ardent and tropical treble note leaving its own proper sphere and snuggling cozily down in the bass staff. But they were husband and wife, therefore the phrases are intertwined sufficiently, but not too much for pleasure.

Finally, there are the "Hochzeitsreise (Bridal-tour)" and "Flitter-wochen (Honey-moon)" motives.

They make up the most exquisitely tender act of the music-drama, and are especially interesting to us, since they are built upon one of our national songs—"Home, Sweet Home." This can only be regarded as a flattering recognition of our support of German opera in this country.

The Issues

Until the early seventies Americans learned about Wagner through music journals like *Dwight's* and through the daily and periodical press, which often conveyed not only items from abroad but also the reports and impressions of American travelers and immigrant German musicians, such as A. R. Parsons' report on the Berlin Wagner Festival of 1871 in E. E. Hale's *Old and New*. It was typical of journalistic style at that time for news items to be loaded with interpretations and opinions, and so the inherently polemical character of Wagnerism was emphasized from the very beginning. In 1871, for example, the foreign correspondent for the *Century's* Culture and Progress department reported the Bayreuth scheme with a remark calculated to give American readers a clear point of reference and a basis for prejudice: "Richard Wagner, the great musical composer, has a marvelous 'event' on his hands—one that smacks a little of Gilmore" (C-II, 661). Details of Wagner's ideas and activities were meager and disconnected, but the drift seemed to be clear. In 1872 the *Century's* home columnist for the same department observed that the Reverend Hugh Reginald Haweis' book, *Music and Morals,* "takes strong grounds against the modern Wagnerian school, which aims at definite expression, by melodies and harmonies, of events, scenes, situations, or distinct thoughts" (C-IV, 645). Obviously, Wagnerism was very much on the reviewer's mind, for Haweis had referred to Wagner in only about a dozen sentences in nearly as many different places throughout his long and provocative book. Furthermore, although the Englishman conceded Wagner's genius, he confessed he did not fully understand the composer's theories at that time.[5]

The *Gesammelte Schriften und Dichtungen* appeared in nine volumes beginning in 1871, and by 1873 competent critics had at hand a tool that would measurably enhance their ability to understand and assess the new movement. Apthorp, who had published an excerpt

5. Hugh Reginald Haweis, *Music and Morals* (London, 1872), p. 424.

from the *Zukunftsmusik* for readers of the *Atlantic* in November, 1873,[6] objectively summarized its significance in February of the following year:

> Whether we regard his artistic career as an enchanting vision of an esthetic and social millennium now made possible, or as a hideous nightmare of chaos regained, we may be assured that for good or for evil he has done and been something real; that his existence is more than a sham (A-XXXIII, 252).

Unfortunately, however, the Carlylean style of Wagner's prose prevented all but expert German linguists from penetrating its meanings. Dwight, the firmness of whose convictions compelled him to reject Wagner's theory of the connection between poetry and music,[7] had already made his own quite adequate translation of Wagner's note on the Ninth Symphony as early as 1853 and had published several more translations thereafter, including excerpts from *Oper und Drama,* but these had been forgotten by the seventies or had been superseded by more recent writings by Wagner. Then, in 1875, Edward L. Burlingame published his translations of a baker's dozen of essays from the collected works, with a list of Wagner's published compositions compiled by Apthorp, under the title *Art Life and Theories of Richard Wagner.*[8] A new era could now begin in American musical life, according to Apthorp, for "all that is absolutely indispensable for the intelligent music-lover to know about Wagner's theories is contained in the two chapters, The Music of the Future [1850], and The Purpose of the Opera [1871]" (A-XXXVI, 254;

6. From the translation by Edward Dannreuther, the founder of the London Wagner Society, which appeared in the *Monthly Musical Record* (London) in 1872.

7. See *Dwight's Journal of Music,* January 21, 1854.

8. The table of contents lists the following titles: Autobiography; The Love-Veto . . . ; A Pilgrimage to Beethoven; An End in Paris; Der Freischütz in Paris (I. . . . an Address to the Parisian Public; II. "Le Freischütz" . . .); The Music of the Future; . . . Tannhäuser in Paris; The Purpose of the Opera; Musical Criticism . . . ; The Legend of the Nibelungen; The Opera-House at Bayreuth (in two parts).

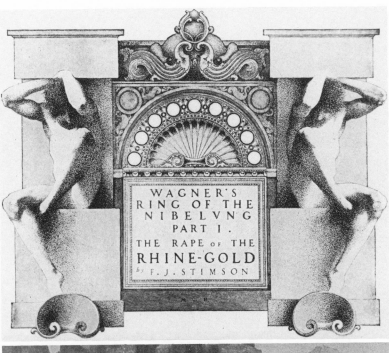

PLATE 5. Chromolithographs by Maxfield Parrish for Frederic Jesup Stimson's translation of *Das Rheingold* (S-XXIV, 693–708).

see also C-X, 520–21). Burlingame's collection was especially admired for the excellence of the translations, and it remained unsur-
passed in American Wagnerian literature until Ashton Ellis' eight-
volume edition of the *Prose Works* began to appear in London in
1893.

In the introduction to *Art Life and Theories* Burlingame urged that
someone else undertake to translate the complete text of Wagner's
Der Ring des Nibelungen into English. It is no coincidence, then, that
while he was editor of *Scribner's* it was begun (though never com-
pleted) by the lawyer, diplomat, and, like Burlingame, expert lin-
guist, Frederic Jesup Stimson, with illustrations by Maxfield Parrish
(S-XXIV, 693–708; see Plate 5).

It is indicative of the vigor and force of opinion in America that
the first two essayists on Wagnerism in the literary magazines were
emphatically opposed to the new movement. Alice Asbury, a young
American writer on music and translator of one of Hermann Mendel's
books on Meyerbeer, reviewed "Wagner's arrogant new school" in the
Atlantic for August, 1872, concluding,

> A reformer he is not, in the particular he asserts, for the theory
> he calls his own was shared by Gluck, Mozart, Beethoven,
> and Weber. He carries out the principle, however, in his own
> perverted and extravagant fashion, which must almost make
> those venerated fathers turn in their graves (A-XXX, 146).

The same tone, part of the argument, and the devotion to Viennese
classicism were also to be found in John Knowles Paine's study of
important parts of the first four volumes of the *Gesammelte
Schriften* which appeared in the *North American Review* in 1873.[9]
Paine's analysis was far more exhaustive and methodical than Americans had yet read, even in the music journals. After summarizing the
biographical contents of the first volume and setting forth clear, ob-

9. John Knowles Paine, "The New German School of Music," *North American Review*, CCXXXIX (April, 1873), 217–45.

jective résumés of *Art and Revolution, The Future Work of Art* [*sic*],
and *Opera and Drama,* he enumerated some of the "counterviews and
criticisms" which the three essays had evoked, citing August Ambros,
Otto Jahn, Adolph Marx, and even Friedrich Schlegel to reinforce his
own not inconsiderable authority among American readers. This is not
to say that many, or even any, of his remarks were original with him.
They had in fact been common currency among European critics—
and certain American critics and musicians, like William Henry Fry
—for a number of years; readers of *Dwight's,* for example, had
encountered most of them nearly two decades earlier (see *Dwight's,*
October 18, 1856, and November 27, 1858). Nor would they have
been agreed upon by all opponents of Wagner.

Paine assailed the doctrines of *Art and Revolution* in behalf of all
"rational and sober-minded" readers. He called Wagner a wild
dreamer, a reckless iconoclast who was "out of joint with the world"
and was bent upon effecting a revolution in religious, social, political,
and artistic life by sheer intellectual force, in futile defiance of the
evolutionary laws of history and the causal processes of organic progress. He scoffed at the concept of a *Gesamtkunstwerk* as unoriginal
and derivative and reasserted the Hegelian proposition that "every fine
art is complete in itself." "The conception of a universal art," he
wrote, "interests us on account of its superficiality rather than its
profundity." He even rejected the idea of a balanced union of poetry
and music on the grounds that the temporal dimension of music tends
to exceed that of poetry, and, "if the music follows the poem strictly,
syllable after syllable, word after word, without the privilege of
dwelling here and there upon the sense of a passage, it cannot fulfill
its highest object, which is to express the emotional principle to the
utmost." He dismissed "infinite melody" as a contradiction in terms,
since melody, by definition, "in order to give the sense of form and
proportion to the ear and move the feelings powerfully, must conform
to the laws of symmetry and design, by a certain imitative progression
of the phrases." He approved the practice of employing characteristic
motives to signify persons as Weber did; but Wagner's excesses in
that regard, he said, "must be termed pedantic and tiresome." He

found in Wagner's music generally a lack of "refined beauty . . . not compensated for by a real grandeur of style" as well as a lack of "the spiritual or religious element" (*Parsifal* had not yet been written). He denigrated the subjects of *Tannhäuser, Lohengrin,* and the *Ring* as entirely foreign to modern taste and understanding, and he found the librettos lacking in "poetic truth," faulty in rhetoric, versification, and characterization.

"What, then, is the secret of Wagner's present popularity and ascendancy?" Paine listed only four factors: mastery of all the externals of the stage, unity of dramatic effect (though the respective arts were thus weakened) the coincidence of poetic prosody and musical meter, and a consummate technical command of the orchestra.

The significance of Paine's essay lay partly in its appearance in a periodical as venerable as the *North American Review* at a time in American history when Wagnerism was a fit subject for serious consideration. Still, the *Review* was a stodgy, expensive, provincial journal compared with the *Atlantic, Harper's,* or the *Century;* its contents were seldom quoted and thus had no far-reaching effects upon American opinion. What is more, few Cultured readers were quite thoughtful enough to suffer a thirty-page magazine article, even about Richard Wagner. Rather, Paine's arguments were indicative of the attitudes Harvard graduates might have been *expected* to learn (and Gustav Stoeckel of Yale published a comparable essay in the *New Englander* in 1877). Most important of all, Paine's critique comprised a catalogue of some of the main issues which were forthwith exposed to the intense, if not always refining, fire of Cultured criticism in the literary magazines. Such criticism was sometimes incidental to that of performances of Wagner's music; sometimes, as in analytical essays like Paine's, it was included in an article unrelated to specific musical events. The critics included musicians as astute as Paine, who was an eminent composer and pedagogue; intellectual charlatans; and dilettantes whose passionate opinions betrayed an uncertainty of "scientific" knowledge. But the issues were always discussed with intensity and conviction, lending a vitality to the literary side of American musical life that has rarely been surpassed. Moreover, the bulk of both reason and opinion in the literary magazines favored rather than opposed Wagner, his music, and his theories.

Co-worker with the Culturists

Wagner's advocates in America were certainly aware of his characteristics as a citizen. A biographical sketch by "J. L. G." in 1876 contained the observation that at that time—at age sixty-four—he had "not a few of the eccentricities of genius, in dress and manner" (C-XII, 365). Nevertheless, Americans were inclined to accept objective, rational explanations for his erratic political behavior and, of course, in the name of "seemliness," politely ignored such episodes as the cuckolding of Bülow. Francis Hueffer, the *London Times* critic who did more than any other individual to popularize Wagnerism in England and who first translated *The Art Work of the Future* into English (1874), explained to readers of the *Century,* in November, 1874, that Wagner had participated in the revolution of 1848–49 more from a sense of antagonism to things existing than from any distinct political persuasion; and he pointed out that the ensuing period of exile had been more of a blessing than a disgrace, for it proved to be one of his most creative periods. Henry T. Finck was perhaps the most passionate of Wagner's American advocates, and Apthorp, who was the most rational, regarded Finck's characterization of the composer in *Wagner and His Works* (1893) as

> probably the best and most lifelike that has yet been given to the public; it shows Wagner as essentially a noble, high-souled nature, furiously concentrated upon one single aim in life, terribly sensitive to criticism, and ever yearning for sympathy. His volcanic petulancy, which often seemed like spite, was but a symptom of persistent ill health. Mr. Finck flatly denies the charge of meanness and ingratitude often brought against him (A-LXXII, 559).

When Wagner was unheroic, he was merely human.

There were certain qualities about Wagner, discerned by American critics in his life and career, which resembled Yankee "push"; he was thus, to some, an exemplar to inspire ambitious Americans, musicians or not. Josiah Gilbert Holland interpreted the consummation of the Bayreuth scheme as a moral lesson of life:

> The power that rules the world is the power of ideas. Any man with genius enough to conceive a vital and germinal idea, and vitality enough to push it, is a master, sure of his triumph. He has that within him which gives a crowning significance to his life. To possess a great idea is to have a mission. It is to know what to do. It is to have a path and a goal (C-XIII, 125).

As early as 1871 the Culture and Progress editor for the *Century* had discerned in Wagner, via the *Tannhäuser* Overture, "the rare gifts of a great intellect and fine sensibilities" (C-II, 215). Thus it was evident that American Wagnerians believed themselves to be following a genuine Culture-hero even before 1879, when Wagner confirmed it by addressing American readers of the *North American Review* as "my earnest co-workers in the domain of ideal, spiritual progress." Clearly he was speaking their language. Some Americans even found that they had something particular in common with the great reformer when they read of his strictures upon late-comers and other audience disturbances at Bayreuth. Wagner seriously considered moving to America in 1880, and Culturists speculated that he would surely have been more enthusiastically welcomed than anywhere in Europe [10]—in Paris, for example, he was said to have been made the scapegoat in the political agitation against the Empire (A-LI, 712).

By showing Wagner to possess features a thoughtful gentleman could admire—by discovering in him, as Apthorp put it, "quite phe-

<hr>

10. See George Willis Cooke, *John Sullivan Dwight, Brook-Farmer, Editor and Critic of Music* (Boston, 1898), p. 230.

nomenal general culture" (A-XLIII, 147)—it could be implied that he was not at all out of phase with the contemporary world but integral with it and that he would be a desirable and even valuable citizen in a country whose manifest destiny was to supplant all the old institutions with organically superior ones. And by further revealing positive connections with the past, it could be shown that Wagnerism was a logical issue of the evolutionary process in music. Krehbiel likened the Chinese composer to the Greek dramatist and called them the prototypes of Wagner because of their insistence on the intimate union of words and music (C-XLI, 451–53). Most critics were satisfied with demonstrations of simple correlations between Wagnerism and the venerated classicists. Dvořák, for example, explained in the *Century* to what extent, and precisely how, Wagner had been anticipated by Schubert (C-XLVIII, 341–46), while John Rose Green Hassard traced his aim of freedom of emotional expression to Beethoven (C-XXIV, 620).

It was especially fashionable to regard Wagner as Mozart's great modern successor. Grieg identified himself as a friend of the "true and genuine admirers" of Wagner as opposed to the "howling horde" of Wagnerians. He traced Mozart's influence on Wagner through Gluck and Weber on the strength of Wagner's own testimony and thus reproved and disarmed all those Wagnerians who had forsaken the Olympian Viennese. Writers like William Mason and Apthorp, however, while admitting the continuity between Mozart and Wagner, tried to clarify the essential differences between the two composers. Apthorp, for instance, always believed that, whereas Mozart seized all experience by its musical side, "making all that he had observed or learned go to further musical ends, . . . in Wagner we feel that his music is the servant of his culture" (A-XLIII, 147).

The American Destiny of Wagnerism

The Darwinian thought which dominated the entire era affected nearly all interpretations of Wagnerism. Furthermore, the realization that a totally flawless species could not possibly evolve any further prompted thoughtful critics to try to identify the anomalies in Wagnerism in order to determine the possibilities for the future of the movement. Some critics in America, as well as in Europe, believed that Wagner's later theories and words represented a deviation from the mainstream of musical evolution and that, in order to progress logically, succeeding composers would have to use *Lohengrin* as their point of departure in order to arrive at a type of musical theater such as Reginald de Koven foresaw, in which the text and the music would be truly separate but equal in aesthetic weight, the one "material," the other "emotional" in its province.[11]

A Contributor to the *Atlantic* refuted the possibility of a return to the idea of opera by appealing to Darwinian logic: "In that case we shall see for the first time in the history of art a genuine return to a form that existed before certain things were discovered" (A-LIX, 571). Those "certain things" were, in many minds, the ideas which had motivated the origins of opera; and, interested as the generation was in origins, the relationships between Wagnerian music drama and the conceptions of the Florentine Camerata were naturally examined in order to clarify and affirm the evolutionary, historical foundations of the modern movement and thus to prove that it was not a new and revolutionary tendency but a necessary reform in order to assure genetic continuity.

In all of American critical literature, perhaps the most thorough application of Darwinian principles to the analysis of Wagnerism is the article written by Apthorp for *Scribner's* in April, 1890. In it, Apthorp, a lifelong Wagnerian but never a fanatic, exhibited the kind of open-minded but tightly logical criticism the Cultured class admired, not merely to win followers for Wagnerism but to provide an objective assessment of Wagner's permanent place in history and to predict the probable course of the subsequent evolution of opera.

Apthorp began by establishing the integrity of Wagnerism with

11. See S-XXIII, 81; Eduard Hanslick, "Richard Wagner's Stage Festival in Bayreuth," in *Music Criticisms 1846–99*, trans. and ed. Henry Pleasants (Baltimore, 1950), p. 152.

natural order by pointing out that Wagner's theories coincided essentially with those of the Florentine Camerata, the group of literary men, musicians, and amateurs who had conceived the idea of lyric drama, or opera, around 1600.

> It is . . . a little curious that Richard Wagner, to whom all authority was as nothing, and who believed firmly that the artist's instinct was an authority to itself, should, in the nineteenth century, have arrived at almost precisely the same conclusions concerning the art of music that the old Florentines did, and this, too, by a perfectly free, spontaneous, and untrammelled process of natural selection. It is one of the most striking confirmations of a philosophic theory in all history; for what more brilliant confirmation could a philosophic theory of art ask for than to find itself mirrored in the unprompted instincts and actual practice of the originally creative artist?

The aims of the Florentine reformers, Apthorp explained, had been to make music serve only to heighten the emotional implications of the words and at the same time to efface its own nature. But the "eternal principle" of organicism would not be permanently suppressed, and operatic music soon began to develop according to its own potency, producing for a while "musical forms of very low organism," such as the *da capo* aria and, later, the operatic fantasies of Liszt and Thalberg. Wagner, said Apthorp, had been the first to try to reestablish both clauses of the original Florentine formula and had again imposed *dramatic* form upon music in defiance of natural law. The fallacy of Wagnerism thus was identical with that of the Camerata: "It is not true that, in order to be dramatic, music must be inorganic, and take what semblance of form it can from the poetry alone. The second finale (statue scene) of Mozart's 'Don Giovanni' proves this," said Apthorp. In other words, he insisted, "Wagner's famous dictum, that the composer in lyric drama must remember not to be too musical, will give way to Von Bülow's far truer and profounder counter-apophthegm, that a composer cannot, in any case, possibly be musical enough." Yet the future would be indebted to Wagner for his contribution to the evolution of opera: "Undramatic or unscenic music is now, and will henceforth forever be, a solecism in the lyric drama, not to be endured; and this we owe to Wagner."

The widespread opinion that Wagner's dramas overshadowed his music was, of course, a point on which there was by no means a unanimity of conviction. Arlo Bates, a poet and novelist, insisted that, in spite of Wagner's intention to maintain a balance between music and word, the libretto was, "by the exigencies of musical composition, forced into the subordinate place of becoming practically a running commentary" upon the music (S-I, 638). On the other hand, Wagner's importance as a theatricalist was obvious to nearly everyone, whether they approved of his music dramas or not. In the *Atlantic,* in 1878, Sylvester Baxter remarked on the influence that Wagner's efforts in behalf of sincerity and truth to nature had had upon the tradition of the spoken drama in Germany. Apthorp instructed his readers in these matters from the beginning of his career, especially in his criticisms of Wagnerian performances, until he wrote a summary explication of the subject for *Scribner's* in 1887 (S-II, 515–31), detailing the ways in which scenery, stage setting, stage management, acting, singing, and orchestral performance were intended by Wagner to contribute to "the most exact, perfect, and life-like expression and embodiment of the poet's thought."

No less convincing than Apthorp's analyses of the intrinsic organicism of Wagner's music dramas was John Comfort Fillmore's ostensibly scientific demonstration of the cosmic connections between Indian music and Wagner's harmonic vocabulary, melodic style, and structural procedure. First, he observed the presence of "major-third relationships" in the melodies of Omaha Indian songs, and noted that the phenomenon also is found in the music of Beethoven, Schubert, Schumann, and Chopin, but "most of all in Wagner and Liszt."

It shows, I take it, simply this: that the great romantic writers, in going outside of the accepted harmonic limits (there are a very few text-books on harmony, even to-day, which account for their practice, still less sanction it), made a genuine discovery of natural harmonic relations.

Second, he confessed that, during the time he spent among the Omahas studying their music,

> in the absolute supremacy of the imaginative and emotional elements which dominated every moment of the Indian's criticism of my work, I was continually reminded of [German romanticism]. Here, as with . . . Wagner, the all-important matter was the feeling to be expressed (C-XLVII, 619, 623).

There was no question in his mind but that the Indians' music was "absolutely natural." The logical implications for Wagnerian criticism were self-evident.

Melody and Morality

Wagner's concept of melody was the basis of the most prolonged and vigorous debate among his devotees, as well as between them and the adherents of Italian operatic traditions. Both intellectual and musical—specifically, vocal—factors were at issue. The most common basis for the rejection of Wagnerian melody was that enunciated by Paine: that it was not constructed according to classical precepts; it did not consist of balanced, symmetrical phrases. Finck responded by belittling as "dance tunes" the melodies of Mozart, Beethoven, and Weber, but Apthorp countered that that was no more logical "than . . . calling Wagner an ape because he probably had simian ancestors" (A-LXXII, 558).

Certain reasonable critics like Hueffer explained that Wagner had merely evolved his *melos* from the latent melody of spoken language; it merely required the exertion of the intellect to appreciate that fact and to recognize the superiority of the new melody over the old. It was difficult, however, to change the minds of individuals, like some voice-teachers whose educated ears belied the arguments and who liked to claim that Wagner did not write real melody because he did not understand it and had "no proper conception of the capabilities and limitations of the human voice" (A-LXIII, 569). His music, they believed, compelled singers to shout over the noise of the orchestra and to force the "chest tones," stressing volume rather than quality and reinforcing a separation of the "registers," which went against the teaching of the "old Italian school"; and because of all this some singers "lost their voices and their health, and died insane" (A-LXIX, 429).[12] More charitable critics were prone to insist—encouraged, perhaps, by Adelina Patti's confessed fondness for Wagnerian music drama (H-LXIV, 308)—that the best singers of Wagner's music were those who had been trained in the old Italian school and had developed through the practice of Italian opera, though their type was disappearing, and their successors had "neither their training nor their practice to fortify them against the demands of 'the music of the future' " (A-LXII, 848).

The moral and ethical implications of Wagner's music and dramas also prompted a great deal of public debate. Unreconstructed classicists, of course, were always inclined to charge Wagner with sensualism; in the absence of the intellectually comprehensible elements of symmetrical melody, thematic development, and logical form, harmony and tone color appeared as pure flesh, without structure or purpose. After the Bayreuth Festival in 1876, however, and again after the *première* of *Parsifal,* in 1882, the dramas themselves became part of the problem. The *Century*'s reviewer of Paul Lindau's *Nüchterne Briefe aus Bayreuth* (1876) recommended to the readers of the magazine the author's emphatic denial of any "bad tendency or inherent naughtiness" in the music. But the style of the poetry, the

---

12. This reference may have been specifically to the aftereffects of the first performance of *Tristan* (1865), although there were other similar episodes, too. See Elliott Zuckerman, *The First Hundred Years of Wagner's Tristan* (New York, 1964), p. 33.

complexity of the plots, and especially the quality of some of the characterizations made many thoughtful Americans reluctant to accept the later works—those after *Lohengrin*—without reservations. Hassard deplored "the gross divinities and incestuous heroes of the 'Nivelung,'" which, he thought, were "now and then unfit for decent company." But, he wrote, "the most appalling example of Wagner's growing insensibility to causes of offense is seen in 'Parsifal,'" in which "the dances of disheveled wantons lead up to the most solemn act of divine worship; the can-can and the holy communion are represented on the same boards, without a thought that there can be an impropriety in acting either" (C-XXIV, 624).

On the other hand, Charles Dudley Warner was equally convinced of the seemliness of *Parsifal*. "There was no one who witnessed it," he wrote after returning from Bayreuth, "and heard the strains of melting music which interpreted it, who was not moved to the depths of his better nature, or for a moment thought that the drama passed the limits of propriety." "I, for one," he continued, "did not feel that I had assisted at an opera, but rather that I had witnessed some sacred drama, perhaps a modern miracle play" (A-LI, 85, 86). His reaction was typical of those who thenceforth looked upon Wagner as, at least in this particular work, a priest and paladin of super-Christianity. Dvořák, for instance, believed that Wagner had "struck the true ecclesiastic chord" in *Parsifal* (C-XLVIII, 342), and Haweis regarded the *Bühnenfestspiel* as "the long-sought link between the oratorio and the stage" and the precursor, along with Rubinstein's sacred operas (see C-L, 31–32), of the truest music of the future—envisioned by Liszt and Berlioz as early as the 1830's—which would ultimately "celebrate the reconciliation of the church and the world" (H-LXXX, 109–15).

"Disinterested" Wagnerism

Apthorp, in another of the essays that prove him to have been the most scholarly and intellectually meticulous of all American

Wagnerians, elucidated the meanings of some of Wagner's works and the significances of certain characters for the readers of *Scribner's* in 1889 (S-V, 331). *Tristan, Parsifal,* and the projected *Die Sieger,* said Apthorp, were meant to illustrate, respectively, the three cardinal points of Schopenhauer's philosophy: The Affirmation of the Will to Live, Altruism, and Renunciation.[13] These points, said Apthorp, were also illustrated "as a whole, if with less completeness and clearness," in the *Ring.* Apthorp subjected to his typically penetrating scrutiny certain characters in whose being and actions metaphysical truths were incarnated and illustrated, including *Parsifal* (compassion) and *Kundry* (self-sacrificing feminine love and ruinous feminine seduction). A few other critics seized the idea of metaphysical analysis; Marion Couthouy Smith, a minor poetess, explored it in "At the Concert: A Wagner Number" (A-LXXIII, 339):

> A CRASH of the drum and cymbals
> A long, keen, wailing cry;
> A throb as of wings of mighty things,
> That with whirring din sweep by.
>
> They come, with their thunder-chorus,
> Vast shapes, of a stronger race;
> An alien throng from some star of song
> In the undiscovered space.
>
> I thrill to their eager calling,
> I shrink from their fierce control.
> They have pressed and pried the great doors wide
> That were closed to guard my soul.

---

13. See also Elizabeth Wendell Barry, "What Wagner Found in Schopenhauer's Philosophy," *Musical Quarterly,* XI (January, 1925), 124–37. William J. Henderson also tried to explain that in all the operas and music dramas (except *Tristan*) Wagner's portrayal of love was more than a mere passion—it illustrated his theory of life: "It is the theory celebrated in Goethe's 'Faust,' where the poet sings 'The woman-soul ever leadeth us upward and on.' Even in those stories of Wagner's which are indefensible on moral grounds this theory is to some extent a key to the personal force of his heroines. . . . Their influence over man is always inspiring. They ennoble his manhood and mould his heroism. Wagner's hero is always greater because of his heroine" (*Preludes and Studies* [New York, 1891], p. 40).

Of course there was opposition to Wagnerism, but after Paine's relatively obscure essay it was limited mainly to the laments of the voice-teachers and the warnings of a few moralists, and it generally lacked the intellectual armament wielded by the proponents of Wagnerism. There was nothing in the literary magazines that equaled the anti-Wagner literature to be found in comparable British periodicals,[14] and Wagner's German and Viennese detractors, like Nietzsche and Eduard Hanslick, were seldom quoted. A reaction to Wagnerism gained momentum in the nineties, but it was a somewhat timid, powerless trend. Henderson, an expert on the voice, although unwilling to admit in the *Century* in 1893 that the music of the future was a thing of the past, emphasized that "The New School of Italian Opera" represented the new taste, a combination of the "powerful expressiveness of the Teutonic declamation with all of the vocal elegance and essentially singable qualities of the Neapolitan manner." The remarkable success of *Cavalleria* and *Pagliacci* were attributed, he said, to a widespread public demand for dramatic brevity and tragic intensity. Krehbiel, recounting the history of Bayreuth up to 1892, was objective, as only a Cultured Wagnerian could be, about the situation there at the mecca but claimed that elsewhere, practically speaking, "anti-Wagnerism is only a phrase; it stands for nothing" (S-XI, 99).

The insistence of the Cultured critics upon a "disinterested" pursuit of Wagnerism is attested in their occasional protests against doctrinaire partisanship. Writing in the *Atlantic* in 1876, Thomas Sergeant Perry thought he discerned a basic insecurity among Wagnerian zealots:

14. Edmund Gurney ("Wagner and Wagnerism," *Nineteenth Century,* XIII [March, 1883], 434–52) and Felix Weingartner ("The Symphony since Beethoven," *Contemporary Review,* LXXV [February, 1899], 271–89 [March, 1899], 418–38) exerted strenuous efforts to discredit the music and the musician of the future, J. F. Rowbotham concluded triumphantly that "the [Wagner] bubble has at last burst, and in a few years' time, except perhaps the little opera of *Lohengrin,* there will be no tongue left to call attention to the high and inflated pretensions which it has been the object of these pages to describe" ("The Wagner Bubble," *Nineteenth Century,* XXIV [October, 1888], 501–12). C. V. Stanford was moved to a dignified but comparatively unconvincing rebuttal in the following issue of the same magazine ("The Wagner Bubble: A Reply," *ibid.* [November, 1888], 727–33).

It may be begging the whole question to say that Wagner belongs among those whose position on Parnassus is not yet assured; but, on the other hand, it is fair enough in view of the way in which his supporters are continually alleging his greatness, and thus betraying their uneasiness.

Apthorp, despite his own genuine commitment to Wagnerism, appealed to the logic of historicism in order to disarm the fanatics. The principal fault that he found in Finck's biography was that "he shuts his eyes to the fact that Wagner and his works are still too recent to be viewed in due historic perspective" (A-LXXII, 558).

No one was more "disinterested" than Curtis, who, impelled by his refined but sensuous appreciation of Italian opera and by the vehemence of the Wagnerian polemecists, was constrained now and then to appeal for catholicity in musical taste. "Wagner is still upon probation," he wrote a month before his own death in 1892. "He is beatified, but not yet canonized, and the *advocatus Diaboli* is very busy" (H-LXXXV, 314). Earlier, he had mocked the more rigidly cerebral among the Wagnerians: "Do you think that you hear music sufficiently with your mind?" he chided. "Instead of being absorbed in the *Leitmotiven,* are you not really hankering for the flesh-pots of melody —of gross *tune?*" (H-LXXVI, 961).

Chapter X

Music in the Sanctuaries: Parlor and Church

AS WE HAVE SEEN, the Cultured class worked zealously throughout the last several decades of the nineteenth century to establish in America the professional symphonic and operatic traditions, already evolved in Europe, which appeared to be proper and necessary for the conduct of the highest and best type of musical life. However, these were complex, expensive public institutions requiring elaborate apologia, and it seemed that virtually the entire population would ultimately have to be educated to their values and mustered to their support.

Meanwhile a vigorous nonprofessional musical life flourished in America. It was larger than the other, in terms of the number of citizens involved, the total financial investment, and the breadth of the social spectrum it drew upon; and from it, especially in the cities, most of the participants in the public musical life were undoubtedly recruited. It required no apologia and thus was far less a musicointellectual mystique than an actively musical life, though it deserved and received a fair amount of judicious criticism. It was carried on mainly in the parlors, the club rooms, and the churches—the private, social, and spiritual sanctuaries of the American people. In addition, amateur singers enthusiastically supported a vigorous choral tradition in astounding numbers. Finally, the unique requirements of amateur musical life in America called forth from numerous composers thousands of new works every year in appropriate forms and styles, which were marketed through a large and prosperous publishing industry.

The Parlor Piano

By mid-century the conduct of amateur musical life in American parlors was almost entirely dependent upon the piano. James Parton, writing in the *Atlantic* in July, 1867, impressed that fact upon his readers. "Almost every couple that sets up housekeeping on a respectable scale considers a piano only less indispensable than a kitchen range," he wrote. During the preceding year twenty-five thousand new pianos, valued at approximately fifteen million dollars, were manufactured and sold in the United States, and perhaps ten second-hand instruments had been sold for every new one; piano rental, on a short-term basis, at from six to twelve dollars a month, was an extremely profitable, large-scale business. The volume of sales was so tremendous that some observers were moved to wonder aloud just what was becoming of worn-out instruments.

In addition to the quantity, the craftsmanship of American pianos was a matter of national pride. "No man," Parton wrote of Jonas Chickering,

> has . . . so nobly illustrated the character of the American mechanic, or more honored the name of American citizen. He was the soul of benevolence, truth, and honor. When we have recovered a little more from the infatuation which invests "public men" with supreme importance, we shall better know how to value those heroes of the apron, who, by a life of conscientious toil, place a new source of happiness, or of force, within the reach of their fellow-citizens.

The music-publishing industry was fully commensurate with the instrument industry. Parton noted that the current Oliver Ditson catalogue contained about thirty-three thousand compositions designed to be performed wholly or in part on the piano. A dozen years later Julius Wilcox, a dilettante like Parton, remarked that possibly more than two hundred thousand compositions for the piano had been published in this country (H-LVIII, 863).

The statistics Parton and Wilcox cited might not have been entirely accurate; manufacturers, like publishers, in those pre-income-tax years were inclined to exaggerate rather than depreciate the extent of their successes, for that was good advertising. But the trend was unmistakable. It was no coincidence that in 1890 Daniel Spillane's *History of the American Pianoforte: Its Technical Development and the Trade* was published in New York; the time of the piano was fulfilled, and the facts were present to prove progress. The history of the instrument in America was to be updated more than once by others, but never again would it be told with quite as much satisfaction.

The popularity of a given genre has nearly always been interpreted by the intellectual and Cultural elite as a symptom of inferiority, so the Cultured class in America, with its transcendental ideals, was understandably suspicious of the financial success of the parlor piano and its repertoire, especially when evidence was present that an appreciable amount of interest was based on the appeal of fashion. Almost without exception, every Cultured critic who wrote of parlor music at all felt constrained to deplore the debasement of Cultural ideals by doting parents who forced the study of the piano upon their idle young daughters merely to satisfy a thirst for "gentility." "In countless towns," complained the Home and Society editor of the *Century* in 1878,

> the acquisition of the proper rank in gentility involves the necessity of "piano-lessons" for the girls. The instrument is bought after much saving and stinting in other matters. Nelly is brought, through sore tribulations, to hammer out a half-

dozen dashing marches or waltzes, and that is the end of it. After she marries, she neither plays for her own pleasure nor for her husband's, and she is not competent to teach her own daughter. But the piano is there, a big assertant token of social rank.

Wilcox was no less critical of parental motives but was more optimistic about the real benefits to the pupil:

Judged by any artistic standard, or by the hard rule of worldly sense, the waste in all this is enormous, yet pleasure and culture are relative, and out of "Bonnie Doon," "Money Musk," the "Virginia Reel," and others of "mother's tunes," people who can not distinguish a tuned from an untuned instrument may perhaps derive a satisfaction, unlike that of the ambitious mamma who is the business support of the piano-maker, which makes the investment profitable (H-LVIII, 855).

Obviously, the trivial motivation of "gentility" and the shabby pedagogy which it bred were ever present, and they were not peculiar to American musical life, as was pointed out by *Harper's* reviewer of Friedrich Wieck's *Piano and Song* (1853; 2d ed., 1875; first American edition, 1875). Wieck, who was the teacher of Bülow and the father-in-law of Robert Schumann, was writing of circumstances in Germany, of course, but the reviewer recognized with sympathetic interest the author's description of the two classes of innocent sufferers to whom the piano was an instrument of torture: "the young ladies who are taught the instrument without being taught music," and "the comparatively small number in society who have really learned to love music" but who must occasionally listen to and pretend to like the playing of the "bangers" (H-LI, 601–2).

The moral pitfalls of popularity and gentility notwithstanding, persons who analyzed the circumstances from a reasonable perspective realized that the function and influence of the parlor piano was beneficent in the long run. Frederick Nast observed that the widespread use of the instrument had created an ever-growing audience for piano recitals by professional artists. "Unless mismanaged," he wrote, "hardly any engagement in New York, or tour through the country, has failed to be profitable to the performer and to art" (H-LXII, 813). Wilcox, summoning the testimony of the great pianist Sigismund Thalberg, pointed out that amateurs in communities remote from the great musical centers could acquaint themselves with all the great orchestral and operatic literature through the study of suitable transcriptions. Another value attributable to the presence of the piano in the parlor was the refining effect on the daily life of the citizen. As Thalberg had said, "Many a man engaged in commercial and other active pursuits finds the chief charm of his drawing-room in the intellectual enjoyment afforded by the piano" (H-LVIII, 854). Finally, and perhaps most important, it was the duty, if not always the pleasure, of the parlor pianist to accompany parlor singers.

Since the beautification and refinement of the domestic atmosphere was primarily a woman's responsibility, the practice of parlor music was dominated by women, and the piano was regarded as a woman's instrument, even though some thoughtful persons felt that men needed the benefit of keyboard facility more than the gentler sex. "No business man who works as intensely as we do," Parton wrote, "can keep alive the celestial harmonies within him—no, nor the early wrinkles from his face—without some such pleasant mingling of bodily rest and mental exercise as playing upon an instrument." He expressed the hope that Mason and Hamlin's new cabinet organ might soon become as popular as the piano, for it seemed to him "peculiarly the instrument for *men*" (A-XX, 97–98).

Parlor Singing

Amateur singing, on the other hand, was certainly an acceptable pastime for men as well as women. In fact, there were moral contingencies that made male vocalists even more welcome in the parlor than some women. As Wilson Flagg explained in an essay for the *Atlantic* in October, 1869:

> Nobody would say that the voices of men are intrinsically as musical and agreeable as those of women. But we listen to a woman's voice as we look upon her face and observe her manners: a defect in either is more easily perceived, and is more disagreeable, than in the rougher sex.

Flagg was writing of "the music of the parlor, which ought always to be of a simple but tasteful character, and which is spoiled when it either sinks into vulgarity, or attempts to accomplish feats that are within the power of those only who have given their life to the art and have been trained for public performance." The best parlor singer was one who could "enter into the spirit of a good composition so as to perfect or improve the design of the author" and display "a certain power of expression that should deeply affect the heart and penetrate the soul"; at the same time, the singer should retain a genuine simplicity and naïveté of tone and style that would betoken "a purer transcript of nature than in one of equal gifts modified to a greater extent by musical education and practice in concert."

Flagg related an interview he had had with just such a singer in 1862, and in reviewing her tastes he enumerated the criteria applicable to the evaluation of parlor songs. With respect to musical style, there were four categories. The first and lowest on the qualitative scale included tunes in the minor mode, which, like some of the old Scottish melodies, "soon pall upon a sensitive ear." The next-best category included songs with a very measured cadence, "singsong airs in which the rhythm, or swing of the movement, is not sufficiently varied to conceal its uniformity," like "Long Ago," by Thomas Haynes Bayly, a hit of 1840. Next were "songs by ordinary composers, which are neither intrinsically melodious, nor capable of being rendered so by a superior vocalist"; they were "full of musical platitudes and plagiarisms," though they often were immensely popular for a season on account of the attractiveness of their lyrics. The fourth and highest level was occupied by "tunes in which the rhythm is not formal or very apparent, and which . . . are extraordinary in their effects when their character is brought out by a superior performer."

Flagg listed twelve classifications of songs according to the sentiments conveyed by the words, including *Songs of Cheerful Humor,* such as "The Musical Wife"; *Songs of Home,* like "Home, Sweet Home"; *Elegiac Songs,* celebrating our sorrows for the dead, like "Long, Long, Weary Day"; *Amatory Songs,* like "Juanita" or "Sweet Afton"; *Songs of Memory,* such as "Oft in the Stilly Night"; *Songs of Fancy,* "in which the interest turns on some imaginary incident," as in "Araby's Daughter"; *Ethical Songs,* inculcating a moral, like "Love Not" ("Very many stupid songs fall under this head, and a *few* very good ones"); and *Songs of Absence,* which were "songs of regret on account of the separation of friends or lovers, such as 'When the Swallows Homeward Fly.' "

Nearly all of Flagg's examples belonged to the first half of the century; so, while his catalogue might have reflected one kind of popular taste, it did not necessarily summarize the state of the art. William Foster Apthorp, however, placed Flagg's songs in their proper perspective as he traced the history of the genre up to 1872 (A-XXIX, 763–66), beginning with the "Dempster ballads" and "passing over, as not worthy of note, the vast amount of music of the sentimental Negro-minstrel stamp." William Richardson Dempster was a Scottish song-writer who emigrated to the United States; his "Lament of the Irish Emigrant" shared the hit parade during the early 1840s with other Irish ballads like "Kathleen Mavourneen" and "Sheila, My Darlin' Colleen." Dempster's fame was soon eclipsed by that of Franz Abt, a German song-writer, whose best effort, "When the Swallows Homeward Fly" (*ca.* 1850), seems to have marked a slight advance beyond the level of the Scotchman in subtlety and technical skill. Abt does not now rate even passing mention in histories of art song, but neither does he appear in studies of popular music along with Dempster.[1] A third source of inspiration for writers of popular songs before mid-century was the opera music of Bellini and Donizetti.

All three styles shared a "purely melodic character" and accompaniments of rudimentary harmonic progressions. Apthorp pointed out that they "would have been rather embarrassed than helped by any so-called *learned* harmonizing, or contrapuntal elaboration in the instrumental part." A consequence of this was a rather casual attitude toward the stylistic appropriateness of the accompaniment to a given tune. "Almost all singers have found out a certain simple series of chords in several keys," said Apthorp, "and in accompanying themselves are too prone to forget that the proper efficacy of a chord, like that of the decimal point, depends in a great measure upon its coming in the right place."

During the 1850s the influence of Schubert, Schumann, and, a little later, Robert Franz, began to take effect, according to Apthorp, not only upon public taste but also upon compositional technique in popular song.[2] Those three, like Dempster and Abt, drew upon the melodic inspiration of the *Volkslied,* but they added "a richness of harmony and a variety in modulation" to the accompaniment. "Instead of the old rum-ti-tum guitar chords, we now find songs written with something that deserves the name of an accompaniment," said Apthorp. Furthermore, the integrity of the vocal and instrumental parts, and the intricacy of the latter, now precluded improvisation.

The definition of modern popular song which Apthorp supplied and which was subscribed to by the Cultured arbiters of musical taste was well illustrated in the *Atlantic* between January and October of 1877, when William Dean Howells published five songs of a

1. Apthorp later said of Abt that in his whole career he had "never given to the world a musical thought that was one jot in advance of the least cultivated of his public" (A-XXX, 503). See also Sigmund Spaeth, *A History of Popular Music in America* (New York, 1948), p. 87.

2. Apthorp was an expert on the songs of Robert Franz. He wrote of the composer in 1893 in "Two Modern Classicists in Music" for the *Atlantic* and edited *Fifty Songs by Robert Franz* (Boston, 1902). He even published his own rather Franzian setting of Edward Lear's poem, "The Owl and the Pussycat" (Boston, 1878).

projected series of twelve in his magazine in an effort to boost lagging circulation (A-XXXIX, 110–11, 236–38, 492–97, 750–51; A-XL, 476–80). The composers who accepted Howells' commissions were John Knowles Paine; Julius Eichberg; Dudley Buck, church musician and composer of the comic opera, *Deseret;* Francis Boott, a part-time expatriate in Florence, Italy, who, when in Boston, was among Howells' circle of close friends; [3] and George L. Osgood, a noted American tenor. The publication of songs in a literary monthly was unusual, though the ladies' magazines had published popular songs frequently in the forties and fifties.[4] *Harper's* tried only twice—in 1883, with a song by the New York composer, violinist, and church musician Joseph Mosenthal, and again in 1884, with one by the Philadelphia choirmaster William Wallace Gilchrist.

We can appreciate the gap that separated the commercially popular repertoire from the songs the Cultured class wished to think of as popular when we compare the *Atlantic's* series and the *Harper's* songs with the "hit-parade" tunes of the day. The former represent what we would now call art-song style, resembling that of Robert Franz, with occasional intimations of Wagner, as in Osgood's piece (see Plate 6). On the other hand, the popular musical theater then was dominated by the team of Harrigan and Hart, whose famous song "The Mulligan Guard," to a march tune by David Braham, was among their best comedy vehicles; and the persistent tradition of what Apthorp had called the "Dempster ballads" produced such hits during the season of 1876–77 alone as "Grandfather's Clock," "I'll Take You Home Again, Kathleen," "The Lost Chord," and "In the Gloaming." It is perhaps indicative of the intrinsic values of the two types of song that the examples cited of the latter have remained in the affections of so many Americans, while virtually all of the American works of the type Howells encouraged are unknown even to devotees of the art song.

3. Boott had once studied under Louis Picchianti, the famous Italian guitarist, whose influence is clearly evident in his songs.

4. See Paul Fatout, "Threnodies of the Ladies' Books," *Musical Quarterly,* XXXI (October, 1945), 565–78.

SONG.

PLATE 6. The opening bars of "Song," by the American singer and voice-teacher, George L. Osgood, the fifth—and last!— of the songs Howells commissioned for the *Atlantic* in 1877 (A-XL, 476).

It was not for lack of encouragement or of conscientious cultivation that the art song failed to take root in America, nor was it mere coincidence that the distinction among levels of quality was widened by the Cultured generation. Flagg's remark that "the music of the parlor would be much improved if it were more generally made the subject of refined criticism" (A-XXIV, 419) may have been what prompted Howells to hire the twenty-four-year-old Apthorp as music critic for the *Atlantic* in 1871. From the beginning the Music Department regularly included reviews of new publications for piano, voice, and chorus, and Apthorp's usually brief notices, under the heading "New Music," constitute a seven-year documentary history of the repertoire and a style manual of capsule criticism.

It was no easy task to try to improve taste among amateur musicians in the early seventies, for the spheres of art and entertainment were not yet as distinct from each other as they were to become by the turn of the century. To be sure, the music of the minstrel shows and *The Black Crook* occupied a clearly defined realm altogether beneath the hierarchy of definable values, and the best songs of the first half of the century had achieved the dignity of "old favorites," with no more than sentimental worth; but there remained the vast limbo between modern songs of the latter type, such as Thomas Paine Westendorf's "I'll Take You Home Again, Kathleen" (1876), and the type represented by John Knowles Paine's "Matin Song" (1877). This middle ground was occupied by innumerable works in a range of qualities and styles so homogeneous as to require the most exacting standards that could be applied in order to distinguish the better from the poorer.

There were, for example, the approximately 350 songs by Harrison Millard, a New York voice-teacher and composer.[5] Apthorp charitably allowed that Millard's "Meeting by the Brookside" belonged to "the would-be piquant sentimental order, in which our best concert singers find many of their most repaying encore pieces"

---

5. In 1867 Millard set to music "Waiting," a poem by Flagg's wife, which suggests that Flagg's interest in parlor song was not casual. Apthorp considered it the best of Millard's songs as of January, 1874 (A-XXXIII, 128).

(A-XXXIII, 512). "Alas" was "weak enough to do ample justice to the meteorological, flimsy woe of the text, a weakness which the very elegant title-page does not satisfactorily compensate for" (A-XXXV, 758). "A Mother's Dream" belonged to "a bygone class of music," since it concluded with "a painful length of roulade and cadenza." "Ave Maria" was found to be a fairly good song but not really "sacred" in character. By comparison, an "Ave Maria" by Hart Pease Danks was dismissed as "still less sacred and still more sentimental" than Millard's (A-XXXVI, 382). Danks's biggest hit, "Silver Threads among the Gold" (1873), had never been mentioned in the Music Department. Neither had Westendorf's "Kathleen" nor any of the other hits of the period 1872–77.[6]

Although Apthorp deplored the "bilious sighings of our modern ballads of the Virginia Gabriel school, and the mock-dramatic 'frenzy tempered by politeness' of Blumenthal and Arditi" (A-XXXVII, 251),[7] he was by no means insensitive to tender sentiment; he found "In the Hushes of the Midnight," by the Bostonian C. Henshaw Dana, to possess "a drowsy, poetical atmosphere . . . that is not wanting in charm" (A-XXXIX, 386). He admired the presence of classical ideals, recognizing in Osgood's "The Sunshine of Thine Eyes" that the composer had studied Franz to good purpose (A-XXXVIII, 640).[8] Still, he was not unwilling to accept a composition as pure sonorous design apart from the tradition of organic formal structure: He greatly admired Carl Tausig's set of piano

---

6. Cf. Spaeth, *Popular Music,* pp. 178–202.

7. Mary Ann Virginia Gabriel was an English composer in whose "Love's Requital" the critic found "queer modulations" and "vague" melody (A-XXXIII, 128); Jacob Blumenthal, a German who spent most of his career in England, whose "Yes" was "about as weak an offering as a sentimental public can well desire" (A-XXXVII, 252); Luigi Arditi, an Italian who settled in London after touring America in the forties and fifties, whom Apthorp never condescended to mention again, but whose *"Il Bacio"* ("The Kiss," 1858) was a perennial favorite and is still heard occasionally.

8. Osgood was indeed a pupil of Franz's. His successful (eight editions) *Guide in the Art of Singing* (1873) Apthorp considered to be "a valuable addition to a class of literature in which there exists little that is really trustworthy, and very much that is bad" (A-XXXIV, 760).

fantasies on themes from Strauss waltzes, entitled *Soirées de Vienne,* meaning to be only complimentary in calling them "nothing but arabesques" (A-XXXVIII, 638).

Being no aesthetic libertine, however, Apthorp was extremely meticulous in his discrimination between good and bad style, and he often found cause to accuse young composers of profligacy in the use of modulations. He approved of Tausig's taking "two bites at a distant key, from no earthly reason but his pleasure in hearing an effective juxtaposition of two foreign harmonies" (A-XXXVIII, 637), but he blamed Francis Korbay, a Hungarian composer who lived in the United States from 1871 to 1894, for "such a constant flying off into distant keys that the impression left on the mind is one of great tonal insecurity" (A-XXXVIII, 639).

Some of Apthorp's strictures upon rule-breaking arouse in the twentieth-century reader the very sense of superiority bequeathed to us by the nineteenth century with its idea of progress. Consider, for example, his review of *The Landing of the Pilgrim Fathers,* a cantata by Otto Singer, a German pupil of Moscheles and Liszt, who came to America in 1867:

> There is some rather mediaeval-sounding harmony, of a somewhat ascetic character, in it, but it is quite in keeping with the Puritan spirit of the subject. We would only protest against such a passage as this next one, as being unnecessarily ugly.

Such a cross-relation as the plain triad of F followed by the plain triad of G is really too much for modern ears to bear, unless insisted upon with the most convincing decision.

Apthorp compared Singer's "hideous" device with a similar passage in Liszt's *The Bells of Strasburg Cathedral* which he found acceptable because of a preferable rhythmic treatment (A-XXXVIII, 252–55):

We may be shocked by Apthorp's dogmatic tone and his immoderate language; but, granting him "disinterested" consideration, we can see that, in the first place, his assessment of the "cross-relation" in Singer's cantata is, by the strictest canons of the tonal system, quite correct and that, in the second place, his conservatism is but a reflection of his Darwinian point of view, according to which evolution, though it may be accelerated, cannot be elided, and rules must not be capriciously overridden but tested and changed under the force of organic necessity. There is no other way to explain the nature of his devotion to Wagnerism or his belief in the inevitability of atonality.[9]

The campaign to improve taste in parlor music was not an unqualified success; for while more thoughtful people may have been led to make obeisance to high art, at the same time they were driven from the heritage of the parlor by embarrassment over the childishness of their former tastes. A Contributor who wrote to the *Atlantic* in 1891 of "The Songs We Used to Sing" was scarcely able to hide his pride in the acquisition of a superior taste behind his sentimental affection for the ballads of the thirties and forties. Moreover, Wagner's music, which lent itself neither to balladic parody nor to the splendid variation techniques applied to Italian opera melodies by

9. He predicted the emergence of a "nullitonic order" in one of the *Entr'Actes* he wrote in 1896 for the Boston Symphony Orchestra programs. See William F. Apthorp, *By the Way*, 2 Vols. (Boston, 1898), I, 156–57.

the Lisztian school, drew many music-lovers from the parlor to the
literary and musical shrines of the music drama and gave profound inferiority complexes to all genuine dilettantes who wavered
in their allegiance to the domestic tradition. "The Wagnerian fervor,"
wrote the same Contributor,

> which looks down upon all Italian and French opera as poor
> and trivial, the wealthy leisure which delights only in that
> which costs vast sums, will scorn or be indifferent to that
> which comes not up to their exclusive tastes or exclusive
> purses. They set the fashion, and much I fear that the coming
> generation will lose one of the delights and comforts of the
> last—the song which in the home circle moved to tears or
> smiles, and which thrilled with simple pathos or noble senti-
> ment the hearts of those who were "not too bright or good
> for human nature's daily food" (A-LXVIII, 575).

Wagnerism and the strivings of the Culturists toward high art
were not the only trends that distracted amateur musicians from the
performance of music in the parlor. By the spring of 1879, *Pinafore*
had become the starting point of a veritable craze that spawned a
sizable bibliography of articles in the literary magazines alone. The
practical consequence of the enthusiasm for Gilbert and Sullivan's
operettas was the stimulation of amateur comic opera productions;
but the very nature of their medium and style tended to breed dis-
unity and discontinuity in the organizations that produced them, and
the activity never constituted more than a minor facet of American
musical life. Nevertheless, for a while, amateur comic-opera companies were as important socially as they were musically (H-LXII,
810).

The Choral Tradition

Far more important, both socially and musically, was the
choral tradition in America. Unlike parlor music, interest in it did

not deteriorate during the postwar period; on the contrary, the great festivals of the seventies and eighties, beginning with the Peace Jubilee of 1869, were said to have greatly stimulated interest in the choral idiom from coast to coast.[10] From then on through the early nineties, George William Curtis, who had a personal interest in the choral medium and who served as president of the New York Music Festival Association in 1882, recorded with pride the accomplishments of the Mendelssohn Club, the Oratorio Society, and the Sylvania Vocal Society, while the *Century* followed the fortunes of such local groups as the short-lived Church Music Association (1869–73), a predecessor of the Oratorio Society.[11] Apthorp documented in the *Atlantic* some of the major achievements of the venerable Handel and Haydn Society and the younger and more adventuresome Cecilia and Apollo societies, and he also reviewed new choral publications, applying to them the same rigorous standards he used on songs and piano works, deriding commonplace or shabby or merely sentimental efforts in either performance or composition whenever they came before his scrutiny. Cantatas and oratorios composed the main body of the repertoire, supplemented by English, German, and American part songs and anthems. A very few of the more esoteric groups sang madrigals and glees from the sixteenth through the nineteenth centuries.

The number of amateur singers participating in choral societies was heartening to observers of American musical life. Choruses of from 500 to 600 singers were considered normal in size for minor festivals. That a chorus of that size was considered desirable was perhaps an indication of the limited qualifications of the individual singers, and that it was possible was perhaps an indication that the

10. Even Boise, Idaho had a Jubilee in 1873, conducted by Mason W. Chapman, a miner and violinist, featuring the Anvil Chorus complete with cannon! See Marvin E. Stallcop, *Music in Boise, Idaho, 1863 to 1890* (Master's thesis, University of Montana, 1968), pp. 47–48.

11. C-III, 758–59. See also Henry E. Krehbiel, *Notes on the Cultivation of Choral Music and the Oratorio Society of New York* (New York, 1884), pp. 51–54.

singers were motivated as much by social allurements as by the glories of Art.

According to George P. Upton, Chicago's first music critic and a founder of the famed Apollo Club (1872), the choral tradition in America had originated as a reaction against the "Billings school of church music—a school characterized by its antiquated treatment and excessive fuguing" (S-XIV, 68–83). Upton sketched the histories of the thirty-eight choral societies from twenty-four different cities which Theodore Thomas had invited to take part in his grandiose but ill-fated scheme for the Chicago World's Fair. Several of them, like the New York Deutscher Liederkranz Society (founded in 1847), belonged to the German Sängerbund tradition, which, by virtue of both the numbers and the musical discipline of its participants and in spite of its nationalistic and social preoccupations, had been the foundation of choral activity in America since before 1850.[12] The choruses of the regular festival associations, such as that at Worcester, Massachusetts (1857), were outgrowths of the "conventions" of music educators like Lowell Mason, Isaac Woodbury, and William Bradbury. Organizations like Boston's Cecilia (1874) were established as private music-study clubs whose concerts originally were open only or mainly to the friends and relatives of the singers.

Choral performances were primarily the responsibility of the broader middle class, though the intellectual elite and the wealthy class were frequently drawn upon for organizational leadership and financial support. Men like Frederick A. P. Barnard, president of Columbia College, who presided over New York's Oratorio Society during its first season, and Andrew Carnegie, who served as the same society's president and chief benefactor for several years beginning in 1888, undoubtedly lent prestige to the tradition, even if they did not always succeed in maintaining perfect amicability among the

12. The Eighteenth National Singing Festival of the Northeastern Sängerbund, held in Philadelphia in 1897, involved 6,000 singers from 400 separate German singing societies (*Boston Evening Transcript*, June 21, 1897; see also H-LXI, 144–45).

performing members. In any case, we may perhaps interpret the stormy and uneven continuity of the histories of American choral societies as an indication of the intensity with which the passions and energies of their members were engaged.

The musical leadership of the American choral tradition during the last generation of the century continued to be, as it had been before the war, in the hands of some of the most important musicians in the country, nearly all of whom were composers and teachers as well as conductors. The men who led the societies involved in the Chicago fair, for example, included Frank and Walter Damrosch, sons of Leopold Damrosch, who had introduced German opera at the Metropolitan; Frank van der Stucken, who measurably furthered the fortunes of American composers both here and in Europe; Joseph Mosenthal, violinist in the New York Philharmonic for forty years; Dudley Buck, one of the country's leading church musicians; Carl Zerrahn, who came to America as flutist with the Germania Orchestra and conducted the Handel and Haydn Society for forty-two years and the Harvard Musical Association for seventeen; Benjamin Johnson Lang, pupil of Liszt and teacher of Arthur Foote and Ethelbert Nevin; George W. Chadwick, pupil of Rheinberger, teacher at the New England Conservatory from 1880, and director of it from 1897; William Wallace Gilchrist, Philadelphia church musician and another champion of American composers;[13] and Theodore Thomas himself.

Church Music

Since many of the conductors of the choral societies were also church organists and choir directors, it is reasonable to suspect that a large proportion of the social singers were also church choristers and to infer that vocal music in church was but an extension of the main choral tradition in America. All Cultured music-lovers would have preferred that condition to obtain, but they were confronted

13. See Sumner Salter, "Early Encouragements to American Composers," *Musical Quarterly,* XVIII (January, 1932), 99.

with a logical predicament of their own making that seemed to defy resolution. They wanted both the public and the private musical lives of the American people to be devoted solely to music worthy of the name Art. On the other hand, in church they expected to hear a "devotional music so sung and played that it will certainly call . . . [worshipers'] minds from the contemplation of earthly to heavenly things" (C-XXVIII, 471), a functional music that would lead "religious hearts" through "a multitude of religious thoughts and emotional exercises" (C-XVIII, 134). The Culturists demanded "artistic execution," but not to the exclusion of congregational participation. They sought a popular congregational music, but not at the expense of literary or musical quality. In other words, having clothed the Muse in the elegant finery of a "higher" type for the parlor and the concert hall, they proposed that she should exchange it on Sunday mornings for a dress fit for the handmaid of religion and behave like an obedient servant, not a matinee matron.

The subject first appeared among the literary magazines in 1873; the last word there was uttered in 1893. The situation during those two decades does not easily lend itself to analysis, for, as Josiah Gilbert Holland put it in 1875,

> there are so many tastes to be consulted in it, it is so complicated with economical questions, it is so overloaded with theories, it presents so many difficulties of administration in its simplest forms, that a church may be accounted happy which can go on one or two years without a row or a revolution.

Inexplicably, he said, "nothing seems to be learned by experience, as in other departments of human effort and enterprise" (C-X, 242–43).

Holland, among others, addressed himself to the contemporary state of Christian hymnody. The evangelical revival that began after the war had produced the "praise meeting," stressing spontaneity in prayer and preaching and summoning a hymnody to match, consisting of rather colloquial rhymes dealing with the gospel call, aspiration, and the future life, set to jingling tunes typified by those of Dwight Moody's chorister, Ira D. Sankey. Holland, whose sense of seemliness was offended by such hymns, submitted that "to stand up and sing them is an absurd performance, especially when it takes place in public" (C-XVIII, 134). Others were troubled by the fact that the decidedly secular character of the tunes tempted young people to profane them further by singing them in purely social settings.[14] It was the poor quality of congregational music and singing, Holland contended, that had made "public worship very much less attractive to the great world which it is the church's duty and policy to attract and to influence." He urged the pursuit of "higher" musical ideals: "The churches are full, as a rule, where the music is excellent" (C-XVIII, 135).

The use of even the best opera and concert music, in parody, paraphrase, or *contrafactum,* was unacceptable on moral grounds. As an *Atlantic* Contributor put it,

> That music can, per se, be sacred or profane will not be urged even by a devotee. That verbal or circumstantial associations can cast a distinctively devotional or secular color over an air forever is quite another matter; and in this hypothesis lies the sole moral separation between Coronation or Windham and The Widow Nolan's Goat or an adagio of Beethoven's.

The writer discovered, to his profound distaste, in "a well-known collection, adopted by several of the most important Protestant denominations in the country, and the music in which purports to be

14. A-XLIV, 253–54. One observer found nothing in modern hymnody to surpass some of "grandfather's hymns" for ludicrous diction and forced prosody. He cited, as an example, a version of "While shepherds watched their flocks," from *Hymns and Spiritual Songs* (Palmer, Mass., 1816):

> As shepherds in Jewry were guarding their sheep,
> Promiscuously seated estranged from sleep.

the selection of three experienced musicians," the hymn "O Love Divine, How Sweet Thou Art" set to a duet from *Die Zauberflöte* and three hymns, including "Eternal Father, Strong to Save," wedded to "Consolation"—one of Mendelssohn's *Songs without Words* (A-LI, 282).

Gottlieb Federlein, the New York organist and vocal pedagogue, asserted that, though Italian opera had led New Yorkers to a fondness for beautiful voices and an appreciation of refined execution in singing, it had "exerted a perverting influence upon church music, in so far as our composers have adopted its forms for sacred songs and church services" (C-XXVII, 158–59; see also H-LVIII, 736–37). Stylistic extravagances combined with topical irrelevance in church music was execrable to men like the Reverend Charles S. Robinson, who complained that " 'high art' kills the spirit of the gospel in a preacher's heart more quickly than anything else in the world" (C-XXVIII, 470). Robinson placed the blame for artistic oppression not only upon musicians but also upon Cultured ministers and music committees who were anxious to hear "good music" in the sanctuary at any cost (C-XXVII, 946). The problem of excessive Cultural ambition was compounded by insufficient understanding of the possible relationships of art and religion. In 1884 one observer documented the lack of preparation of ministers in the field of music: "Inquiry made of thirteen of our leading theological seminaries develops the remarkable fact that in *not one* of them does music form any part of the studies of its course" (C-XXIX, 157). Waldo Selden Pratt, the distinguished music-teacher and historian, found a comparable lack of theological study in the education of musicians: "There is a noble opening," he wrote in 1893, "for a school exclusively devoted to training 'church musicians' " (C-XLVI, 317). John Finley Williamson's school was still a full generation away.[15]

---

15. The Westminster Choir was founded in 1926. See Leonard Van Camp, "The Formation of A Cappella Choirs at Northwestern University, St. Olaf College, and Westminster Choir College," *Journal of Research in Music Education,* XIII (Winter, 1965), p. 236.

In 1873, Apthorp had identified "sentimentalism" as the pervading evil in church music in America and had indicted the nonmusical churchgoing public for the exercise of bad taste; more than ten years later the situation had not altered appreciably. A correspondent to the *Century* took a more positive, even if pessimistic, point of view:

> Ask yourself what are the real objects which engage the thoughts and attention of the persons whom you yourself actually know. Unless your experience differs vastly from mine, you will admit that these objects are, at one end of the church, dignified and polished oratory; at the other, sensuous and ravishing strains of music; and in the territory between, unexceptionable manners and rich and stylish apparel. . . . And if people want fine music, good oratory, and brave millinery, why should they not have them? (C-XXVIII, 638).

Yet a change was definitely under way by the early eighties, which may well have been precisely what made possible such vigorous discussion as that which took place in the *Century* in 1884–85. As soon as alternatives were recognizable, debate could take place. Nast, reviewing the history of church music in New York in his 1881 article for *Harper's,* had recalled that, during the period before the war,

> the true function of church music was lost sight of, light secular music, arranged according to the fancy of the organist or leader, was introduced, gifted vocalists rivalled to the extent of their ability in brilliancy and effects the artists on the stage, and propriety was very often disregarded. This state of confusion was transitory only, and a change for the better has already taken place; but great diversity of opinion and practice still exists. . . . The vexed question of quartette or chorus choirs has been generally solved by the employment of both (H-LXII, 813).

The "quartette choir," consisting of four salaried soloists, had become fashionable in urban churches before 1850.[16] Ideally, it was supposed to assure the maintenance of professional standards in the choir loft; but, as Robinson pointed out in the *Century* for March, 1884, the dogmatic pronouncements of critics like Richard Storrs Willis, demanding immunity of church musicians from nonprofessional interference, had been interpreted by too many of the former as license to impose their tastes upon ministers and congregations ex cathedra, though Willis had specifically granted clergy and congregation the prerogative of dismissing unsatisfactory musicians.[17] Evidently, in the meantime, the Culturists had succeeded in convincing faithful Christians of their musical Philistinism.

By 1885, Edward Witherspoon, father of the great American basso and pedagogue, was confident that the quartet choir had "seen its palmy days" and would soon be a thing of the past, and with it would die "many a disturbing element" (C-XXIX, 475). One of the most disturbing elements attendant upon the professionalization of church music was "candidating"—the annual auditioning before music committees of wealthy and influential laymen for the sometimes lucrative positions in the quartets—which often bred a decidedly un-Christian atmosphere of unfriendly competition, petty jealousy, and gross venality.

Lutheran churches with primarily German congregations were relatively free from musical strife, according to Apthorp, and the Episcopal church witnessed a revival of the "surpliced" choir of men and boys that generally assured a predictable measure of excellence in the choice of repertoire—mainly English cathedral music—and modesty and innocence, if not perfect propriety, in the conduct of the participants.[18] In other Protestant churches, however, so-called chorus

16. See Robert Stevenson, *Protestant Church Music in America* (New York, 1966), pp. 112–13.

17. Robinson quoted from Willis' *Our Church Music: A Book for Pastors and People* (New York, 1856).

18. See A-XXXI, 118; H-LXXVII, 65–73. By the nineties, festivals of parish choirs were annual affairs in certain parts of the country, and they exhibited notably high standards in performance and repertoire. For a summary of one such festival, see the *Boston Evening Transcript,* May 18, 1892.

choirs were the only alternatives to quartets, though they were as unsatisfactory then as now; for volunteers could not be depended upon to attend rehearsals or services regularly. "In the city, where life is full," Holland pointed out, "especially at that season of the year when rehearsals are practicable, . . . a volunteer choir . . . is one of the most difficult things to maintain that can be imagined" (C-X, 243).

The long hegemony of the quartet choir had relieved amateurs of the responsibility for music in the worship service, and the taste for performances of professional caliber which it had fostered undoubtedly discouraged amateurs from assuming that duty again. The trend away from popular adult music-making was clearly evident by the early nineties. "There must have been—there *was*—a time when the title [amateur] carried with it respect, dignity, and worth," wrote a Contributor. However,

> amateur has collided with professional, and the former term has gradually but steadily declined in favor; in fact, it has become almost a term of opprobrium. The work of an amateur, the touch of the amateur, a mere amateur, amateurish, amateurishness—these are different current expressions which all mean the same thing, bad work (A-LXXIII, 859).

During the ensuing generation, tin-pan alley would begin to route itself through the American parlor, the secondary schools and the colleges would commence a new choral tradition, and diffident church choirs of "volunteers" would endlessly repeat anthems by Dudley Buck and excerpts from Gounod's *The Redemption*.

Chapter XI

The Legacies of
the Cultured Generation

THE INTEGRATION of the art of music with life in America was the principal musical ambition of the class of individuals that composed the audience of the quality monthly literary magazines such as the *Atlantic, Harper's,* the *Century,* and *Scribner's* between 1870 and 1900. It is indicative of the essential nature of the Cultured remnant that merely permitting the two spheres to achieve concentricity by their own organic powers was not enough; the process had to be thoughtfully monitored, if not rationally controlled.

The doctrines of Culture, through the offices of Reason, were employed toward the resolution of all the practical artistic predicaments that issued from the basic theoretical and societal ones. Simple human delight in irrational, pleasurable perceptions was opposed by the principle of the superiority of the mind over the senses; faith in democratic individualism fostered a kind of artistic laissez-faire, which contradicted the old-world idea of authoritarianism in art, dominated by eccentric geniuses; Puritan morality, focusing attention on the artist's personal history, clashed with the traditional primacy of the artist's creative history; middle-class ethics, requiring that

193

every human act and idea have a practical application, conflicted with the romantic concept of music as a language of ideality; the traditional hierarchical standards of musical value collided with the altruistic urge of the Culture-guardians to secure the widest possible subscription to those standards; but all these were reduced to mere phantoms by rationalization and verbalization in the literary climate of the quality monthly magazines. In fact, the natural polarity of art and life, of imagination and cogitation, of intuition and logic, was completely obscured from all but a few reasonable minds.

This very fact of the musical life of the Remnant signified that, far from being economically determined, and equally remote from "gentility" or from mere derivation from European precedent, the musical identity of the class was arrived at independently and self-consciously by strenuous effort. Furthermore, the Cultured class not only was receptive to new ideas; it actively sought them out and examined them in the broad competitive intellectual atmosphere provided by the literary magazines. It may be said that the critical tradition accomplished little; but, after all, solutions were not important. What was important was the testing of ideas before the court of criticism, the exercise of "the free play of the mind." The function of criticism, then, was first to reaffirm the findings of evolution to date and second to clarify the questions. Rarely since the last three decades of the nineteenth century have we experienced such energetic activity in the literary aspects of our musical life.

The End of
the Cultured Generation

What became of the Cultured class after 1900? To be sure, an intellectual elite prevailed that continued to patronize the literary magazines, and the *Century* lasted until the spring of 1930, *Scribner's* until May, 1939; *Harper's* and the *Atlantic,* almost miraculously, continue, now circulating about 300,000 copies each per month. But after 1900 the "word of ambition of the day" was no longer *Culture*.

Irving Babbitt and Paul Elmer More sought to perpetuate certain basic Emersonian ideas in the doctrines of the New Humanism, but transcendentalism and romanticism succumbed to the invincible forces of naturalism and pragmatism. Early twentieth-century critics like George Santayana turned upon the Cultured generation with the cruelest accusation of all, misnaming the Cultured generation "the genteel tradition" and charging it with intellectual, moral, and aesthetic cowardice in the face of the "realities" of American life.

Actually, the critics of the early twentieth century found little with which to accuse the Cultured generation that that noble class had not discovered itself; but a concomitant of Cultural self-awareness had been an optimism manifested in a genuine satisfaction with the good things it recognized about itself and its times and by its immunity to the intimidation of fault-finding:

> This our nineteenth century [wrote Mariana Van Rensselaer in 1883] is commonly esteemed a prosaic, a material, an unimaginative age. Compared with foregoing periods, it is called blind to beauty and careless of ideals. Its amusements are frivolous or sordid, and what mental activity it spares from the making of money it devotes to science and not to art. These strictures . . . have certainly much truth to back them. But leaving out of sight many minor facts which tell in the contrary direction, there is one great opposing fact of such importance that by itself alone it calls for at least a partial reversal of the verdict we pass upon ourselves as children of a nonartistic time. This fact is the place that music—most unpractical, most unprosaic, most ideal of the arts—has held in nineteenth-century life (H-LXVI, 540).

Nevertheless, around 1900 the Cultured generation of music-lovers began to expire as a coherent faction in American society because several of its most cherished precepts lost their force.

First, the concept of the relationship between music and morals that made Mendelssohn a model for all American musicians was invalidated by new understandings of human nature achieved through studies in psychology, which culminated in the idea of the composer as an individual rather than a type. In the recent biography by Eric Werner, *Mendelssohn: A New Image of the Composer and His Age* (New York, 1963), the seraphic figure that served a long and important era in American musical life has been replaced by what this generation prefers to call a more "human" one, complete with anxieties, complexes, and failures. A musician who was once viewed as the transcendent ideal of a genius and a truly gentle man is now imagined to have been an unusual creature indeed, but a mortal one withal.

Second, cosmopolitan nationalism, which enabled Wagner to dominate American musical life and thought during the Cultured generation, gave way to a musical chauvinism comparable to the flag-waving carried on by literary critics like Randolph Bourne.[1] Furthermore, the intellectualization that Wagnerism invited by its very nature led to its own dissipation. By the turn of the century, reaction drove Wagner's literary and musical images into the historical distance, and there were no Cultured music-lovers left to explain how, or even whether, anyone else had taken his place in the evolutionary scheme.

Third, the idea of dilettantism, of skillful amateur participation in the performance and criticism of music, was displaced by the exclusiveness of professionalism. The music of the parlor became implicitly inferior to the music of the concert hall and the opera house; and, whereas thoughtful individuals had once been eager to grapple individually with the maxim *de gustibus non est disputandum,* they became more and more willing to leave the *disputandum* to flamboyant critics like James Huneker and Henry L. Mencken.

---

1. See Randolph Bourne, "Our Cultural Humility," *Atlantic,* CXIV (October, 1914), 505.

The Cultured Tradition

Hierarchical standards were among the several ideas that did not expire with the Cultured generation but were bequeathed to the twentieth century. One result has been that music is still taught principally as a historical study of styles; selected idioms from the past are elevated to the status of high art without regard for their functions in their original social milieu, while the mundane or functional idioms of the present—"popular" music, folk music, the music of the films and television, and certain types of ritual music—are relegated to an aesthetic and academic limbo. Fortunately for themselves, those musics do not require for their existence the intellectual patronage of the academies.

The desire of the Cultured class to extend the benefits of "the genius of song" throughout all social and economic levels of American society also continues undiminished into the twentieth century. Recent studies have suggested, however, that the apparent gains made in this direction have been illusory and that audiences are still drawn from the very small "thoughtful" segment of our population.[2]

The persistent Cultured conviction that the purpose of music education in the elementary and secondary schools is primarily to prepare children for a maturer musical existence as adults has long prevented us from entertaining the possibility that musical activity in the schools might well be regarded as a complete and sufficient musical life in itself. Furthermore, the proposition that musical life in America should be chiefly public and that it should take place mainly within the precincts of the concert hall and the opera house has so long been unquestioned that we now find ourselves largely unprepared to consider the efficacy of any other mode or medium. Purely functional music, for example, hardly qualifies as art. Meanwhile, we are con-

2. See William J. Baumol and William G. Bowen, *Performing Arts—The Economic Dilemma* (New York, 1966), chap. 4.

strained to pursue the course a distant generation set out for us, even though the economic problems it poses are compounded by the very tenacity of the tradition.[3]

The Culturists' dream of federal subsidy to support the public musical life finally became a reality of modest proportions when the National Foundation for the Arts and Humanities was established in 1965. Thus music, along with the other arts, is at last an item in the national budget and is incontrovertibly a fact of everyday life. Actually, of course, ever since the beginning of the Cultured generation, music has been securing its own place in the economic existence of the American people, not only as part of the "gross national product" but also in terms of the ever-growing amounts of local and state tax monies that have been devoted to musical activities in colleges and universities, which now are the true centers of musical life in the United States.

Perhaps the most durable legacy of the Cultured generation is the Hellenization of our musical life. One recent manifestation of this bequest is to be found in the Tanglewood Symposium of 1967–68, which, in its most advanced aspect, involved a new breed of thoughtful individuals, an aesthetic elite from all spheres of musical activity, as well as music-lovers from the other humanities and from the sciences, and which in its most traditional aspect served to remind the latter-day Barbarians, the Populace, and the Philistines that one must know something *about* music in order to appreciate it properly; and *that,* for better or for worse, still keeps the Remnant separated from the Rest.

3. See the various articles on "The Business of Culture" in the *Saturday Review,* February 28, 1970, esp. Amyas Ames, "The Silent Spring of Our Symphonies."

Appendix I

Articles Pertaining to Music in
the *Atlantic Monthly*, 1857–1900

Volume	Pages	Month	Year
I	125–28	November	1857
———	378–79	January	1858
———	634–36	March	———
———	847–61	May	———
II	152–56	July	———
IV	131	———	1859
V	364–70	March	1860
———	497–505	April	———
VI	759–61	December	———
IX	763–75	June	1862
X	580–85	November	———
XI	756–66	June	1863

Symbols: Music Department (M), Contributors' Club (CC), Book Review (R), Fiction (F), Art Review (AR), Song (S), Poem (P).

A solid line indicates the repetition of the preceding information (volume, month, etc.); brackets enclose the name of the author to whom an unsigned article has been attributed; a broken line indicates that the author is unknown.

Author	Title
— — — — — —	"Outlook in October, 1857"
— — — — — —	"Schoelcher's *Life of Handel*" (R)
— — — — — —	"Retrospect in March, 1858"
[Alexander W. Thayer]	"Beethoven: His Childhood and Youth (*From Original Sources*)"
[W. Mitchell]	"Songs of the Sea"
[F. H. Underwood]	"*The Choral Harmony,* by Baker and Perkins" (R)
[Alexander W. Thayer]	"Marx's *Beethoven*" (Part I) (R)
———————	——————— (Part II) (R)
— — — — — —	"Chappell's *Popular Music of Olden Time*" (R)
[H. E. Prescott]	"The Author of *Charles Auchester*"
[R. B. Harding]	"Blind Tom"
[Gail Hamilton]	"Camilla's Concert" (F)

Volume	Pages	Month	Year
XII	82–94	July	1863
——	285–91	September	——
XIV	116–23	July	1864
XV	126–27	January	1865
——	177–81	February	——
——	350–52	March	——
——	573–75	May	——
——	718–23	June	——
XVIII	740–45	December	1866
XIX	685–94	June	1867
XX	82–98	July	——
——	608–16	November	——
XXI	503–6	April	1868
——	638–39	May	——
XXII	150–54	August	——
XXIII	635–44	May	1869
XXIV	245–54	August	——
——	410–20	October	——
XXVI	321–31	September	1870
——	614–25	November	——
XXIX	118–20	January	1872
——	120–21	——	——

Author	*Title*
[L. Hale]	"The Musician" (F)
[Moncure D. Conway]	"Robert and Clara Schumann"
[Francis Williams]	"Meyerbeer"
[W. Leonard Gage]	"Mendelssohn-Bartholdy's Letters" (R)
[Louis M. Gottschalk]	"Notes of a Pianist"
————————	"Notes of a Pianist"
————————	"Notes of a Pianist"
[Anne M. Brewster]	"Schumann's Quintette in E Flat Major" (F)
[H. H. Weld]	"The Singing-School Romance" (F)
[Thomas W. Higginson]	"Negro Spirituals"
[James Parton]	"The Piano in the United States"
[Robert P. Nevin]	"Stephen C. Foster and Negro Minstrelsy"
[John S. Dwight]	"Matheiu's Busts of the Composers" (AR)
— — — — — —	"Seiler's *The Voice in Singing*" (R)
[Charles Dawson Shanly]	"Convivial Songs"
[William Dean Howells]	"The New Taste in Theatricals"
————————	"Jubilee Days"
[Wilson Flagg]	"Parlor Singing"
John S. Dwight	"Music as a Means of Culture"
————————	"The Intellectual Influence of Music"
[William F. Apthorp]	"The Season" (M)
————————	"New Music" (M)

Volume	Pages	Month	Year
XXIX	247	February	1872
——	247–48	——	——
——	248–49	——	——
——	249	——	——
——	378–79	March	——
——	379–80	——	——
——	508–10	April	——
——	510	——	——
——	510–11	——	——
——	635–37	May	——
——	637	——	——
——	763–66	June	——
——	766	——	——
XXX	122–24	July	——
——	140–46	August	——
——	249	——	——
——	249–51	——	——
——	251	——	——
——	376–79	September	——
——	502–5	October	——
——	625–26	November	——
——	635–38	——	——
——	755–58	December	——
XXXI	117–18	January	1873
——	118–19	——	——
——	119–20	——	——
——	129–45	February	——
——	247–49	——	——

Author	*Title*
[William F. Apthorp]	"Wachtel" (M)
————	"The Dolby Troupe in Oratorio" (M)
————	"Thomas's Concerts and Wagner's Music" (M)
————	"New Musical Publications" (M)
————	"Gaertner's *Art of Singing*" (M)
————	"New Songs and New Piano Music" (M)
————	"Offenbach's Music and Success" (M)
————	"Opéra Bouffe in General" (M)
————	"Raff's Symphony in C" (M)
————	"Thomas's *Mignon*" (M)
————	"Bülow's Beethoven's Works" (M)
————	"Improvement in Popular Music" (M)
————	"New Music" (M)
————	"New Publications" (M)
Alice Asbury	"Wagner and the Pianist Bülow"
[William F. Apthorp]	"Stage Elocution" (M)
————	"Dressing and Mise-en-scène" (M)
————	"Ballet" (M)
————	"The Jubilee" (M)
————	"New Music" (M)
————	"Haweis's *Music and Morals*" (R)
————	"Orchestral Music in our Theatres" (M)
————	"The Season" (M)
————	"Eichberg's *Fourth Music Reader*" (M)
————	"Church Music" (M)
————	"Wieniawski" (M)
James V. Blake	"English Folk Songs"
[William F. Apthorp]	"Thomas's Orchestra" (M)

Volume	Pages	Month	Year
XXXI	249	February	1873
——	——	——	——
——	——	——	——
——	374–76	March	——
——	376	——	——
——	——	——	——
——	420–28	April	——
——	505–6	——	——
——	506	——	——
——	——	——	——
——	506–8	——	——
XXXII	120–23	July	——
——	248–51	August	——
——	379–82	September	——
——	382–83	——	——
——	383	——	——
——	384	——	——
——	633–35	November	——
——	635	——	——
——	756–59	December	——
——	759	——	——
——	759–60	——	——
XXXIII	112–13	January	1874
——	124	——	——
——	124–25	——	——
——	125–26	——	——

Author	*Title*
[William F. Apthorp]	"Miss Mehlig" (M)
———————	"Osgood" (M)
———————	"Mrs. Moulton" (M)
———————	"Lucca in Opera" (M)
———————	"New Music" (M)
———————	"National College of Music" (M)
Amanda R. Gere	"Frederick [sic] Chopin"
[William F. Apthorp]	"Madame Rudersdorff" (M)
———————	"Varley" (M)
———————	"Miss Liebe" (M)
———————	"Paine's Oratorio of *St. Peter*" (M)
———————	"Letter from London" (M)
———————	"Performance of Mr. Paine's Oratorio of *St. Peter* at Portland" (M)
———————	"Concert of the London Wagner Society" (M)
———————	"The Italian Opera in Athens" (M)
———————	"The Athenian Ballet" (M)
———————	" 'Characteristic' Turkish Music" (M)
———————	"Promises of the Season" (M)
———————	"New Music" (M)
———————	"What Are the Symphony Concerts For?" (M)
———————	"As to Piano Stools" (M)
———————	"M. Frédéric Boskowitz" (M)
Z. F. Peirce	"Moscheles' *Recent Music and Musicians*" (M)
[William F. Apthorp]	"Lucca" (M)
———————	"Di Murska" (M)
———————	"Rudersdorff"

Volume	Pages	Month	Year
XXXIII	127	January	1874
——	127–28	——	——
——	252–56	February	——
——	256	——	——
——	380–83	March	——
——	383–84	——	——
——	384	——	——
——	417–29	April	——
——	509	——	——
——	510	——	——
——	511–12	——	——
——	512	——	——
——	632–33	May	——
——	633	——	——
——	633–34	——	——
——	634–35	——	——
——	757–59	June	——
——	759–60	——	——
XXXIV	247–52	August	——
——	453–65	October	——
——	758–61	December	——
XXXV	113–14	January	1875

Author	Title
[William F. Apthorp]	"Good Opera and High Prices" (M)
———————	"New Music" (M)
———————	"Wagner's Works" (M)
———————	"New Music" (M)
———————	"Popular and Classic Entertainments" (M)
———————	"Raff's *Lenore* Symphony in Boston" (M)
———————	"Rubinstein's *Ivan der Grausame*" (M)
———————	"Buck's Overture" (M)
"A.F." [Amy Fay]	"In Weimar with Liszt: From a Young Lady's Letters Home"
[William F. Apthorp]	"Strakosch Troupe in Boston" (M)
———————	"Verdi's *Aïda*" (M)
———————	"Meyerbeer's *Huguenots*" (M)
———————	"Buck's *Te Deum*" (M)
———————	"New Music" (M)
———————	"Eclectic and Naturalist School" (M)
———————	"Saran's *Fantasies*" (M)
———————	"Bach's *Passions-Musik* for the Piano" (M)
———————	"New Music" (M)
———————	"Ambros's Bunte Blätter" (M)
———————	"New Music" (M)
———————	"Händel and Haydn Triennial in Boston" (M)
"A.F." [Amy Fay]	"Some Great Contemporary Composers"
[William F. Apthorp]	"Buck's *Legend of Don Munio,* and Other Recent Publications" (M)
[Harriet W. Preston]	"Hiller's *Mendelssohn*" (R)

Volume	Pages	Month	Year
XXXV	122–24	January	1875
——	378–80	March	——
——	380–81	——	——
——	633–34	May	——
——	634–35	——	——
——	635–36	——	——
——	636	——	——
——	753–58	June	——
XXXVI	253–56	August	——
——	256	——	——
——	——	——	——
——	377–80	September	——
——	380–82	——	——
——	382	——	——
——	——	——	——
——	634–37	November	——
——	763–64	December	——
XXXVII	251–52	February	1876
——	509–10	April	——
——	510–12	——	——
——	512	——	——
——	633	May	——
——	633–35	——	——

Author	Title
[William F. Apthorp]	"Musical Education and Popular Concerts" (M)
———————	"*Lohengrin* by the Strakosch Troupe" (M)
———————	"Recent Music" (M)
———————	"Schumann's *Paradise and the Peri* by the Cecilia Club" (M)
———————	"Chomet's *Influence of Music*" (M)
———————	"Ritter's *History of Music*" (M)
———————	"Recent Music" (M)
———————	"Symphony Concerts by the Harvard Musical Association and by Theodore Thomas" (M)
———————	"Burlingame's *Art Life and Theories of Richard Wagner*" (M)
———————	"Recent Music" (M)
———————	"Tytler's *Musical Composers and Their Works*" (M)
———————	"Liszt's *Die Glocken des Strassburger Münsters*" (M)
———————	"Bennett's *The Maid of Orleans*" (M)
———————	"Wieck's *Piano and Song*" (M)
———————	"Recent Music" (M)
———————	"Ignorance of Musical Terminology in the United States" (M)
———————	"Von Bülow's Concerts in Boston" (M)
———————	"Recent Music" (M)
———————	"Circulating Musical Libraries" (M)
———————	"Von Bülow's Concerts in Boston" (M)
———————	"Recent Music" (M)
———————	"Paine's New Symphony" (M)
———————	"Bach's *Magnificat* in Boston" (M)

Volume	Pages	Month	Year
XXXVII	635–36	May	1876
——	636	——	——
——	744–45	June	——
——	763–64	——	——
XXXVIII	122	July	——
——	122–24	——	——
——	124	——	——
——	252–55	August	——
——	372–73	September	——
——	377–79	——	——
——	379–80	——	——
——	451–60	October	——
——	635–40	November	——
——	640	——	——
——	759–63	December	——
——	763	——	——
——	763–64	——	——
XXXIX	110–11	January	1877
——	122	——	——

Author	Title
[William F. Apthorp]	"Saint-Saëns' Deuxième Concerto" (M)
——————	"Recent Music" (M)
John G. Whittier, John K. Paine	"Hymn Written for the Opening of the International Exhibition, Philadelphia, May 10, 1876" (words by John G. Whittier, music by John K. Paine) (S)
[John Fiske]	"Paine's Symphony" (M)
[William F. Apthorp]	"Wagner's *Centennial March*" (M)
——————	"Dudley Buck's Centennial Cantata" (M)
——————	"Paine's Centennial Hymn" (M)
——————	"Otto Singer's Cantata" (M)
[Thomas S. Perry]	"Hauslick's [*sic*] *Die Moderne Oper*" (M)
[William F. Apthorp]	"Snap-Judgment in Musical Criticism" (M)
——————	"Bach's *St. Matthew Passion*" (M)
Harriet W. Preston	"The Songs of the Troubadours"
[William F. Apthorp]	"Tausig's *Nouvelles Soirées de Vienne*" (M)
——————	"New Songs" (M)
——————	"Large and Small Concert Halls" (M)
——————	"Massenet's *Poème d'Avril* and *Poème du Souvenir*" (M)
——————	"Weber's Piano-Forte Compositions from Liszt's Edition" (M)
Bayard Taylor, John K. Paine	"Matin Song" (words by Bayard Taylor, music by John K. Paine) (S)
[William F. Apthorp]	"Belocca" (M)

Volume	Pages	Month	Year
XXXIX	122–23	January	1877
——	236–38	February	——
——	252–53	——	——
——	253–54	——	——
——	254–56	——	——
——	256	——	——
——	385–86	March	——
——	386	——	——
——	492–97	April	——
——	513–16	——	——
——	517–29	May	——
——	603–10	——	——
——	750–51	June	——
XL	106–7	July	——
——	125–28	——	——
——	128	——	——
——	——	——	——
——	236–37	August	——
——	476–80	October	——

Author	*Title*
[William F. Apthorp]	"Harvard and Thomas Concerts" (M)
Celia Thaxter, Julius Eichberg	"Sunset Song" (words by Celia Thaxter, music by Julius Eichberg) (S)
[William F. Apthorp]	"First Concert at Saunders Theatre" (M)
————————	"Madame Essipoff's Concerts" (M)
————————	"Stainer and Barrett's *Dictionary of Musical Terms*" (M)
————————	"Thallon's 'Boat of My Lover' " (M)
————————	"Christmas Performance of Handel's *Messiah*" (M)
————————	"New Songs" (M)
Edmund C. Stedman, Dudley Buck	"Creole Lover's Song" (words by Edmund C. Stedman, music by Dudley Buck) (S)
[William F. Apthorp]	"Unwarrantable Liberties of Performers" (M)
Edward H. Knight	"Crude and Curious Inventions at the Centennial Exhibition"
Henry T. Finck	"The Wagner Music-Drama"
W. W. Story, F. Boott	"A Dream" (words by W. W. Story, music by F. Boott) (S)
— — — — — —	"The Musical Critic" (CC)
[William F. Apthorp]	"The Wagner Festival of Music in Boston" (M)
————————	"The Exhibition of the Violin Pupils of the Boston Conservatory" (M)
————————	"Recent Music" (M)
— — — — — —	"Mr. R. G. White among the Composers" (CC)
G. P. Lathrop, Geo. L. Osgood	"Dear Love, Let This My Song Fly to You" (words by G. P. Lathrop, music by Geo. L. Osgood) (S)

Volume	Pages	Month	Year
XLI	32–42	January	1878
XLII	177–87	August	——
——	321–32	September	——
——	371–73	——	——
——	488–96	October	——
——	749–61	December	——
——	769–70	——	——
XLIII	12–24	January	1879
——	124–25	——	——
——	145–53	February	——
——	397	March	——
——	452–58	April	——
——	814	June	——
——	825–26	——	——
XLIV	252–54	August	——
——	444–51	October	——
——	670–71	November	——
——	683–84	——	——
——	807	December	——
XLV	253–65	February	1880
——	699–702	May	——
XLVI	410–12	September	——
XLVII	285–90	February	1881

Author	Title
[William F. Apthorp]	"An Episode in the Life of an Artist"
Sylvester Baxter	"The Stage in Germany"
William F. Apthorp	"Additional Accompaniments to Bach's and Handel's Scores"
——————	"Negro Hymns" (CC)
Richard G. White	"The Meaning of Music"
————	"The Nature of Music"
——————	"The Quality of Boston Music Culture" (CC)
Harriet W. Preston	"The Latest Songs of Chivalry"
[Horace E. Scudder]	"Goodrich's *Young Folks' Opera*" (R)
William F. Apthorp	"Musicians and Music Lovers"
——————	"Immorality of Violin Collecting" (CC)
[Arthur G. Sedgwick]	"New York Theatres"
——————	"Horace on Violin Collecting" (CC)
[Thomas S. Perry]	"Berlioz's *Correspondance Inédite*" (R)
——————	"Missionary Work of *Pinafore*" (CC)
William F. Apthorp	"Giacomo Meyerbeer"
——————	"Selections in Art" (CC)
——————	"Pole's *The Philosophy of Music*" (R)
[William F. Apthorp]	"Emery's *Elements of Harmony*" (R)
Richard G. White	"Antonius Stradivarius and the Violin"
[Arthur J. Mundy]	"Hector Berlioz" (R)
[William F. Apthorp]	"Music" (R)
[Hjalmar H. Boyeson]	*"The Spell-Bound Fiddler"* (R)

Volume	Pages	Month	Year
XLVII	362–71	March	1881
——	431–32	——	——
XLVIII	138	July	——
——	280–81	August	——
——	576	October	——
——	719	November	——
——	746–51	December	——
——	855–57	——	——
——	859	——	——
XLIX	242	February	1882
——	286	——	——
——	336–46	March	——
——	461–69	April	——
——	562–64	——	——
L	741–50	December	——
——	813–23	——	——
——	858	——	——
LI	75–86	January	1883
——	282–84	February	——
——	285	——	——
——	404–8	March	——
——	542–43	April	——
——	709–14	May	——
——	714–15	——	——
——	769–74	June	——
LII	851–53	December	——

Author	*Title*
[Arthur G. Sedgwick]	"New York Theatres"
[William F. Apthorp]	"Challoner's *History of Music*" (R)
— — — — — —	"Value of Dedications in Musical Compositions" (CC)
— — — — — —	"Applause in the Wrong Places" (CC)
— — — — — —	"Holbrook's *Hymns and Tunes*" (R)
— — — — — —	"Johnson's *Our Familiar Songs*" (R)
Theodore Child	"Shakespeare and Berlioz"
— — — — — —	"Nature and Music" (CC)
— — — — — —	"Gottschalk's Journals" (R)
Owen Wister	"Beethoven" (P)
— — — — — —	"Hensel's *Mendelssohn Family*" (R)
A. P. Hitchcock	"Hymns and Hymn-Tinkers"
Amelia E. Barr	"Shakespearean Operas"
[Sylvester Baxter]	"The Mendelssohn Family" (R)
Octavius B. Frothingham	"Art and Wealth"
John S. Dwight	"Our Dark Age in Music"
	"Nohl's *Life of Haydn*" (R)
Charles D. Warner	"Wagner's *Parsifal*"
— — — — — —	"Cantemus Domino" (CC)
— — — — — —	"Sara Bull's *Ole Bull*" (R)
[William W. Newell]	"The English and Scottish Popular Ballads" (R)
[Horace E. Scudder]	"Sara Bull's *Ole Bull*" (R)
— — — — — —	"Richard Wagner in Paris" (CC)
— — — — — —	"Notes from a Norse Musician" (CC)
Amelia Barr	"The Biography of Two Famous Songs"
— — — — — —	"Nature's Music" (CC)

Volume	Pages	Month	Year
LIII	739–53	June	1884
LIV	76–79	July	——
——	288	August	——
——	575	October	——
LV	495–507	April	1885
——	640–52	May	——
LVII	286	February	1886
LVIII	137–39	July	——
——	144	——	——
——	284–86	August	——
LIX	568–71	April	1887
——	720	May	——
LX	142	July	——
LXI	573	April	1888
LXII	595	November	——
——	715–18	——	——
——	720	——	——
——	848–50	December	——
LXIII	256–61	February	1889
——	267–71	——	——
——	568–69	April	——
——	573	——	——
——	846–50	June	——
LXIV	288	August	——
——	572–75	October	——
——	714–16	November	——

Author	Title
— — — — — —	"Paris Classical Concerts"
A. F. Matthews	"Chimes and How They Are Rung"
— — — — — —	"Ritter's *History of Music,* Haweis's *Musical Memories*" (R)
— — — — — —	"Butterworth's *Great Composers*" (R)
John S. Dwight	"George Frederick Handel: 1685–1885"
————————	"Johann Sebastian Bach: 1685–1885"
— — — — — —	"Macfarren's *Musical History*" (R)
— — — — — —	"The Management of the Mind while Hearing Music" (CC)
— — — — — —	"Upton's *Woman in Music*" (R)
— — — — — —	"Can Tunes Be Inherited?" (CC)
— — — — — —	"Republican Opera" (CC)
— — — — — —	"Naumann's *History of Music*" (R)
— — — — — —	"Upton's *Standard Oratorios*" (R)
— — — — — —	"Brooks' *Olden-Time Music*" (R)
Lucy C. Bull	"The Fifth Symphony" (P)
— — — — — —	"A Warning Note" (CC)
— — — — — —	"Wilson's *Musical Yearbook*" (R)
— — — — — —	"German Opera and the Voice" (CC)
Philip G. Hubert	"The New Talking Machines"
[George E. Woodbury]	"Letters of Felix Mendelssohn" (R)
— — — — — —	"Vocal Culture Once More" (CC)
— — — — — —	"Upton's *Standard Symphonies*" (R)
[William F. Apthorp]	"Hector Berlioz" (R)
— — — — — —	"Finck's *Chopin and Other Musical Essays*" (R)
— — — — — —	"The Lark and the Gamut" (CC)
— — — — — —	"The Rock and the Singing Tree" (CC)

Volume	Pages	Month	Year
LXV	718–19	May	1890
LXVI	716	November	——
LXVII	421	March	1891
LXVIII	428	September	——
——	572–74	October	——
——	574–75	——	——
LXIX	429–30	March	1892
——	489–501	April	——
——	712	May	——
——	843–46	June	——
LXX	422–23	September	——
——	677–88	November	——
LXXI	711	May	1893
LXXII	488–503	October	——
——	557–61	——	——
——	638–49	November	——
——	650–55	——	——
LXXIII	207–9	February	1894
——	332–39	March	——
——	339	——	——

Author	Title
— — — — — —	"Whiting's Music Readers" (R)
— — — — — —	"Wilson's *Musical Yearbook*" (R)
— — — — — —	"McCaskey's *Franklin Square Song Collection*" (R)
— — — — — —	"Ritter's *Two Lectures*" (R)
— — — — — —	"The Songs We Used to Sing" (CC)
— — — — — —	"Set to Music" (CC)
— — — — — —	"The Fatal Effects of False Voice Training" (CC)
Alfred M. Williams	"American Sea Songs"
— — — — — —	"Krehbiel's *Studies in the Wagnerian Drama*" (R)
[Frederic M. Bird] ·	"*A Dictionary of Hymnology*" (R)
— — — — — —	"Statham's *Thoughts on Music and Musicians*, Matthew's *Manual of Musical History*, Stanford's *Child's Garland of Songs*" (R)
Theodore Bacon	"Some Breton Folk-Songs"
— — — — — —	"Zahm's *Sound and Music*" (R)
William F. Apthorp	"Two Modern Classicists in Music— Part I"
[William F. Apthorp]	"Finck's *Wagner and His Works*, Zahm's *Sound and Music*, Rogers' *Philosophy of Singing*" (R)
William F. Apthorp	"Two Modern Classicists in Music— Part II"
Owen Wister	"Catholicity in Musical Taste"
Benjamin J. Lang	"From Literature to Music"
Edith Brower	"Is the Musical Idea Masculine?"
Marion Couthouy Smith	"At the Concert: A Wagner Number" (P)

Volume	Pages	Month	Year
LXXIII	419	March	1894
——	855–60	June	——
LXXIV	794–800	December	——
LXXV	39–45	January	1895
——	135	——	——
——	286–88	February	——
——	565	April	——
LXXVI	422	September	——
LXXVII	138–40	January	1896
——	394–402	March	——
——	720	May	——
——	786–96	June	——
——	853	——	——
LXXVIII	347–51	September	——
LXXIX	283–85	February	1897
LXXX	534–47	October	——
LXXXIV	828–34	December	1899
LXXXV	143–44	January	1900
LXXXVI	761–66	December	——
——	826–32	——	——

Author	Title
— — — — — —	"Holland and Rockstro's *Jenny Lind*" (R)
— — — — — —	"The Decline of the Amateur" (CC)
Aline Gorren	"The New Criticism of Genius"
Philip H. Goepp	"The Symphony Illustrated by Beethoven's Fifth in C Minor"
— — — — — —	"Booth's *Everybody's Guide to Music,* Apthorp's *Musicians and Music Lovers*" (R)
— — — — — —	"Rossini, Composer and Gourmet" (CC)
— — — — — —	"Raymond's *Two Essays in Comparative Aesthetics,* Hadow's *Studies in Modern Music*" (R)
— — — — — —	"Walker's *Letters of a Baritone*" (R)
— — — — — —	"State Summer-Evening Open-Air Schools" (CC)
Edith Brower	"New Figures in Literature and Art: IV—E. A. MacDowell"
— — — — — —	"The National Hymn" (CC)
William F. Biddle	"The Opera before the Court of Reason"
— — — — — —	"Humphreys' *Evolution of Church Music*" (R)
Lafcadio Hearn	"Out of the Street: Japanese Folk-Songs"
— — — — — —	"Of Melody" (CC)
Henry B. Fuller	"The Upward Movement in Chicago"
Elia W. Peattie	"The Artistic Side of Chicago"
— — — — — —	"Notes from Our Grandfather's Hymns" (CC)
Owen Wister	"The Bird of Passage: An Ode to Instrumental Music" (P)
Waldo S. Pratt	"New Ideas in Musical Education"

Appendix II

Articles Pertaining to Music in
Harper's New Monthly Magazine, 1850–1900

Volume	Pages	Month	Year
I	703–4	October	1850
——	850	November	——
II	67–68	December	——
III	488–89	September	1851
IV	132	December	——
——		——	
——	844	May	1852
V	127	June	——
——	266–67	July	——
——	414	August	——
——		——	
——	843	November	1852

Author	Title
——————	"Arrival of Jenny Lind" (M)
——————	"Jenny Lind's Concerts" (M)
——————	"Street Music in London"
——————	"Mems for Musical Misses"
——————	"Biscaccianti; Opera; Music for the Million; Proposed Opera House Seating 5,000" (C)
——————	"Rossini and Lumley" (C)
——————	"Jenny (Lind) Goldschmidt" (C)
——————	"Jenny Lind Goldschmidt" (C)
——————	"Ole Bull" (C)
——————	"Alboni; with a Hint to Musical Critics" (C)
——————	"Monkeys at the Opera House" (C)
——————	"The Opera and Concerts; Alboni, Sontag, and Paul Jullien" (C)

Volume	Pages	Month	Year
VI	271–72	January	1853
——	559	March	——
——	704–5	April	——
VII	557	September	——
——	557–58	——	——
——	702	October	——
——	707	——	——
VIII	132	December	——
——	695–96	May	1854
IX	119–21	June	——
——	123	——	——
——	124	——	——
——	137	——	——
——	523–24	September	——
——	693	November	——
X	123–24	December	——
——	251–53	January	1855
XI	269–71	July	——
——	846–47	November	——
XII	116–17	December	——
XIV	127–28	December	1856

Author	Title
——————	"The Music Mania" (C)
——————	"Sontag and Alboni in Opera" (C)
——————	"The Opera" (C)
——————	"The Opera and the Ravels" (C)
——————	"Anecdotes of Sontag" (C)
——————	"Street Music and Reminiscences" (C)
——————	"Jullien" (C)
——————	"The Wishy-Washy School in Literature and Music" (C)
——————	"The Opera House; Basis of the Opera; Musicians' Speculations" (C)
——————	"Charity Concerts; Polyhymnia Baggs" (C)
——————	"Music Coming; Mario and Grisi" (C)
——————	"Re-opening of the Crystal Palace— The Music and Speeches" (C)
——————	"A History of the Old Hundredth Psalm Tune" (L)
——————	"Posthumous Adventures of Paganini"
——————	"Grisi and Mario; Characteristics of Grisi; Grisi and Rachel" (C)
——————	"The New Opera House; Reception of Grisi; No Jenny Lind Furor; The Singers Going South" (C)
——————	"The Singer's Dream" (F)
——————	"The Mystery of the Opera; The Opera Never Pays; Why and Wherefore" (C)
——————	"The Opera; Miss Hensler" (C)
——————	*"Plymouth Collection of Hymns and Tunes"* (R)
——————	"The Opera War" (C)

Volume	Pages	Month	Year
XIV	128	December	1856
——	270–72	January	1857
——	272–73	——	——
——	564	March	——
——	702–3	April	——
——	849–50	May	——
XV	83–85	June	——
——	224–31	July	——
——	499–504	September	——
XVIII	560–61	March	1859
XIX	268–69	July	——
——	323	August	——
XXII	413–14	March	1861
XXIII	415	August	——
——	706–7	October	——
XXV	418–19	September	1862
——	420–21	——	——
——	616–18	October	——
XXVI	97–101	December	——
——	420–21	February	1863
——	423	——	——
——	495–501	March	——
——	563	——	——
——	853–54	May	——
XXVII	855	November	——
XXVIII	275–76	January	1864
——	567	March	——
XXIX	190	June	——

Author	*Title*
— — — — — —	"Thalberg" (C)
— — — — — —	"The Opera War" (C)
— — — — — —	"Thalberg" (C)
— — — — — —	"Talking at Concerts" (C)
— — — — — —	"Music and the Press" (C)
— — — — — —	"Thalberg" (C)
— — — — — —	"Animal Love of Music"
— — — — — —	"The Story of a Piano" (F)
— — — — — —	"Handel"
[George W. Curtis]	"Street Music" (C)
——————	"Opera; *Don Giovanni*" (C)
— — — — — —	"The Musicians of Our Woods"
[George W. Curtis]	"Poor Opera, High Costs and Prices" (C)
——————	"Patti, Lind, Grisi" (C)
——————	"National Hymn" (C)
——————	"Gottschalk" (C)
——————	"Mme. Borchard in Summer Opera" (C)
— — — — — —	"A Monthly Concert at Tampa Bay"
Dennar Stuart	"A Camp-meeting in Tennessee"
[George W. Curtis]	"Effects of the War—On Opera" (C)
——————	"Patti in Paris" (C)
Charlotte Taylor	"Musicians of Field and Meadow"
[George W. Curtis]	"The Past Season; Effects of the War" (C)
——————	"Opera—Effects of the War" (C)
——————	"Opera and Theatre during Wartime"
——————	"Boston's Music Hall"
——————	"Stephen Foster" (C)
[A. C. Wheeler]	"Doomed to Music" (F)

Volume	Pages	Month	Year
XXX	48	December	1864
——	123	——	——
XXXI	533	October	1865
XXXIII	259–60	July	1866
——	666–67	October	——
——	803–5	November	——
XXXIV	265	January	1867
XXXV	626–30	October	——
——	803–5	November	——
XXXVI	259	January	1868
——	809–11	May	——
XXXVII	753–59	November	——
XXXVIII	557–59	March	1869
XXXIX	148–49	June	——
——	447–48	August	——
XL	450–55	February	1870
XLI	144	June	——
——	299–300	July	——
——	453–54	August	——
XLII	295–96	January	1871
XLIII	451–52	August	——

Author	Title
[Elizabeth Stoddard]	"Music in a Crowd" (P)
[George W. Curtis]	"Bilingual Opera" (C)
————————	"German Influences in America" (C)
[George W. Curtis]	"Fire at the Academy of Music" (C)
————————	"Concert Manners" (C)
————————	"Popular Ballads" (C)
— — — — — —	"Beethoven's Letters (tr. Wallace)" (R)
[J. V. C. Smith]	"Giving Lessons on the Piano" (H)
[George W. Curtis]	"English Opera at the Park Theatre" (C)
————————	"Kellogg's Success in London" (C)
————————	"Ballet at Niblo's" (C)
[Moncure D. Conway]	"Handel Festival at the Crystal Palace"
[George W. Curtis]	"Madrigal Concert" (C)
— — — — — —	"Reminiscences of Felix Mendelssohn-Bartholdy (Polko)" (R)
[George W. Curtis]	"Peace Jubilee in Boston" (C)
[Maximilian] Schele De Vere	"A Chat on Bells"
— — — — — —	"Tone Masters" (L)
[George W. Curtis]	"The New York Madrigal Society" (C)
————————	"The Beethoven Centennial in New York" (C)
————————	"Nilsson" (C)
————————	"Vocal Society Concerts" (C)

Volume	Pages	Month	Year
XLIV	458–59	February	1872
——	615–16	March	——
——	641–58	April	——
——	752–60	——	——
XLV	134–35	June	——
——	142	——	——
——	618–20	September	——
XLVI	454–55	February	1873
——	831–52	May	——
——	926–29	——	——
XLVII	771–75	October	——
XLVIII	291–93	January	1874
——	739	April	——
——	628–42	——	——
XLIX	130–32	June	——
LI	136–38	——	1875
——	295–96	July	——
——	601–2	September	——
——	736–44	October	——
LII	142	December	——

Author	Title
[George W. Curtis]	"Nilsson" (C)
——————	"Wachtel" (C)
Moncure D. Conway	"The City of the Little Monk"
H. W. [sic] Haweis	"Music, Emotion, and Morals"
[George W. Curtis]	"Opera" (C)
— — — — — —	"Haweis's *Music and Morals*" (L)
[George W. Curtis]	"The Boston Peace Jubilee of 1872" (C)
——————	"Classicism in Boston's Harvard Concerts" (C)
Moncure D. Conway	"Vienna"
Samuel Osgood	"Social Art" (C)
——————	"The Appreciation of Art" (C)
[George W. Curtis]	"The Spirit of '27" (C)
Titus Munson Coan	"Orchestral Music" (P)
Olive Logan	"The Secret Regions of the Stage"
[George W. Curtis]	"New York Vocal Society; Wagnerism" (C)
——————	"Good Manners in Public" (C)
——————	"May Festival in Cincinnati" (C)
— — — — — —	"Wieck's *Piano and Song*" (L)
"Ellis Gray" [Louisa T. Cragin]	"The Mission of Music"
[George W. Curtis]	"Italian Opera" (C)

Volume	Pages	Month	Year
LII	298	January	1876
——	610–12	March	——
——	882	May	——
LIV	1–18	December	——
——	206–9	January	1877
——	463–64	March	——
LVI	462–63	February	1878
LVII	113–21	June	——
——	787	October	——
——	934–35	November	——
LVIII	56–75	December	——
——	229–34	January	1879
——	426–43	February	——
——	687–98	April	——
——	735–40	——	——
——	777–78	——	——
——	778–79	——	——
——	854–63	May	——
——	931–32	——	——
——	932–33	——	——
LIX	138–39	June	——
——	620–21	September	——

Author	Title
— — — — — —	"The Sunlight of Song" (L)
[George W. Curtis]	"History of Music in New York; Rubinstein and von Bülow" (C)
Celia Thaxter	"To a Violin" (P)
O. M. Spencer	"The Home of Columbus"
Moncure D. Conway	"Félicien David"
[George W. Curtis]	"Baltimore's Peabody Institute" (C)
———————	"The Philharmonic under Thomas" (C)
Matilda Despard	"Music in New York Thirty Years Ago" (C)
— — — — — —	"Ella's *Musical Sketches at Home and Abroad*" (L)
[George W. Curtis]	"Farewell to Theodore Thomas" (C)
Lucy White Lillie	"Mendelssohn and Moscheles"
W. P. Garrison	"Rousseau"
— — — — — —	"Mendelssohn's Letters to Madame Moscheles"
Olive Logan	"The Ancestry of Brudder Bones"
Mrs. A. B. Blake	"Church Music in America"
[George W. Curtis]	"The Violinist Wilhelmj" (C)
———————	*"Pinafore"* (C)
Julius Wilcox	"The Piano and Its Antecedents"
[George W. Curtis]	"Gerster in *Sonnambula*" (C)
———————	*"Pinafore* Once More" (C)
———————	"Mapleson's Italian Opera in New York; Gerster" (C)
———————	"On Deference to Europe" (C)

Volume	Pages	Month	Year
LIX	947	November	1879
LX	235	January	1880
——	411–17	February	——
——	463–64	——	——
——	501–8	March	——
——	629–30	——	——
——	641–55	April	——
——	778–83	——	——
——	793	——	——
——	827–43	May	——
——	938–39	——	——
LXI	144–45	June	——
——	307–8	July	——
LXII	238–47	January	1881
——	305–6	——	——
——	468–69	February	——
——	475	——	——
——	803–18	May	——
——	945–46	——	——
LXIII	52–61	June	——
——	286–88	July	——

Author	*Title*
[George W. Curtis]	*"Pinafore* Once More" (C)
A. H. Louis	"Music and Words" (P)
Emily Royall	"Hector Berlioz"
[George W. Curtis]	"Manners at Public Entertainments" (C)
J. Brander Matthews	*"Pinafore's* Predecessor"
— — — — — —	"Songs from the Published Writings of Alfred Tennyson" (L)
Mrs. John Lillie	"Music and Musicians in England—Part I"
A. Bowman Blake	"Madrigals"
— — — — — —	"Ferris's *Great Singers*" (L)
Mrs. John Lillie	"Music and Musicians in England—Part II"
[George W. Curtis]	"The Season of 1879–80; Thomas's Return" (C)
———————	"Amateur Choral Singing: A German Contribution" (C)
———————	"Ole Bull" (C)
Barnet Phillips	"Some Great Violins"
[George W. Curtis]	"Opera; Gerster" (C)
———————	"Premiere of Boito's *Mephistophele*" (C)
— — — — — —	"Franz's Album of Songs" (L)
Frederick Nast	"Music and Musicians in New York"
[George W. Curtis]	*"Don Giovanni"* (C)
Amelia E. Barr	"Ballads and Ballad Music Illustrating Shakespeare"
S. Austin Pearce	"The Music of the Spheres"

Volume	Pages	Month	Year
LXIII	304–5	July	1881
——	306–7	——	——
——	634	September	——
——	947–48	November	——
——	952–53	——	——
LXIV	1–29	December	——
——	308–9	January	1882
——	309–10	——	——
——	467–68	February	——
——	577–88	March	——
——	786–87	April	——
——	825–36	May	——
LXV	242–48	July	——
——	281–86	——	——
——	306–8	——	——
——	798–99	October	——
LXVI	540–56	March	1883
——	631–32	——	——
——	793–94	April	——
——	954–55	May	——

Author	*Title*
[George W. Curtis]	"Choral Music in New York" (C)
———————	"Festivals" (C)
— — — — — —	"Amy Fay's *Music Study in Germany*" (L)
[George W. Curtis]	"Dwight and the Journal" (C)
— — — — — —	"Franklin Square Song Collection" (C)
Zadel B. Gustafson	"The Bernadottes"
[George W. Curtis]	"The Next May Festival" (C)
———————	"Madame Materna" (C)
———————	"Patti's Return" (C)
William L. Gage	"The Mendelssohn Family"
[George W. Curtis]	"New Morality in the Theatre" (C)
Mary Alice Seymour	"Music and Musicians in Austria"
"Octavia Hensel" [Mary Alice Seymour]	"Franz Liszt"
William C. Alden	"Sailor Songs"
[George W. Curtis]	"The Festival of 1882" (C)
———————	*"Parsifal"* (C)
Mariana G. Van Rensselaer	*"Parsifal* at Baireuth"
[George W. Curtis]	"Success of Madame Scalchi" (C)
———————	"Public Manners at Concerts" (C)
———————	"Wagner and Beethoven at the May Festival" (C)

Volume	Pages	Month	Year
LXVII	143–44	June	1883
——	245–65	July	——
——	292–96	——	——
——	877–89	November	——
LXVIII	142	December	——
——	313–14	January	1884
——	641–42	March	——
——	968–69	May	——
LXIX	154	June	——
——	307–8	July	——
——	309–10	——	——
——	388–404	August	——
——	962–63	November	——
LXX	157–64	December	——
——	807–8	April	1885
LXXI	135–39	June	——
LXXII	476–77	February	1886
——	643–45	March	——

Author	Title
[George W. Curtis]	"John Howard Payne" (C)
Olive Logan	"Cincinnati"
George Cary Eggleston	"The Education of Women"
Montgomery Schuyler	"The Metropolitan Opera House"
R. J. de Cordova, J. Mosenthal	"The Hunger of the Heart" (words by R. J. de Cordova, music by J. Mosenthal) (S)
[George W. Curtis]	"Italian Opera in New York" (C)
———————	"The Contest of Nightingales" (C)
———————	"The Old and the New Singers" (C)
— — — — — —	*"The Franklin Square Song Collection"* (L)
[George W. Curtis]	"The Wagner Concerts in New York" (C)
———————	"Vulgar Manners at Public Amusements" (C)
Ernest Ingersoll	"Salt Lake City"
[George W. Curtis]	"The Coming Opera Season" (C)
Mrs. Margaret Sangster, W. W. Gilchrist	"The Dear Long Ago" (words by Mrs. Margaret Sangster, music by W. W. Gilchrist) (S)
[George W. Curtis]	"German Opera in New York" (C)
Mary Tucker Magill	"A Georgian at the Opera"
[George W. Curtis]	"The Gilbert and Sullivan Comic Operettas" (C)
———————	"American Opera in New York" (C)

Volume	Pages	Month	Year
LXXII	802–3	April	1886
——	804–5	——	——
——	969–70	May	——
LXXIV	475–76	February	1887
——	977–79	May	——
LXXVI	474–75	February	1888
——	812	April	——
——	960	May	——
——	961–62	——	——
LXXVII	65–73	June	——
LXXVIII	454–58	February	1889
——	484–86	——	——
——	820–21	April	——
LXXX	109–15	December	——
——	314–16	January	1890
——	317–18	——	——
——	530–36	March	——
LXXXI	147–48	June	——
LXXXII	190–202	January	1891
——	564–72	March	——

Author	*Title*
[George W. Curtis]	"Good Manners at the Opera" (C)
	"Mr. Gilbert on His Pedestal" (C)
————————	"The Dethronement of Italian Opera in New York" (C)
————————	"The American Opera in the Field" (C)
————————	"A Concert by the Sylvania Vocal Society" (C)
————————	"The Musical Season in New York" (C)
Walter Pelham	"A Musical Concert" (D)
[George W. Curtis]	"The Winter Music" (C)
————————	"Opera and the Concerts" (C)
Henry E. Krehbiel	"Surpliced Choirs in New York"
Emilie Christina Curtis	"The Training of Children's Voices in Public Schools"
[George W. Curtis]	"The Charm of Music" (C)
[William Dean Howells]	"Brown's *Musical Instruments and Their Homes*" (L)
Hugh Reginald Haweis	"Oratorio and Drama"
[George W. Curtis]	"Street Musicians" (C)
————————	"The New and the Old Opera" (C)
Henry E. Krehbiel	"How to Listen to Wagner's Music"
[George W. Curtis]	"Musical Notes from Barataria" (C)
"F. Anstey" [Thomas Anstey Guthrie]	"London Music Halls"
Francis Korbay	"Nationality in Music"

Volume	Pages	Month	Year
LXXXII	636–38	March	1891
——	797–98	April	——
LXXXIII	309–10	July	——
——	633–34	September	——
——	637–38	——	——
LXXXIV	16–26	December	——
——	637–38	March	1892
——	960–62	May	——
LXXXV	313–14	July	——
LXXXVI	801–2	April	1893
LXXXVII	476–79	August	——
LXXXVIII	385–91	February	1894
——	802–3	April	——
XC	429–34	February	1895
——	492	——	——
XCI	505–9	September	——
XCIII	316–21	July	1896
——	622–35	September	——
XCIV	471–75	February	1897
XCVI	473–78	——	1898

Author	*Title*
[George W. Curtis]	"A Great Opera Night" (C)
———————	"The Humors of the Opera" (C)
———————	"Theodore Thomas's Farewell" (C)
———————	"Jenny Lind" (C)
———————	"Mozart's Music" (C)
William Wallace Gilchrist	"A Maid's Choice; A Musical Pastoral"
[George W. Curtis]	"A Critical Nightingale" (C)
———————	"The Musical Hero of the Winter" (C)
———————	"The Semicentenary of the Philharmonic Society" (C)
[Charles Dudley Warner]	"Hampton's Colored Students in *Esther*" (ES)
———————	"Ruskin and Wagner" (ES)
Jean Forsyth	"A Singing-Student in London"
[Charles Dudley Warner]	"A National School of Music" (ES)
Antonín Dvořák	"Music in America"
— — — — — —	"The Trombonist and the Fishes" (D)
David Graham Adee	"The Story of a Song"
Kate Douglas Wiggin	"Bluebeard: Lecture Recital on a Posthumous Music-Drama by Richard Wagner" (D)
William Von Sachs	"Musical Celebrities of Vienna"
Hugh Reginald Haweis	"Composers and 'Artistes' "
George P. Upton	"Recent Development of Musical Culture in Chicago"

Volume	Pages	Month	Year
XCVII	313–16	August	1898
XCIX	823–46	November	1899
C	969–71	May	1900
CI	797–801	October	——
CII	163–66	December	——

Author	Title
[Charles Dudley Warner]	"Mexican Love of Architecture, Music, and Flowers" (ES)
Sylvester Baxter	"Boston at the Century's End"
Anne Warrington Witherup	"With the Libretti: I—Tannhäuser" (D)
———————	"With the Libretti: II—Lohengrin" (D)
———————	"With the Libretti: III—Fafner" (D)

Appendix III

Articles Pertaining to Music in
*Scribner's Monthly–Century Illustrated Monthly
Magazine,* 1871–1900

Volume	Pages	Month	Year
I	266–67	January	1871
——	680	April	——
——	683	——	——
——	685–86	——	——
II	107–8	May	——
——	211	June	——
——	214–16	——	——
——	555–56	September	——
——	661	October	——
——	——	——	——
III	247–48	December	——
——	377–78	January	1872
——	——	February	——
——	497	——	——
——	502	——	——

Symbols: Culture and Progress (CP), Topics of the Time (T), Home and Society (HS), World's Work (W), Nature and Science (NS), Literature (L), Communications (Comm), Open Letters (O), Poem (P), Etchings (E), Bric-À-Brac (B), Fiction (F), Song (S), In Lighter Vein (V).

A solid line indicates the repetition of the preceding information (volume, month, etc.); brackets enclose the name of the author to whom an unsigned article has been attributed; a broken line indicates that the author is unknown.

Author	Title
"K.C.B."	"Tartini's Dream-Music"
— — — — — —	"Beethoven's Centennial" (CP)
— — — — — —	"Gounod" (CP)
— — — — — —	"Kellogg" (CP)
— — — — — —	"Nilsson" (CP)
— — — — — —	"Abbé Liszt" (CP)
— — — — — —	"Wagner in the Bowery" (CP)
— — — — — —	"Auber's Death" (CP)
— — — — — —	"The *Ring* at Baireuth" (CP)
— — — — — —	"Weber's *Freischütz*" (CP)
— — — — — —	"Wachtel" (CP)
— — — — — —	"Opera in New York" (CP)
Mrs. R. S. Greenough	"Christine Nilsson and Her Maestro"
— — — — — —	"Hiller's *Tone-Life of Our Times*" (CP)
— — — — — —	"Santley" (CP)

Volume	Pages	Month	Year
III	512	February	1872
——	633–34	March	——
——	758–59	April	——
——	759	——	——
IV	121–22	May	——
——	253–54	June	——
——	503–4	August	——
——	511	——	——
——	645–46	September	——
V	129–31	November	——
——	393–94	January	1873
VI	372–73	July	——
VII	557	March	1874
——	735	April	——
VIII	245–46	June	——
IX	81–89	November	——
——	458–66	February	1875
——	501–2	——	——
——	537–45	March	——
——	759	April	——
——	773	——	——
X	9–20	May	——
——	110–11	——	——
——	242–43	June	——
——	254	——	——
——	390	July	——

Author	Title
— — — — — —	"Matinée at the Academy of Music" (E)
— — — — — —	"The Concerts" (CP)
— — — — — —	"The Church Music Association" (CP)
— — — — — —	"Santley" (CP)
— — — — — —	"Music" (CP)
— — — — — —	"The Great Quartette" (CP)
— — — — — —	"The Jubilee" (CP)
— — — — — —	"Bible Music" (CP)
— — — — — —	"Haweis's *Music and Morals*" (CP)
— — — — — —	"Music" (CP)
— — — — — —	"Italian Opera" (CP)
— — — — — —	"Music in New York" (CP)
John Fraser	"To Christine Nilsson" (P)
Edward King	"Parepa-Rosa" (P)
— — — — — —	"Music" (CP)
Franz [Francis] Hueffer	"Richard Wagner"
J. R. G. Hassard	"Theodore Thomas"
[Josiah G. Holland]	"Theaters and Theater-going" (T)
Ita Aniol Prokop	"How the Opera of 'Dante' Was Written"
— — — — — —	"To the Unmusical" (HS)
— — — — — —	"Musical Notes of Waterfalls" (NS)
Frederick A. Schwab	"A Temple of Song"
[Josiah G. Holland]	"Popular Arts" (T)
————————	"The Music of the Church" (T)
— — — — — —	"Musical Medicine" (CP)
— — — — — —	"A New Hymn and Tune Book" (CP)

Volume	Pages	Month	Year
X	510–11	August	1875
——	520–21	——	——
——	700–7	October	——
XI	98–107	November	——
——	739–40	March	1876
——	912	April	——
XII	361–67	July	——
XIII	124–25	November	——
——	419	February	1877
——	427–28	——	——
——	545–47	——	——
XIV	573	August	——
XVI	432–33	July	1878
——	437	——	——
XVII	32	November	——
——	59–76	——	——
——	148–49	——	——
——	309–10	December	——
——	438–39	January	1879

Author	Title
[Josiah G. Holland]	"Cincinnati" (T)
— — — — — —	"Richard Wagner" (CP)
"L.L.L."	"Recollections of Liszt and von Bülow"
J. Bunting	"The Old Germania Orchestra"
[Josiah G. Holland]	"Public Halls" (T)
— — — — — —	"Song of the Horse-Car Conductor" (words and music by Winkelried Wolfgang Brown) (B)
"J.L.G."	"Wagner at Bayreuth"
[Josiah G. Holland]	"Wagner at Bayreuth" (T)
[Richard W. Gilder]	"Essipoff" (P)
[Charles Barnard]	"Recent Researches in Orchestration" (W)
Neña Sturgis	"Traditional Music of the Spanish Pyrenees"
[Charles Barnard]	"Improvements in Organ Building" (W)
[Josiah G. Holland]	"Culture and Christianity" (T)
— — — — — —	"Music and Drawing at Home" (HS)
Celia Thaxter	"Beethoven" (P)
J. D. Osborne	"A Modern Playwright" [Eugène Scribe]
[Josiah G. Holland]	"Mr. Theodore Thomas" (T)
[Charles Barnard]	"Automatic Device for Reproducing Music" (W)
[Josiah G. Holland]	"Art as a Steady Diet" (T)

Volume	Pages	Month	Year
XVII	904–6	April	1879
XVIII	111–16	May	——
——	134–35	——	——
——	751–55	September	——
——	904–10	October	——
XIX	897–904	April	1880
——	941–42	——	——
XX	159	May	——
XXI	293–95	December	——
——	583–86	February	1881
——	777–80	March	——
XXII	120–32	May	——
——	307–8	June	——
——	627–29	August	——
——	949	October	——
XXIII	686–703	March	1882
——	865–82	April	——
XXIV	31–43	May	——
——	193–210	June	——
——	317–18	——	——
——	619–24	August	——
——	956	October	——
XXV	156	November	——
——	796–97	March	1883
——	958	April	——
XXVI	194–97	June	——

Author	Title
— — — — — —	*"H.M.S. Pinafore,* for Amateurs" (HS)
J. R. G. Hassard	"Wilhelmj and Remenyi"
[Josiah G. Holland]	"Church Music" (T)
Kate Field	"W. S. Gilbert"
———————	"Arthur Sullivan"
Sidney Lanier	"The Orchestra of To-day"
— — — — — —	"Operas for Amateurs" (HS)
[Charles Barnard]	"Transposing Piano" (W)
Gustav Kobbé	"The Musician's Ideal" (F)
Eugene Thayer	"The Music of Niagara"
Theodore Thomas	"Musical Possibilities in America"
Sir Julius Benedict	"Jenny Lind"
L. Y. Schermerhorn	" 'The Music of Niagara' " (Comm)
Hosea E. Holt	"Mr. Theodore Thomas and Music in American Public Schools" (Comm)
J. Spencer Curwen	" 'Music in American Public Schools': A Reply" (Comm)
Richard Grant White	"Opera in New York" (Part I)
———————	——————— (Part II)
———————	——————— (Part III)
———————	——————— (Part IV)
[Charles Barnard]	"Recording Music" (W)
J. R. G. Hassard	"How Wagner Makes Operas"
— — — — — —	"Jenny Lind's Courtship" (HS)
[Charles Barnard]	"The Music Electrograph" (W)
———————	"Women as Piano Tuners" (HS)
— — — — — —	"Sara Bull's *Ole Bull*" (L)
William L. Tomlins	"On the Training of Children's Voices"

Volume	Pages	Month	Year
XXVI	798	September	1883
XXVII	158–59	November	——
——	632–34	February	1884
——	787–89	March	——
——	946–48	April	——
——	948–54	——	——
XXVIII	221	May	——
——	306–9	June	——
——	209–11	——	——
——	311–12	——	——
——	468–71	July	——
——	471	——	——
——	——	——	——
——	638	August	——
——	950–52	October	——
XXIX	156–57	November	——
——	474–76	January	1885
XXXI	414–24	——	1886
——	477–78	——	——

Author	Title
J. Spencer Curwen	"The Training of Children's Voices" (O)
Gottlieb Federlein	"Opera in New York" (O)
Charles S. Robinson	"Artistic Help in Divine Service" (O)
————————	"Organs and Orchestras in Church" (O)
————————	"Worshiping by Proxy" (O)
Richard Grant White	*"Music in America"* (O)
Richard Watson Gilder	"Music and Words" (P)
Charles S. Robinson	"What the Choirs Say" (O)
Frédéric L. Ritter	*"Music in America"* (O)
Richard Grant White	*"Music in America"* (O)
Charles S. Robinson	"The Minister and the Music" (O)
"W.H.S."	*"In Re* Church Music" (O)
Frederick W. Wodell	"An Ideal Church" (O)
"A Pew-Owner"	"Church Music: A Letter to the Rev. Dr. Robinson" (O)
Eugene Thayer	"Congregational Singing" (O)
"Diapason"	"A Word from the Organ-Loft" (O)
Edward Witherspoon	"A Voice from the Choir-Loft" (O)
Frederick A. Schwab	"Verdi, the Composer"
"G."	"A National Conservatory of Music" (O)

Volume	Pages	Month	Year
XXXI	517–32	February	1886
——	804	March	——
——	807–28	April	——
XXXII	162–63	May	——
——	655–69	September	——
——	967–68	October	——
XXXIII	493–94	January	1887
——	494	——	——
——	975	April	——
XXXIV	413–17	July	——
——	619–29	August	——
——	629–30	——	——
XXXV	314–17	December	——
——	317–19	——	——
——	724–31	March	1888

Author	*Title*
George W. Cable	"Creole Slave Dances: The Dance in Place Congo; with Arrangements of Creole Music by H. E. Krehbiel, Miss M. L. Bartlett, and John A. Broekhoven"
Margaret Vande-grift	"The Music-Stool" (B)
George W. Cable	"Creole Slave Songs; with Arrangements of Creole Music by Miss M. L. Bartlett, Mme L. Lejeune, and H. E. Krehbiel"
— — — — — —	"The American Opera Company" (O)
Albert Morris Bagby	"A Summer with Liszt in Weimar"
E. W. B. Canning	"The Singing-Schools of Olden Time" (O)
Charles Barnard	"The Cultivation of the Cantata" (O)
Paul David	"Liszt and David" (O)
George H. Wilson	"The Cantata and American Composers" (O)
William J. Henderson	"The Sportsman's Music"
Brander Matthews	"The Songs of the War"
Julia Ward Howe	"Note on the 'Battle Hymn of the Republic'"
Theodore F. Seward	"The Tonic Sol-Fa System: Opinions of a Teacher" (O)
Henry E. Krehbiel	"The Tonic Sol-Fa System: Opinions of a Critic" (O)
Albert Morris Bagby	"Some Pupils of Liszt"

Volume	Pages	Month	Year
XXXV	845–48	April	1888
XXXVI	147–49	May	——
——	254–56	June	——
——	416–17	July	——
——	718–19	September	——
——	894	October	——
——	908–11	——	——
XXXVII	318–19	December	——
——	637–39	February	1889
XXXVIII	158–59	May	——
——	234–35	June	——
——	958–59	October	——
XLI	449–57	January	1891
XLII	475–76	July	——
XLIII	155	November	——
——	203–20	December	——
——	388–95	January	1892
——	475	——	——
——	720–24	March	——
——	724–26	——	——

Author	Title
Simeon Pease Cheney	"Bird Music" (Part I)
————————	———————— (Part II)
————————	———————— (Part III)
————————	———————— (Part IV)
————————	———————— (Part V)
Harriet P. Spofford	"O Music" (P)
Charles Allen	"Bird Music"
Mary L. Lewis	"The Holt Method of Teaching Music" (O)
— — — — — —	"Coming from the Fields" (words by H. S. Edwards, music by A. L. Wood) (S) (B)
Philip G. Hubert, Jr.	"The Abuse of Applause" (O)
Simeon Pease Cheney	"Bird Music"
George H. Wilson	"A Tenor Farm" (O)
Henry E. Krehbiel	"Chinese Music"
Richard Hoffman	"Similar Musical Phrases in Great Composers" (O)
Auguste Vianesi	"The Paris Opera" (O)
Amelia Gere Mason	"Mozart—After a Hundred Years"
Charles François Gounod	"Gounod in Italy and Germany"
Henry Krehbiel	"M. Gounod and His Ideals" (O)
William Mason	"Paderewski: A Critical Study"
Fanny Morris Smith	"Paderewski: A Biographical Sketch"

Volume	Pages	Month	Year
XLIII	727	March	1892
XLIV	657–60	September	——
XLV	122–26	November.	——
——	207–10	December	——
——	312–14	——	——
——	517–24	February	1893
——	628–31	——	——
——	735–36	March	——
XLVI	152–54	May	——
——	237–44	June	——
——	317	——	——
XLVII	150–52	November	——
——	304–10	December	——
——	421–31	January	1894
——	440–49	——	——
——	616–23	February	——
——	701–4	March	——
XLVIII	341–46	July	——
——	358–63	——	——
XLIX	670–73	March	1895
——	935–38	April	——
L	28–33	May	——

Author	Title
Richard Watson Gilder	"How Paderewski Plays" (P)
Henry E. Krehbiel	"Antonín Dvořák"
Jules Massenet	"Autobiographical Notes by the Composer Massenet"
Ronald J. McNeill	"Jenny Lind"
William J. Henderson	"To Persons Desiring to Cultivate a Taste in Music" (O)
Camille Saint-Saëns	"Franz Liszt"
Fanny Morris Smith	"How Pianists May Be Different and Yet Each Be Great" (O)
Henry E. Krehbiel	"Camille Saint-Saëns"
Philip G. Hubert, Jr.	"What the Phonograph Will Do for Music and Music-Lovers" (O)
Henry T. Finck	"An Hour with Robert Franz"
Waldo S. Pratt	"Wanted, Specialists in Church Music" (O)
William J. Henderson	"The New School of Italian Opera" (O)
Ernest Reyer	"Hector Berlioz"
Alice C. Fletcher	"Indian Songs"
Edvard Grieg	"Robert Schumann"
John Comfort Fillmore	"A Study of Indian Music"
William Mason	"Edvard Grieg"
Antonín Dvořák	"Franz Schubert"
John C. Carpenter	" 'The Star-Spangled Banner' "
Henry E. Krehbiel	"Eugene Ysaye"
Henry T. Finck	"Bernhard Stavenhagen"
Alexander McArthur	"Rubinstein: The Man and the Musician"

Volume	Pages	Month	Year
LI	257–59	December	1895
——	707–12	March	1896
LII	461–66	July	——
——	474–76	——	——
LIII	448–54	January	1897
——	476–77	——	——
LIV	554–58	August	——
——	558–59	——	——
LV	140–46	November	——
——	719–27	March	1898
——	768–79	——	——
——	797	——	——
LVI	3–14	May	——
——	537–43	August	——
LVIII	164–65	May	1899
——	577–81	August	——
LIX	63–76	November	——
——	158–59	——	——
——	747–54	March	1900

Author	Title
Bernhard Stavenhagen	"Humperdinck's *Hänsel und Gretel*"
H. C. Mercer	"On the Track of 'The Arkansas Traveler' "
Bernard Boekelman	"Recollections and Anecdotes of Bülow"
John Knowles Paine, Horatio Parker, and Edward McDowell [*sic*]	"American Musical Authorities against the Treloar Bill" (O)
Henry T. Finck	"An American Composer: Edward A. MacDowell"
Fanny Morris Smith	"The Kingdom of Rosenthal"
Henri Appy	"Characteristics of Jenny Lind"
Fanny Morris Smith	"What Jenny Lind Did for America"
Edvard Grieg	"Mozart"
John Burroughs	"Songs of American Birds"
Rupert Hughes	"Women Composers"
— — — — — —	"Boldoni's Pastel of Verdi" (O)
Henry E. Krehbiel	"The Beethoven Museum at Bonn"
Gustav Kobbé	"The Trumpet in Camp and Battle"
Gelett Burgess	"A Musical Fable" (V)
Marion Alexander Haskell	"Negro 'Spirituals' "
Gustav Kobbé	"Wagner from behind the Scenes"
Henry Mayer	"High C, and How They Take It" (V)
Moritz Moszkowski	"The Composer Meyerbeer"

Volume	Pages	Month	Year
LX	438–49	July	1900
——	569–74	August	——
——	763–76	September	——
——	848–64	October	——

Author	*Title*
William Mason	"Memories of a Musical Life" (Part I)
———————	——————— (Part II)
———————	——————— (Part III)
———————	——————— (Part IV)

Appendix IV

Articles Pertaining to Music in
Scribner's Magazine, 1887–1900

Volume	Pages	Month	Year
I	637–40	May	1887
II	379–84	September	——
——	515–31	November	——
III	131–50	February	1888
——	331–49	March	——
IV	435–54	October	——
V	331–48	March	1889
VII	487–96	April	1890
XI	98–104	January	1892
——	350–65	March	——

Point of View (P), About the World (W).

Symbols: A solid line indicates the repetition of the preceding information (volume, month, etc.); brackets enclose the name of the author to whom an unsigned article has been attributed; a broken line indicates that the author is unknown.

Author	Title
Arlo Bates	"Words and Music"
Maurice Thompson	"The Motif of Bird-Song"
William F. Apthorp	"Wagner and Scenic Art"
————————	"Mendelssohn's Letters to Moscheles" (Part I)
————————	———————— (Part II)
Gustav Kobbé	"Behind the Scenes of an Opera-House"
William F. Apthorp	"Some of Wagner's Heroes and Heroines"
————————	"Wagnerianism and the Italian Opera"
Henry Krehbiel	"Bayreuth Revisited"
William F. Apthorp	"Paris Theatres and Concerts: The Opéra, the Opéra-Comique, and the Conservatoire"

Volume	Pages	Month	Year
XI	482–96	April	1892
——	628–43	May	——
XIV	68–83	July	1893
——	712–13	December	——
XV	130–31	January	1894
XVII	384–92	March	1895
XIX	525–26	April	1896
XXIII	78–84	January	1898
——	757–59	June	——
——	763–64	——	——
XXIV	693–708	December	——
XXV	622–33	May	1899
——	745–52	June	——
XXVII	194–99	February	1900
XXVIII	250–51	August	——

Author	Title
William F. Apthorp	"Paris Theatres and Concerts: The Unsubventioned Theatres and Orchestral Concerts"
————————	"Paris Theatres and Concerts: Theatre-going Habits and Customs; the Café Chantant; Symphony Concerts; Musical and Dramatic Criticism"
George P. Upton	"Musical Societies of the United States and Their Representation at the World's Fair"
William Wallace Gilchrist	"January and May"
— — — — — —	"Music and the Author" (P)
William F. Apthorp	"Orchestral Conducting and Conductors"
— — — — — —	"An Epoch of Opera" (W)
Reginald de Koven	"Some Tendencies of Modern Opera"
Henry Krehbiel	"Anton Seidl"
— — — — — —	"Music and General Culture" (P)
Frederic Jesup Stimson	"Wagner's *Ring of the Nibelung:* Part I—*The Rape of the Rhine-Gold*" (translation illustrated by "M. P." [Maxfield Parrish])
Sidney Lanier	"A Poet's Musical Impressions" (Part I)
————————	———— (Part II)
James Huneker	"Frédéric François Chopin: Poet and Psychologist"
— — — — — —	"The Teaching of Music in the Schools" (P)

Bibliography

Books

ABRAM, GERALD. *A Hundred Years of Music.* 3d ed. Chicago, 1964.

ALLEN, WARREN DWIGHT. *Philosophies of Music History.* New York, 1962.

APTHORP, WILLIAM FOSTER. *By the Way.* 2 Vols. Boston, 1898.

————. *Musicians and Music Lovers, and Other Essays.* New York, 1894.

ARNOLD, MATTHEW. *Civilization in the United States.* Boston, 1888.

————. *Culture and Anarchy.* Edited by R. H. SUPER. Ann Arbor, Mich., 1965.

————. *Discourses in America.* New York, 1894.

————. *Lectures and Essays in Criticism.* Edited by R. H. SUPER. Ann Arbor, Mich., 1962.

————. *Mixed Essays.* New York, 1894.

AUSTIN, JAMES C., ed. *Fields of the "Atlantic Monthly."* San Marino, Calif., 1953.

BAUMOL, WILLIAM J., and BOWEN, WILLIAM G. *Performing Arts— The Economic Dilemma.* New York, 1966.

BEARD, CHARLES A. and MARY R. *The American Spirit.* New York, 1942.

Bio-Bibliographical Index of Musicians in the United States of America from Colonial Times. Washington, D. C., 1941.

BRIDGES, ROBERT. *Suppressed Chapters.* New York, 1895.

BROOKS, VAN WYCK. *Howells: His Life and World.* New York, 1959.

————. *New England: Indian Summer, 1865–1915.* New York, 1940.

BURLINGAME, EDWARD L. *Art Life and Theories of Richard Wagner.* 2d ed. New York, 1909.

CADY, EDWIN. *The Gentleman in America: A Literary Study in American Culture.* Syracuse, 1949.

CALVOCORESSI, MICHAEL D. *Musical Taste.* Oxford, 1925.

CARPENTER, FREDERIC IVES. *Emerson Handbook.* New York, 1953.

CHASE, GILBERT. *America's Music.* 2d ed. rev. New York, 1966.

CLARK, JOHN SPENCER. *The Life and Letters of John Fiske.* 2 Vols. Boston, 1917.

COOKE, GEORGE WILLIS, ed. *Early Letters of George William Curtis to John S. Dwight; Brook Farm and Concord.* New York, 1898.

———. *John Sullivan Dwight, Brook-Farmer, Editor and Critic of Music.* Boston, 1898.

Copyright in Congress. Copyright Office Bulletin no. 8. February, 1905.

COWELL, FRANK RICHARD. *Culture in Private and Public Life.* New York, 1959.

EKIRCH, ARTHUR ALPHONSE, JR. *The Idea of Progress in America, 1815–1860.* New York, 1944.

ELLINWOOD, LEONARD. *The History of Ameircan Church Music.* New York, 1953.

ELLSWORTH, WILLIAM WEBSTER. *A Golden Age of Authors.* Boston, 1919.

ELSON, LOUIS C. *The History of American Music.* Rev. ed. New York, 1915.

EMERSON, RALPH WALDO. *The Works of Ralph Waldo Emerson.* 5 Vols. New York, n.d.

FARNSWORTH, PAUL R. *The Social Psychology of Music.* New York, 1958.

FIELDS, ANNIE ADAMS. *James T. Fields: Biographical Notes and Personal Sketches.* Boston, 1881.

FIRKINS, OSCAR W. *William Dean Howells: A Study.* Cambridge, Mass., 1924.

FISHER, WILLIAM ARMS. *One-Hundred-and-Fifty Years of Music Publishing in the United States.* Boston, 1933.

GILBERT, KATHERINE E., and KUHN, HELMUT. *A History of Esthetics.* Rev. ed. Bloomington, Ind., 1953.

GILDER, ROSAMUND, ed. *Letters of Richard Watson Gilder.* Boston, 1916.

GRAF, MAX. *Composer and Critic: Two Hundred Years of Musical Criticism.* London, 1947.

GREENSLET, FERRIS. *Life of Thomas Bailey Aldrich.* Boston, 1908.

HANSLICK, EDUARD. *Music Criticisms 1846–99.* Translated and edited by Henry Pleasants. Baltimore, 1950.

HARAP, LOUIS. *The Social Roots of the Arts.* New York, 1949.

HARPER, J. HENRY. *The House of Harper.* New York, 1912.

HAWEIS, HUGH REGINALD. *Music and Morals.* London, 1872.

————. *Travel and Talk, 1885–93–95: My Hundred Thousand Miles of Travel through America, Canada, Australia, New Zealand, Tasmania, Ceylon, and the Paradise of the Pacific.* 2 Vols. New York, 1896.

HENDERSON, WILLIAM J. *Preludes and Studies.* New York, 1891.

HENDRICK, BURTON J. *The Training of an American: The Earlier Life and Letters of Walter H. Page.* New York, 1829.

HOFSTADTER, RICHARD. *Social Darwinism in America.* Rev. ed. Boston, 1955.

HOWE, M. A. DEWOLFE. *The "Atlantic Monthly" and Its Makers.* Boston, 1919.

HYDE, A. R. *The Story of "Harper's Magazine."* New York, 1931.

JOHNSON, ROBERT UNDERWOOD. *Remembered Yesterdays.* Boston, 1923.

KOLODIN, IRVING. *The Metropolitan Opera, 1883–1966.* Rev. ed. New York, 1967.

KROEBER, A. L., and KLUCKHOHN, CLYDE. *Culture: A Critical Review of Concepts and Definitions.* Papers of the Peabody Museum of American Archaeology and Ethnology, Harvard University, Vol. XLVII, no. 1. Cambridge, Mass., 1952.

LANG, PAUL HENRY, ed. *One Hundred Years of Music in America.* New York, 1961.

LOESSER, ARTHUR. *Men, Women and Pianos.* New York, 1954.

MATHEWS, W. S. B., and HOWE, GRANVILLE L., eds. *A Hundred Years of Music in America.* Chicago, 1889.

MILNE, GORDON. *George William Curtis and the Genteel Tradition.* Bloomington, Ind., 1956.

MOTT, FRANK LUTHER. *A History of American Magazines.* 5 Vols. Cambridge, Mass., 1938–68.

MUELLER, JOHN HENRY. *The American Symphony Orchestra: A Social History of American Taste.* Bloomington, Ind., 1951.

————, and HEVNER, KATE. *Trends in Musical Taste.* University of Indiana Publications, Humanities Series, no. 8. Bloomington, Ind., 1951.

MYERS, GUSTAVUS. *The History of American Idealism.* New York, 1925.

PERRY, BLISS. *Park Street Papers.* Boston, 1908.

RALEIGH, JOHN HENRY. *Matthew Arnold and American Culture.* Berkeley, Calif., 1957.

RUSKIN, JOHN. *Ruskin on Music.* Edited by A. M. WAKEFIELD. London, 1894.

RUSSELL, CHARLES EDWARD. *The American Orchestra and Theodore Thomas.* New York, 1927.

RYAN, THOMAS. *Recollections of an Old Musician.* New York, 1899.

SANTAYANA, GEORGE. *The Genteel Tradition at Bay.* New York, 1931.

SCHNEIDER, HERBERT W. *A History of American Philosophy.* 2d ed. New York, 1963.

SCHOLES, PERCY A. *The Mirror of Music, 1844–1944: A Century of Musical Life in Britain as Reflected in the Pages of the "Musical Times."* 2 Vols. London, 1947.

SCHWAB, ARNOLD T. *James Gibbons Huneker: Critic of the Seven Arts.* Stanford, 1963.

SHACKLETON, ROBERT. *The Story of "Harper's Magazine."* New York, 1917.

SHAFTER, ALFRED M. *Musical Copyright.* 2d ed. Chicago, 1939.

SILBERMANN, ALPHONS. *The Sociology of Music.* Translated by CORBET STEWART. London, 1963.

SMITH, HENRY NASH, and GIBSON, WILLIAM M., eds. *Mark Twain–Howells Letters.* 2 Vols. Cambridge, Mass., 1960.

SMYTH, ALBERT H. *Bayard Taylor.* Boston, 1896.

SPAETH, SIGMUND. *A History of Popular Music in America.* New York, 1948.

SPALDING, WALTER RAYMOND. *Music at Harvard: A Historical Review of Men and Events.* New York, 1935.

TASSIN, ALGERNON. *The Magazine in America.* New York, 1916.

THOMAS, THEODORE. *A Musical Autobiography.* Edited by GEORGE P. UPTON. 2 Vols. Chicago, 1905.

TRILLING, LIONEL. *Matthew Arnold.* New York, 1949.

UPTON, WILLIAM TREAT. *Art-Song in America.* Boston, 1930.

VINCENT, LEON HENRY. *American Literary Masters.* Boston, 1906.

WHITE, MORTON. *Social Thought in America.* Boston, 1957.

WOOD, JAMES PLAYSTED. *Magazines in the United States.* 2d ed. New York, 1956.

ZUCKERMAN, ELLIOTT. *The First Hundred Years of Wagner's "Tristan."* New York, 1964.

Articles in Periodicals, Essays in Collections, and Documents

ALDEN, HENRY MILLS. "An Anniversary Retrospect: 1900–1910. *Harper's,* CXXI (June, 1910), 38–45.

ALLEN, A. V. G. "Horace E. Scudder: An Appreciation." *Atlantic,* XCI (April, 1903), 549–60.

ALLEN, FREDERICK LEWIS. "Fifty Years of *Scribner's Magazine.*" *Scribner's,* CI (January, 1937), 19–24.

"The American Gentleman of Leisure." *Century,* VII (December, 1873), 239.

"American Literature." *Blackwood's,* CXXXIII (January, 1883), 136–61.

AMES, AMYAS. "The Silent Spring of Our Symphonies." *Saturday Review,* February 28, 1970, pp. 81–83.

"An Apology for Workers." *Scribner's,* XVIII (October, 1895), 394–95.

BARNES, EARL. "The Feminizing of Culture." *Atlantic,* CIX (June, 1912), 770–76.

BATES, ERNEST S. "Henry Mills Alden." In *Dictionary of American Biography,* I, 144–45.

BEAUX, CECELIA. "Mr. Gilder's Public Activities: His Relation to the Arts." *Century,* LXXIX (February, 1910), 631.

BICKNELL, ANNA. "French Wives and Mothers." *Century,* LV (January, 1898), 339–54.

———. "The Pretenders to the Throne of France." *Century,* XXVII (December, 1883), 251–56.

BOURNE, RANDOLPH. "Our Cultural Humility." *Atlantic,* CXIV (October, 1914), 503–7.

BRIDGES, ROBERT. "Edward L. Burlingame." In *Dictionary of American Biography,* III, 290–91.

BROOKES, VAN WYCK. "America's Coming of Age." In *Three Essays on America,* pp. 15–112. New York, 1934.

BROWNELL, W. C. "French Traits: The Art Instinct." *Scribner's,* V (February, 1889), 241–51.

CABLE, GEORGE WASHINGTON. "Home Culture Clubs." *Century,* XXXVI (August, 1888), 497–507.

CAIRNS, WILLIAM B. "Josiah Gilbert Holland." In *Dictionary of American Biography,* IX, 147–48.

———. "Richard Watson Gilder." In *Dictionary of American Biography,* VII, 275–76.

CASSOT, ARTHUR. "George William Curtis." *Chautauquan,* XVII (May, 1893), 165–69.

"*Century Magazine.*" *Century,* XXIII (November, 1881), 143–44.

"The *Century Magazine,* 1870–1924." *Pan American Magazine,* XXXVII (July, 1924), 341.

"The *Century's* First Year under Its New Name." *Century,* XXIV (October, 1882), 939.

"The *Century's* Quarter of a Century." *Century,* LI (November, 1895), 155–56.

"The *Century's* Twentieth Anniversary." *Century,* XLI (November, 1889), 148.

CHAMBERLIN, JOSEPH EDWARD. "The Foreign Elements in Our Population." *Century,* XXVIII (September, 1884), 761–70.

CHURCH, FRANCIS P. "Richard Grant White." *Atlantic,* LXVII (March, 1891), 303–14.

"College Men in the World." *Scribner's,* VII (February, 1890), 264.

COOKE, GEORGE WILLIS. "George William Curtis at Concord." *Harper's,* XCVI (December, 1897), 137–49.

COUNTESS OF GALLOWAY. "Wagner at Bayreuth." *Nineteenth Century,* XXXVI (October, 1894), 507–14.

CURTIS, GEORGE WILLIAM. "An Autobiographical Sketch." *Cosmopolitan,* XVIII (October, 1894), 703–4.

DENT, EDWARD J. "The Historical Approach to Music." *Musical Quarterly,* XXIII (January, 1937), 1–17.

DOWNES, EDWARD. "The Taste Makers: Critics and Criticism." In *One Hundred Years of Music in America,* edited by Paul Henry Lang, pp. 230–44. New York, 1961.

DWIGHT, JOHN SULLIVAN. "The History of Music in Boston." In *The Memorial History of Boston, 1630–1880,* edited by Justin Winsor, IV, 415–64. Boston, 1880.

"The Editor of *Harper's.*" *Literary Digest,* October 25, 1919, 32–33.

"Editorial Policy." *Harper's,* LXII (January, 1881), 303.

"On Editorial Policy." *Harper's,* XLVIII (March, 1874), 595.

Editoral Statement. *Scribner's,* XIII (May, 1893), 689.

"Edward Livermore Burlingame." *Scribner's,* LXXIII (January, 1923), 121.

EGGLESTON, EDWARD. "Josiah Gilbert Holland." *Century,* XXIII (December, 1881), 161–67.

EGGLESTON, GEORGE CARY. "The Education of Women." *Harper's,* LXVII (July, 1883), 292–96.

ELIOT, CHARLES W. "What Is a Liberal Education?" *Century,* XXVIII (June, 1884), 203–12.

EMERSON, RALPH WALDO. "Aspects of Culture." *Atlantic,* XXI (January, 1868), 87–95.

———. "Culture." *Atlantic,* VI (September, 1860), 343–53.

"England's Bad Laws." *Century,* II (June, 1871), 212.

FARWELL, ARTHUR. "America's Gain from a Bayreuth Romance." *Musical Quarterly,* XXX (October, 1944), 448–57.

FATOUT, PAUL. "Threnodies of the Ladies' Books." *Musical Quarterly,* XXXI (October, 1945), 464–78.

"The Faults of Culture." *Century,* III (January, 1872), 370–71.

"Fifty Years of *Harper's Magazine.*" *Harper's,* C (May, 1900), 947–62.

FINCK, HENRY T. "If Richard Wagner Came Back." *Century,* LXXXVI (June, 1913), 210.

FLAGG, WILSON. "Parlor Singing." *Atlantic,* XXIV (October, 1869), 410–20.

"The Foreign Critic and the Fair." *Scribner's,* XIV (November, 1893), 658.

"Forty Years of the *Atlantic Monthly.*" *Atlantic,* LXXX (October, 1897), 571–76.

"Forty Years of This Magazine." *Century,* LXXXI (November, 1910), 131–50.

"George William Curtis." *Nation,* September 8, 1892, pp. 180–82.

GEROLD, KATHERINE FULLERTON. "The Plight of the Genteel." *Harper's,* CLII (February, 1926), 310–19.

GLADDEN, WASHINGTON. "Christianity and Popular Amusements." *Century,* XXIX (January, 1885), 384–92.

GOHDES, CLARENCE. "The *Atlantic* Celebrates Its 100th Birthday." *South Atlantic Quarterly,* LVII (Spring, 1958), 163–67.

GORREN, ALINE. "American Popularity." *Scribner's,* XXIV (October, 1898), 497–500.

———. "American Society and the Artist." *Scribner's,* XXVI (November, 1899), 628–33.

"The Greatest Need of the Working Class." *Century,* XXVI (August, 1883), 470–71.

GURNEY, EDMUND. "Wagner and Wagnerism." *Nineteenth Century,* XIII (March, 1883), 434–52.

HATCH, C. "Music for America: A Critical Controversy of the 1850's." *American Quarterly,* XIV (Winter, 1962), 578–86.

HELLMAN, GEORGE S. "George William Curtis." In *Dictionary of American Biography,* IV, 614–15.

HENDERSON, WILLIAM J. "Programme Music Then and Now." *Atlantic,* XCIX (February, 1907), 272–77.

"Herbert Spencer in America." *Century,* XXIV (September, 1882), 789.

"The History of a Publishing House: 1846–1894." *Scribner's,* XVI (December, 1894), 793–804.

HOLLAND, JOSIAH GILBERT. "Art as a Steady Diet." *Century,* XVII (January, 1879), 438.

———. "Theaters and Theater-Going." *Century,* IV (June, 1872), 238–39.

"How to Develop American Sentiment among Immigrants." *Century*, XLI (January, 1891), 471–73.

HOWELLS, WILLIAM DEAN. "George William Curtis." *North American Review*, CVII (July, 1868), 104–17.

———. "In Memoriam [of Henry Mills Alden]." *Harper's*, CXL (December, 1919), 133–36.

———. "Recollections of an *Atlantic* Editorship." *Atlantic*, C (November, 1907), 594–606.

———. "The New Taste in Theatricals." *Atlantic*, XXIII (May, 1869), 635–44.

"International Copyright Accomplished." *Century*, XLII (May, 1891), 148.

ISAACS, LEWIS M. "Mr. Huneker's Musical Essays." *Atlantic*, XCII (June, 1904), 859–60.

IVES, MARION. *"Scribner's*—Surveyor of the American Scene." *Quill*, XXIII (December, 1935), 8, 12–13.

JENKS, FRANCIS H. "Boston Musical Composers." *New England Magazine*, I (January, 1890), 475–83.

"Josiah Gilbert Holland." *Century*, XXIII (December, 1881), 310–16.

KIMBALL, ARTHUR REED. "The Social Menace of Specialism." *Century*, LIV (August, 1897), 475–76.

KIVY, PETER. "Herbert Spencer and a Musical Dispute." *Music Review*, XXIII (November, 1962), 317–29.

LADD, GEORGE T. "The Development of the American University." *Scribner's*, II (September, 1887), 346–60.

LOFT, ABRAM. "Musician's Guild and Union: A Consideration of the Evolution of the Protective Organization among Musicians." Ph.D. dissertation, Columbia University, 1950.

MABIE, HAMILTON WRIGHT. "Art," *Atlantic*, C (November, 1907), 625–35.

MARSHALL, FLORENCE A. "Music and the People." *Nineteenth Century*, VIII (December, 1880), 921–32.

———. "Music for the Masses." *Nineteenth Century*, XXXII (July, 1892), 67–76.

"Matthew Arnold." *English Illustrated Magazine*, I (January, 1884), 241–45.

MATTHEWS, BRANDER. "Richard Watson Gilder." *North American Review*, CXCI (January, 1910), 39–48.

"Men's Women." *Scribner's*, VII (February, 1890), 890.

MILES, EMMA BELL. "Some Real American Music," *Harper's*, CIX (June, 1904), 118–23.

"Mr. Scudder and the *Atlantic.*" *Atlantic,* LXXXIX (March, 1902), 433–34.

MOTT, FRANK LUTHER. "The Magazine Revolution and Popular Ideas in the Nineties." *Proceedings of the American Antiquarian Society,* pp. 195–214. April, 1954.

MUNGER, THEODORE T. "Education and Social Progress." *Century,* XXXIV (June, 1887), 268–75.

"Music Composers and Copyright." *Century,* LXXIII (February, 1907), 639–40.

"National Disinterestedness." *Century,* LVI (May, 1898), 152.

"The New German Empire." *Century,* II (May, 1871), 105–6.

"A New Volume of the *Century.*" *Century,* XXX (May, 1885), 164–65.

NORTH, S. N. D. "The Newspaper and Periodical Press." In *Tenth Census of the United States,* VIII, 1–446. Washington, D. C., 1884.

NORTON, CHARLES ELIOT. "Harvard University in 1890." *Harper's,* LXXXI (September, 1890), 581–92.

"The Organization of Culture." *Nation,* June 18, 1868, pp. 486–88.

"Other Tributes to Dr. Holland." *Century,* XXIII (December, 1881), 315.

"Our Decennial." *Century,* XXI (November, 1880), 151–52.

"Our English Visitors." *Century,* V (December, 1872), 254–55.

"Our New Psychological Quality." *Scribner's,* XVIII (November, 1895), 526–60.

PAINE, JOHN KNOWLES. "The New German School of Music." *North American Review,* CCXXXIX (April, 1873), 217–45.

PARKER, WILLIAM BELMONT. "Thomas Bailey Aldrich." In *Dictionary of American Biography,* I, 158–60.

PHELPS, ELIZABETH S., et al. "Richard Watson Gilder." *Century,* LXXIX (February, 1910), 622–37.

"Point of View in the Labor Question." *Scribner's,* XVII (April, 1895), 527.

"The Present Aspect of the Irish Question." *Century,* XXVI (June, 1883), 305.

"Professor Jevons on Education." *Century,* XXVI (October, 1883), 950–51.

"Retrospect of the *Century.*" *Century,* LXXXI (November, 1910), 151–54.

ROWBOTHAM, J. F. "The Wagner Bubble." *Nineteenth Century,* XXIV (October, 1888), 501–12.

SALTER, SUMNER. "Early Encouragements to American Composers." *Musical Quarterly,* XVIII (January, 1932), 76–105.

"*Scribner's Monthly.*" *Century,* I (November, 1870), 105–6.

"Scribner's Monthly—Historical." *Century,* XXII (June, 1881), 302–3.

[SEDGWICK, ARTHUR GEORGE.] "International Affinities." *Atlantic,* XXXI (January, 1873), 123–25.

"Selections in Art." *Atlantic,* XLIV (November, 1879), 670–71.

"A Service of England to America." *Century,* LVI (June, 1898), 314.

SLONIMSKY, NICOLAS. "The Plush Era in American Concert Life." In *One Hundred Years of Music in America,* edited by Paul Henry Lang, pp. 109–27. New York, 1961.

"Social Life in Print." *Scribner's,* VII (January, 1890), 131.

"Some Facts from England." *Century,* III (December, 1871), 243–44.

"Some Religious Newspapers." *Century,* VII (December, 1873), 236.

"Spencer in America." *Harper's,* LXVI (January, 1883), 303–5.

STANFORD, C. V. "The Wagner Bubble: A Reply." *Nineteenth Century,* XXIV (November, 1888), 727–33.

STANTON, THEODORE. "State Education of Frenchwomen." *Century,* XLVI (October, 1893), 955–56.

STODDARD, JOHN T. "Composite Photography." *Century,* XXXIII (March, 1887), 750–57.

STONE, JAMES H. "Mid-Nineteenth-Century American Beliefs in the Social Values of Music." *Musical Quarterly,* XLIII (January, 1957), 38–49.

THOMPSON, OSCAR. "American School of Criticism: The Legacy Left by W. J. Henderson, Richard Aldrich and Their Colleagues of the Old Guard." *Musical Quarterly,* XXIII (October, 1937), 428–39.

THWING, CHARLES F. "College Instruction." *Century,* XIV (September, 1877), 706–12.

"To Our Readers—In Confidence." *Century,* XXXIII (December, 1886), 318.

"To the Readers of the *Century.*" *Century,* XXXV (November, 1887), 160.

"University Topics." *New Englander and Yale Review,* LII (May, 1890), 466–79.

WAGNER, RICHARD. "The Work and Mission of My Life." *North American Review,* CCLXXIII (August, 1879), 107–24; CCLXXIV (September, 1879), 238–58.

WALTER, WILLIAM E. "The Industry of Music-Making." *Atlantic,* CI (January, 1908), 91–96.

WARNER, CHARLES DUDLEY. "Thoughts Suggested by Mr. Froude's Progress." *Century,* VII (January, 1874), 351–59.

———. "What is Your Culture to Me?" *Century,* IV (August, 1872), 470–78.

————. "A Memorial to George William Curtis." *Harper's,* LXXXIX (August, 1894), 477–78.

WATERS, EDWARD N. "John Sullivan Dwight, First American Critic of Music." *Musical Quarterly,* XXI (January, 1935), 69–88.

WEINGARTNER, FELIX. "The Symphony since Beethoven." *Contemporary Review,* LXXV (February, 1899), 271–89; (March, 1899), 418–38.

WELTER, RUSH. "The Idea of Progress in America." *Journal of the History of Ideas,* XVI (June, 1955), 401–15.

WHEELER, BENJAMIN IDE. "A National Type of Culture." *Atlantic,* XCII (July, 1903), 74–77.

WHIPPLE, E. P. "Richard Grant White." *Atlantic,* XLIX (February, 1882), 214–22.

WHITE, RICHARD GRANT. "Three Periods of Modern Music." *Galaxy,* XXIII (June, 1877), 832–41.

Index

Abbott, Emma, 140
Abt, Franz, 175–76
Academy of Music (New York), 88, 138–39
Aida (Verdi), 131
"Alas" (Millard), 180
Albani, Emma, 129
Alboni, Marietta, 75
Alden, Henry Mills, 10, 15
Aldrich, Thomas Bailey, 15
Allen, Charles, 39
Altruism, 29, 51
Amateur in American musical life, 169–70; decline of, 192, 196–97
Ambros, August Wilhelm, 40, 155
"American" character in American musicians, 58, 68–69, 105, 107, 130
American composer, 106 n, 108–9, 118–19, 122. *See also* Nationalism
American Opera Company, 102, 138–39

Anschutz, Karl, 77
Apollo Club (Boston), 184
Apollo Club (Chicago), 90, 185
Apthorp, William Foster: on Buck, 119; on choral tradition, 184; on church music, 190, 191; on concert hall as classroom, 85–87; as Cultured critic, 21–22, 179, 182; on Eichberg's music books, 94; on evolution in music, 40–42; on Gottschalk, 110; on Mendelssohn, 60; on *Music and Morals* (Haweis), 43; and National College of Music (Boston), 101; on nationalism, 114–15, 122; on opera, 128, 131–34, 136; on *opéra bouffe,* 54–55; on organic nature of music, 40–41; on parlor music, 175–77, 180–82; predicts atonality, 182; on progress of musical taste in U. S., 76, 81; on Wagner, 40, 146, 152, 158–63, 166, 168

Arditi, Luigi, 180
Aristotle, doctrines of, 45, 50, 125
Arnold, Matthew, 21, 34, 51;
    definition of criticism, 26; defini-
    tion of culture, 26–28; and
    nature of genius, 35
Associationist theory, 46–47
Atlantic Monthly, 8–9, 14
Atonality, predicted by Apthorp, 182
Audience conduct, 16, 135–36, 158
aus der Ohe, Adele, 18
Art and Revolution (Wagner), 155
*Art Life and Theories of Richard
    Wagner* (Burlingame), 152, 154
Artôt, Alexandre-Joseph, 75
Asbury, Alice, 154
"Ave Maria" (Danks), 180
"Ave Maria" (Millard), 180

Babbitt, Irving, 195
Bach, Johann Sebastian, 54
Bacon, Theodore, 116
Balatka, Hans, 77
Baltimore, 78, 108
"Barbarians" (Arnold's term), 28–
    29
Barnard, Charles, 74
Barnard, Frederick A. P., 185
Bates, Arlo, 21, 162
Baxter, Sylvester, 162
Bayly, Thomas Haynes, 174
Bayreuth, 72, 82, 145, 151, 164,
    167. *See also* Wagner
Beauty: intellectualization of, 36,
    44–47; not innate in American
    character, 105–6
Beethoven, Ludwig van, 9, 75, 81,
    90, 92; as genius, 67; and
    Wagner, 154, 159, 162, 163
Belle Hélène, La (Offenbach), 54
Bellini, Vincenzo, 71, 132, 176
Bells of Strasburg Cathedral, The
    (Liszt), 182
Belmont, August, 102
Benedict, Sir Julius, 80

Bergmann, Carl, 49, 77, 142
Berlin Akademie, 79
Berlioz, Hector, 145, 165; as genius,
    67, 68; compared with Mendels-
    sohn, 60
Biddle, William F., 20, 125
Billings, William, 185
Birds, songs of, 38–39
Bispham, David, 140
Black Crook, The, 56, 179
Blackwood's, 11
Blumenthal, Jacob, 180
Boekelman, Bernard, 63–64
Boott, Francis, 14, 177
Boston, 89, 101; as musical center,
    20
Boston Symphony Orchestra, 85, 89;
    compared with Parisian orchestras,
    81
Bouhy, Jacques, 102
Bourgault-Ducoudray, Louis-Albert,
    115
Bourne, Randolph, 196
Bradbury, William B., 59, 185
Braham, David, 177
Brahms, Johannes, 81
Bristow, George F., 111
Brooklyn Philharmonic Society, 144
Brook Farm, 15
Brower, Edith, 64, 120
Buck, Dudley, 68, 119, 120, 177,
    186
Bull, Ole, 14, 75
Bülow, Hans Guido von, 63, 64,
    143, 161–62
Bunting, Joseph, 21, 71
Burlingame, Edward L., 18–19, 152
Burroughs, John, 39

Cable, George Washington, 29, 116
Camerata, Florentine, and evolution
    of music, 39 n, 40, 132, 160–61
Carey, Annie Louise, 130
Carnegie, Andrew, 185

Castle Square Opera Company
    (Boston), 140
Cavalleria Rusticana (Mascagni),
    167
Cecilia Society (Boston), 90, 184,
    185
Centennial Meditation of Columbia
    (Buck), 119
Central Park Garden Concerts, 144
*Century Illustrated Monthly
    Magazine,* 11–13
Chadwick, George W., 186
Chamber music, 71, 98
Cheney, Simeon Pease, 39
Chickering, Jonas, 170
Chopin, Frédéric, 67, 114, 162
Choral tradition in American
    musical life, 170, 183–86
Christy Minstrels, 54
Churches, music in, 53–54, 186–92
Church Music Association (New
    York), 184
Cincinnati, 75, 78
Civil War: music of, 110–11; as
    turning point in American
    musical life, 70, 83, 190
Colonne, Edouard, 81
Commercialism, 110, 116. *See also*
    Materialism
Concert halls, American: compared
    with Parisian, 81–82; educational
    function of, 85–91, 98; size of,
    75
Conservatories of music, 100–102,
    108
"Conspicuous leisure" (Veblen's
    term), 135
Contract Labor Act (1887), 119,
    121
Contributors' Club (*Atlantic*), 9
Conway, Moncure D., 21
Copyright, 16, 118
Cosmopolitanism, 32, 115, 123
Cragin, Louisa T. [pseud. Ellis
    Gray], 21, 89, 94, 106

Creole music, 112–13, 116
Criticism; defined by Arnold, 26;
    function of, 119, 194; in news-
    papers, 22; style of, 16, 47. *See
    also* Curtis, George William;
    Apthorp, William Foster
Critics, Cultured, 19–22
Culture and Anarchy (Arnold), 26
Curtis, George William: on audi-
    ence conduct, 135; and choral
    tradition, 184; and copyright,
    118; as Cultured critic, 15–16;
    on ethical value of music, 49; on
    festivals, 86–87; on Stephen
    Foster, 110; on Germans in
    American musical life, 77–78,
    105; on intellect and music, 46;
    and Jenny Lind, 129; on opera,
    128, 131, 133–37, 139; on
    progress of musical taste in U. S.,
    71–72, 74, 79, 81; on Wagner,
    145–46, 168
Curwen, J. Spencer, 96

Damrosch, Frank, 186
Damrosch, Leopold, 77, 85, 87,
    145, 186
Damrosch, Walter, 148, 186
Dana, C. Henshaw, 180
Danks, Hart Pease, 180
Darwin, Charles, and origin of
    music, 39 n
Darwinism: and music, 40, 57–58,
    130–31, 182; and Wagnerism,
    41–42, 159–60
David, Félicien, 67
de Koven, Reginald, 41, 160
Democracy: and music, 36, 51, 62,
    86; and musicians, 82
Dempster, William Richardson,
    175–76
Despard, Matilda, 54, 71
Deutscher Liederkranz Society
    (New York), 185
Diderot, Denis, 39 n

Disinterestedness, 25–26, 58, 98–99
Ditson, Oliver (publishers), 171
Doctor of Alcantara, The (Eichberg), 132
Donizetti, Gaetano, 176
Don Juan (Strauss), 42 n
Dramma per musica, 39 n, 40, 132. *See also* Camerata, Florentine
Dvořák, Anton: and U. S., 104–5, 111, 114, 117; and Wagner, 159, 165
Dwight, John Sullivan: on American Opera Company, 138; as Cultured critic, 15–16, 22; on genius, 67; on Germans in American musical life, 77; on morality in music, 55, 57–58; and nature of music, 36, 37, 45, 47–49, 84, 98; on programing, 88; and progress of musical taste in U. S., 75, 109–10; and Wagner, 152

Economic determinism, 4–5
Economics: and moral musician, 58–59; and music in U. S., 4–5, 103, 194, 198; and high cost of opera, 53, 133–37
Editor's Easy Chair (*Harper's*), 15–16
Education of Cultured class, 27. *See also* Music education
Eichberg, Julius, 94, 132, 177
Eisfeld, Theodor, 77
Electricity in theaters, 81–82
Elijah (Mendelssohn), 62
Ellis, Ashton, 154
Emerson, Ralph Waldo: and Culture, 25–26, 28, 195; and genius, 35, 68; and morality, 32–34; and music, 34, 59
Emersonianism, 195
Emotion and music, 42–45, 64
Empiricism, English, 46

English musicians in U. S., 76
English Opera Company (Parepa-Rosa), 135
Equalitarianism, 24, 51, 74, 97
Ernst, Heinrich, 88 n
Essays in Criticism (Arnold), 26
"Eternal Father, Strong to Save," 189
Ethics and music, 48–51, 62
Etiquette among concert and opera audiences, 16
Europe contrasted with U. S., 32, 80–81, 106–8, 111, 117, 118; genius, 67–68, 108; meliorism, 90; music education, 85, 92–93, 96–97, 101; progress, idea of, 30; standards of musical criticism, 79–81, 118, 120–22; Wagnerism, 143, 147–48, 158
European attitudes toward U. S., 16, 80
Evolution: and nationalism, 107–8, 111, 114–15, 122; and opera, 136–37, 139; and progress, 31, 32, 115, 139; and Wagnerism, 40–42, 159–62

Fadette Ladies' Orchestra (Boston), 65
Falstaff (Verdi), 41
Farwell, Arthur, 75
Faust (Goethe), 166 n
Federlein, Gottlieb, 101, 189
Fétis, François-Joseph, 40
Feuilleton as model of style in criticism, 16
Fields, James T., 14
Fillmore, John Comfort, 44, 162–63
Finck, Henry T.: as critic, 22; on nationalism, 106, 120, 123; and Wagner, 157, 163, 168
First Symphony (Paine), 120
Fiske, John, 20, 120
Flagg, Wilson, 174–75, 179

Fliegende Höllander (Wagner),
144
Flower Queen, The (Root), 74
Folk music: as basis for musical
nationalism, 108–9; in U. S.,
111–17
Foote, Arthur, 186
Form, organic, in music, 41, 45
Formalism in aesthetic theory, 50
Forsyth, Jean, 121
Forty-sixth Psalm (Buck), 119
Foster, Stephen, 110
Franz, Robert, 88, 176, 177
Fraser, John, 129 n
Frontier, musical taste on, 62, 78
Fry, William Henry, 111, 155
Fuller, Henry B., 89
Fursch-Madi, Emma, 102

Gabriel, Virginia, 180
Gage, W. Leonard, 60
Garcia, Manuel, 75
Genius: defined by Emerson, 35;
Mendelssohn as, 59; qualities of,
67–69; Wagner as, 157–59
Genteel tradition, 4, 195
Gentility, 58, 134, 171–72, 194
Gentleman, 28; Mendelssohn as,
62; as musician, 58–59, 67
Gericke, Wilhelm, 77, 85
Germania Orchestra, 76, 78–79,
85, 142, 186
Germans, influence of, on Ameri-
can musical life, 76–78, 105–6,
129, 185, 191
Germany, evolution of, as musical
nation, 122
Gerster, Etelka, 129
*Gesammelte Schriften und Dich-
tungen* (Wagner), 19, 151,
154–56
Gesamtkunstwerk, 147, 155, 159,
162
Gewandhaus (Leipzig), 79
Gigantism, 86

Gilbert, Sir William, 55–56, 118,
183
Gilchrist, William Wallace, 68,
177, 186
Gilder, Richard Watson, 12,
17–18
Gilman, Lawrence, 18
Gilmore, Patrick, 86–87, 151
Gluck, Christoph Willibald, 154,
159
Godefroid, Dieudonné, 88
Goepp, Philip H., 47
Goldmark, Karl, 81
Gottschalk, Louis Moreau, 9, 110,
114
Gounod, Charles, 71, 87, 92–93,
131, 192
Grand-Duchesse de Gerolstein, La
(Offenbach), 54
"Grandfather's Clock," 177
Gray, Ellis. *See* Cragin, Louisa T.
Grétry, André Ernest Modeste, 131
Grieg, Edvard, 81, 82, 159
Grisi, Giulia, 79
Gurney, Edmund, 167 n

Hale, Edward Everett, 151
Halévy, Jacques, 131
Handel, Georg Friedrich, 54, 67
Handel and Haydn Society (Bos-
ton), 184, 186
Hanslick, Eduard, 50, 167
Harper, Fletcher, 11
Harper's New Monthly Magazine,
9–11
Harrigan and Hart, 177
Harvard Musical Association, 85,
186
Harvard University, 20, 27, 43, 98
Hassard, John Rose Green, 71, 80,
159, 165
Hauptmann, Moritz, 37
Hauser, Miska, 88 n
Haweis, Hugh Reginald, 43, 64,
151, 165

Haydn, Franz Joseph, 54, 75, 81
Hearn, Lafcadio, 116
"Hebraism and Hellenism" (Arnold's terms), 26
Hegel, Georg Wilhelm Friedrich, 37, 155
Heinrich, Anthony Philip, 111
Henderson, William J., 22, 39, 92, 166 n, 167
Henschel, George, 14, 77
Herz, Henri, 60
Higginson, Henry L., 117
Higginson, Thomas Wentworth, 116
Historicism, 40, 100, 168
History of the American Pianoforte (Spillane), 171
H.M.S. Pinafore (Gilbert and Sullivan), 56, 118, 183
Hoffman, Richard, 44
Holland, Josiah Gilbert: on church music, 187–88, 192; and copyright, 118; as critic, 17, 21; as editor, 11–12; on morality in opera, 53; on nature of music, 49; on progress of taste in American West, 78; on Wagnerism, 147, 158; on women's role in music, 65–66
Holt, Hosea E., 92, 96
Hornemann, Christian, 88
Howells, William Dean: *Atlantic* song series, 176–78; as editor, 14, 179; and morality in music, 52, 54; on opera, 15, 125; on Parepa-Rosa, 129
Hueffer, Francis, 157
Hughes, Rupert, 22, 64, 80, 122
Huneker, James, 196
Hünten, Franz, 60
Hymnody, 187–89

"I'll Take You Home Again, Kathleen" (Westendorf), 177, 179, 180

Immigration regulations, effect of, on American musical life, 118–19, 121
Indians, music of: not American, 111; not suitable as basis of nationalistic music, 114–15; and Wagnerism, 44, 162–63
Indian Suite (MacDowell), 115
Individualism, 29, 68, 97
Intellect: and genius, 35; of Mendelssohn, 59–60; and moral intellectual, 58; music as exercise of, 45–47, 84, 92, 99–100, 173, 193–94, 198; and Wagnerism, 47, 147–48, 163–64
"In the Hushes of the Midnight" (Dana), 180

Jahn, Otto, 155
James, Henry, 26
"J.L.G.," 157
Johnson, Robert Underwood, 12
Journal of Music (Dwight), 15, 151, 155
Jubilees. *See* World Peace Jubilees
Juch, Emma, 140

Kellogg, Clara Louise, 18, 107, 130, 140
Kepler, Johannes, 38
King, Edward, 129
Kobbé, Gustav, 22
Korbay, Francis, 115–16, 181
Krehbiel, Henry: on American musical taste, 82; as critic, 22; on Dvořák, 105, 114; on the musical experience, 46–47; and music education, 95–97; on nationalism, 106 n; and Wagnerism, 143, 148, 159, 167

Lablache, Luigi, 79
Laboring class, effect of music on, 89–91

Lahee, Henry C., 83
"Lament of the Irish Emigrant" (Dempster), 175
Lamoureux, Charles, 81
Landing of the Pilgrim Fathers, The (Singer), 181–82
Lang, Benjamin Johnson, 72, 92, 186
Lanier, Sidney, 49, 64, 119
La Périchole (Offenbach), 55
Leibniz, Gottfried Wilhelm von, 38
Leipzig Conservatory, 101, 108
Lillie, Mrs. John, 96
Lind, Jenny, 66, 75, 79, 129, 130
Lindau, Paul, 164
Liszt, Franz, 60, 67, 115, 145, 147, 165, 186; and evolution of music, 161–62; compared with Otto Singer, 181–82
Lohengrin (Wagner), 143, 146, 165, 167 n; in evolution of music, 41, 160
"Long Ago" (Bayly), 174
Lucca, Pauline, 128, 130

Mabie, Hamilton Wright, 70
MacDowell, Edward, 18, 68, 115, 118, 120
Magazines, literary, 7–8; *Atlantic,* 8–9, 14; *Century,* 11–13; *Critic,* 148; editors of, 14–19; function of, in American musical life, 23; *Harper's,* 9–11; musical illustrations in, 74; *New Englander,* 156; *North American Review,* 154, 156, 158; *Old and New,* 151; readership of, described, 9, 11–13, 25–35, 66, 78; readership, size of, 24, 194; *Scribner's,* 13; songs in, 176–77; writers in, 19–22
Magill, Mary Tucker, 125
Manliness as an aspect of morality in musicians, 63–64

Mapleson, Col. James H., 135–36
Maretzek, Max, 134
Mario, Giovanni, 79
Marx, Adolph, 155
Mason, Lowell, 185
Mason, Redfern, 57–58
Mason, William, 18, 63, 67, 120, 159
Mason and Hamlin (manufacturers), 173
Materialism in American musical life, 4–5; deplored, 29, 65, 99; transcended by power of beauty, 48
Materna, Amalie, 129, 146
"Matin Song" (Paine), 179
Matthews, Brander, 18, 111
"Meeting by the Brookside" (Millard), 179
Meistersinger, Die (Wagner), 144
Meliorism, 22, 24, 28, 47–51, 84–103, 197
Melting pot, America as, 106, 106 n
Mencken, Henry L., 196
Mendel, Hermann, 154
Mendelssohn-Bartholdy, Felix, 71, 81, 147, 189; image of, in U. S., 59–62, 142, 196; and music education, 101
Mendelssohn Club (New York), 184
Mendelssohn Quintette Club (Boston), 101
Metropolitan Opera, 136–37, 143, 145, 148, 186; conduct of audience, 16, 135–36
Metropolitan Opera House: building of, 75; compared with *Festspielhaus* at Bayreuth, 82
Meyerbeer, Giacomo, 71, 88, 131, 154
Midsummer Night's Dream (Mendelssohn), 62

Mignon (A. Thomas), 131
Millard, Harrison, 179
Minstrel show music, 77, 110,
    175, 179
Mitchell, Donald G., 16
Moody, Dwight, 188
Morality, 52–69, 193, 196; in
    church music, 188–89; defined,
    32–33; and Mendelssohn, 60,
    62; and music, connection re-
    jected, 50, 54; and musicians,
    34–35; and opera, 52–57, 130;
    in parlor music, 172–74; of
    populace, redeemed by music,
    90; and Wagner, 53, 157, 164–
    65
More, Paul Elmer, 195
Moscheles, Ignaz, 60, 181
Mosenthal, Joseph, 77, 177, 186
"Mother's Dream, A" (Millard),
    180
Mozart, Wolfgang Amadeus, 54,
    75, 97, 189; operas of, 132; and
    Wagner, 154, 161, 163
Munger, Theodore T., 27
Munich, 108
Murska, Ilma di, 128
Music and Morals (Haweis), 43,
    151
Music Department (*Atlantic*), 179
Music drama, 132, 141, 146,
    160–63. *See also Dramma per
    musica; Gesamtkunstwerk;* Wag-
    ner, Richard
Music education: of adults, 85–
    89, 92; of children, 92–97, 197;
    in higher institutions, 98–103,
    198; methods, 47, 94–96; and
    musical literacy, 74; private,
    65–66; in seminaries, 189
Music festivals, 71–72, 75, 78, 80,
    86–87, 144–46, 184–85
"Music of the future," 72, 165.
    See also Gesamtkunstwerk;
    Wagner, Richard

"Music of the spheres," 38
Music publishing, 170, 171, 176–
    77, 184

Nast, Frederick, 56, 110; on
    church music, 190; on growth
    of musical taste in U. S., 70,
    102; on nationalism, 106; on
    parlor music, 173
Nation, 10
National College of Music, 101
National Conservatory, 75, 101–
    2, 104, 117, 138
Nationalism, 12–13, 32, 57–58,
    104–23, 196. *See also* "Ameri-
    can" character; Civil War;
    Copyright; Cosmopolitanism;
    Creole music, Folk music; Foster,
    Stephen; Gottschalk, Louis
    Moreau; Indians, music of; Ne-
    groes, music of; Opera; West,
    American, music in
National Opera Company of New
    Jersey, 138
Nature and music, 38–40
Negroes, music of, 110–11, 114–
    17
Neuendorff, Adolf, 146
Nevin, Ethelbert, 186
New England Conservatory, 100,
    186
New Englander, 156
Newman, Ernest, 39 n
Newspapers, music criticism in,
    22–23, 76
New World Symphony (Dvořák),
    114–15
New York City, 108, 125, 133
New York Music Festival Associ-
    ation, 184
New York Philharmonic Society,
    81, 88, 186
Niagara Falls, 38
Nichols, Carrie B., 65
Nietzsche, Friedrich, 167

Nikisch, Arthur, 119
Nilsson, Christine, 129–30, 133
Nordica, Lillian, 129
North, Roger, 39 n
North, S. N. D., 7
North American Review, 154,
    156, 158
Norton, Charles Eliot, 99
Nüchterne Briefe aus Bayreuth
    (Lindau), 164

Oberlin Conservatory, 100
Offenbach, Jacques, 15, 54, 55
"O Love Divine, How Sweet
    Thou Art," 189
Opera: "American," 136, 138–41;
    appreciation of, 125–28; and
    church music, 188–89; comic,
    54–56; English, 132; in English,
    139–40; and evolution, 40–41;
    French, 131, 137, 183; German,
    132, 136–37, 139, 145; and
    growth of musical taste in U. S.,
    71, 80, 128; high cost of, 53,
    134; Italian, "New School of,"
    167; Italian, in U. S., 54, 75,
    121, 133, 135, 137; Italian,
    compared with Wagnerian, 147,
    164, 182–83; and morality, 52–
    56; and parlor music, 176,
    182–83; singers, 128–30; star
    system, 133–35; "symmetry"
    in, 134–35, 140–41; types,
    130–33. *See also* Wagner,
    Richard
Opéra bouffe, 15, 54–56
Operetta, 132, 183
Oper und Drama (Wagner), 152
Oratorio, 62, 110
Oratorio Society (New York), 85,
    184–85
Organicism in music, 37, 40–42,
    45, 47, 108–9, 120
Origin of music, 37–40

Osgood, George L., 177–78, 180
Osgood, Samuel, 49–50, 53

Paderewski, Ignace Jan, 18, 63
Page, Walter Hines, 15
Pagliacci (Leoncavallo), 167
Paine, John Knowles, 68, 98, 120,
    177, 179; and copyright, 118;
    and Wagner, 154–56, 163, 167
Painting and music, 46–47
Parepa-Rosa, Euphrosyne, 129, 135
Paris Conservatoire, 79, 81
Parker, Horatio, 118
Parlor music, 169, 196; piano,
    170–73; song, 173–83
Parrish, Maxfield, 153–54
Parsifal (Wagner), 143, 145,
    147–48, 156, 164–66
Parsons, A. R., 151
Parton, James, 170–71, 173
Patronage of music in U. S.: gov-
    ernment, 117–18, 198; by
    wealthy class, 28–29, 75, 135,
    185–86
Patti, Adelina, 79, 134, 164
Peabody Conservatory, 85, 100
Pearce, S. Austin, 38
Perry, Thomas Sergeant, 9, 15, 167
Phillips, Adelaide, 130
Phonograph, 92
Piano: music of Mendelssohn, 62;
    training, 103. *See also* Parlor
    music
Piano and Song (Wieck), 172
Picchianti, Louis, 177 n
Pinafore. See H.M.S. Pinafore
Planté, Francis, 63
Platonism and music, 48, 62, 84
Poems: on Nilsson, 129 n; on
    Parepa-Rosa, 129; on Wagner,
    166
Poetry and music, 18, 115–16,
    119; Wagner's theory of, 152,
    155

Pratt, Waldo Selden, 47, 48, 56–57; and music education, 98, 99, 189
Program music, 47, 60
Progress, idea of: defined, 29–31; in musical taste in U. S., 70–83, 105, 130–31
Protectionist policies, 118–19, 121
Psalmody, early American, 109–10
Puritan morality, 54, 193
Putnam's, quoted, 11

Racial characteristics in music, 57–58, 106. *See also* Nationalism
Raff, Joseph Joachim, 81, 147
Redemption, The (Gounod), 192
Reid, Thomas, 50
"Remnant" (Arnold's term), 26–29, 198
"Republican opera." *See* Opera, "symmetry" in
Revivalism in church music, 187–88
Rheinberger, Josef, 186
Rheingold, Das (Wagner), 143, 153
Ring des Nibelungen, Der (Wagner), 154, 156, 165–66
Ritter, Alexander, 88 n
Ritter, Frédéric Louis, 109
Robinson, Charles S., 189 ·
Romanticism: and aesthetic theory, 42, 46–47; and composers, 67–68, 82; decline of, 195; and Indian music, 163
Root, George F., 74
Rosa, Carl, 140
Rossini, Gioacchino, 71, 88 n, 132
Rousseau, Jean-Jacques, 39 n, 67
Rowbotham, John Frederick, 167 n
Royall, Emily, 21, 67
Royalties. *See* Copyright
Rubinstein, Anton, 165
Rudersdorff, Hermine, 128

Ruskin, John, 34
Russell, Henry, Jr., 140
Ryan, Thomas, 101

Saint Peter (Paine), 120
San Francisco, 145
Sankey, Ira D., 188
Santayana, George, 195
Santley, Charles, 63, 130
Savage, Henry, 140
Scaria, Emil, 146
Schlegel, Friedrich von, 155
Schopenhauer, Arthur, 166
Schubert, Franz, 67, 81, 88 n, 176; and Wagner, 159, 162
Schumann, Robert, 44, 67, 71, 88 n, 176; and Wagner, 162
Scribner, Charles, 11
Scribner's Magazine, 13
Scribner's Monthly Magazine. See Century Illustrated Monthly Magazine
Scudder, Horace Elisha, 15, 58
Sedgwick, Arthur, 125
"Sea Change, A" (Howells and Henschel), 14
Seelig, Hans, 88 n
Seidl, Anton, 77, 143
Seymour, Mary Alice, 85
Sieger, Die (Wagner), 166
Sight-singing, 95–96
"Silver Threads among the Gold" (Danks), 180
Sing-Akademie (Berlin), 81
Singer, Otto, 77, 181
Singers, 74, 128–30
Singing. *See* Voice
Singing schools, 109
Slave Songs of the United States (Allen, Ware, Garrison), 116
Smith, Fanny Morris, 18
Smith, Marion Couthouy, 166
Smith, Roswell, 11
"Social idea," 27–29
Soirées de Vienne (Tausig), 181

Sonata, 45, 47
Song. *See* Parlor music
"Song" (Osgood), 178
Songs without Words (Mendelssohn), 62, 189
Spencer, Herbert, 20, 31, 39 n, 40, 58
"Spheres, music of the," 38
Spillane, Daniel, 171
Spohr, Ludwig, 71
Spontini, Gasparo, 132
Stadt Theater (New York), 143
Stanford, Charles Villiers, 167 n
Star system. *See* Opera
Stavenhagen, Bernhard, 21
Stimson, Frederic Jesup, 154
Stoeckel, Gustav, 99, 156
Strakosch, Maurice, 146
Strauss, Johann, Jr., 88, 119
Strauss, Richard, 42, 56–57
Studies in the Wagnerian Drama (Krehbiel), 148
Sullivan, Sir Arthur, 55–56, 118, 183
"The Sunshine of Thine Eyes" (Osgood), 180
"Sweetness and light," 26, 66
Sylvania Vocal Society (New York), 77, 184
Symphony Society (New York), 85

Tamberlik, Enrico, 79
Tamburini, Antonio, 79
Tannhäuser (Wagner), 142, 143, 146, 156, 158
Tausig, Carl, 180
Tchaikovsky, Pëtr Ilich, 56–57
Technology, potential benefits of, to music education, 92
Thackeray, William, 16
Thalberg, Sigismund, 75, 161, 173
Thayer, Alexander Wheelock, 9
Thayer, Eugene, 38

Theater: immorality of, 52–54; music in, 77; and opera, 124. *See also* Concert halls, American
Thomas, Ambroise, 131
Thomas, Theodore, 68–69, 81, 101; and American Opera Company, 102, 138–39; and choral tradition, 185–86; and educational programing, 71–72, 88–91; and music education, 95, 105, 121; and progress of musical taste in U. S., 68, 75, 77, 78, 81 n; and Wagnerism, 144–46
Thurber, Mrs. Francis B., 102, 117, 138
Thwing, Charles F., 98
Tomlins, William L., 94–96
"Tonic Sol-fa" system, 96
Tostée, Mlle, 54
Tourjée, Eben, 100
Transcendentalism, 47, 171, 195
Tristan (Wagner), 47, 146, 166
Twain, Mark, 14, 20

Universities and music education, 98–100
Upton, George P., 77, 91, 106, 185

Van der Stucken, Frank, 77, 186
van Dyke, Henry, 17
Van Rensselaer, Mariana, 147, 195
Vassar, 98
Veblen, Thorstein, 4–5, 135
Verdi, Giuseppe, 41, 67, 71, 131–32
Vienna, 85
Vieuxtemps, Henri, 75
Voice, training of: childrens', 95; in Europe, 121; quality of, in U. S., 102–3; and Wagner's music, 146, 164
Volkmann, Robert, 88
von Stosch, Leonora, 18

Wachtel, Theodore, 129
Wagner, Richard: appeal of his music in U. S., 72, 132, 142–47; Apthorp on, 40–41, 160–63, 166; and Christianity, 165; co-worker with Culturists, 157–58; decline of importance in U. S., 196; de Koven on, 41–42; and evolution, 40–42, 159–63; and Indian music, 44; intellectual appeal of his music, 47, 147–48, 163–64; literature on, in U. S., 148–51; and melody, 163–64; and Metropolitan Opera, 136–37; and morality, 53, 157, 164–65; opposition to, in England, 167 n; opposition to, in U. S., 167–68; Paine on, 155–56; and parlor music, 182–83; satire on music drama of, 148–50; and Schopenhauer's philosophy, 166; and singers, 146, 164; writings of, in U. S., 19, 151–55
Wagner and His Works (Finck), 157
"Wagner Verein," 144
"Waiting" (Millard), 179 n
Walküre, Die (Wagner), 146
Warner, Charles Dudley, 20, 31, 114, 165
Weber, Carl Maria von, 71, 81, 132, 144, 154, 155; compared with Wagner, 159, 163
Weingartner, Felix, 167 n
Werner, Eric, 196

West, American, music in, 62, 78, 145, 184 n
Westendorf, Thomas Paine, 179, 180
White, Richard Grant, 20, 21; on American music, 109; denies moral power of music, 50, 54; on history of opera in New York, 74, 86
Whiting, Charles E., 95
Wieck, Friedrich, 172
Wieniawski, Henri, 75
Wiggin, Kate Douglas, 148
Wilcox, Julius, 171–73
Willis, Richard Storrs, 191
Wilson, George H., 74
Winkelmann, Hermann, 146
Witherspoon, Edward, 191
Women and music, 63, 64–66, 171–74
Woodbury, Isaac, 185
Worcester (Mass.) Festival Association, 185
World Peace Jubilees (Boston), 15, 86, 129, 184
World's Columbian Exposition (Chicago), 91, 185, 186

Yale University, Music Department, 99

Zauberflöte, Die (Mozart), 189
Zerrahn, Carl, 77, 186
Zukunftsmusik, Wagner's, 152, 155, 157